COMMANDO MEDIC

DOC HARDEN VC

STEPHEN SNELLING

For Julia, who has given
so much to this book,
in memory of her father,
mother and brother.

First published 2012
by Spellmount, an imprint of

The History Press
The Mill, Brimscombe Port
Stroud, Gloucestershire, GL5 2QG
www.thehistorypress.co.uk

British Library Cataloguing in Publication Data.
A catalogue record for this book is available from the British Library.

ISBN 978 0 7524 7943 9

Typesetting and origination by The History Press
Printed in Great Britain

Contents

Acknowledgements

Any book involving historical research is, necessarily, a collaborative effort and this one is no exception. So many people have helped in so many ways over so many years that it is difficult to know where to begin in thanking them all.

Sadly, the project's protracted gestation has meant that a number of those who helped set me on the path to chronicling the life and death of Doc Harden are no longer with us. I can only hope that I have been able to do belated justice to the memories provided by the likes of Four Five veterans Bobby Cory, Johnny Haville, Neil Patrick and Don Thomas. Happily, a few of the commandos who served alongside Doc almost seventy years ago and who can vividly recall their days training together at Eastbourne and in the Scottish Highlands as well as the more harrowing times on the beaches of Normandy and in the flatlands of Holland are still with us. Great characters such as Derrick 'Cakes' Cakebread, Fred 'Cabbie' Harris and Walter 'Scouse' Bigland have been able to shed glorious light on their shared experiences as members of that grand company Doc was so proud to serve with: A Troop, 45 Royal Marine Commando.

I am grateful also to Harry Bellars for the loan of his precious copies of '45 Vintage', a series of wonderfully entertaining and informative newsletters edited by ex-Four Five troop officer and unit historian John Day. Without them, this book would have been a much drier record.

The same may be said for Ted Finch, who remembered his time in the freezing billets at Harehills Lane, Leeds; and for Pat Higgins, for sharing his knowledge on all things relating to the Royal Army Medical Corps (RAMC) and who generously gifted me his wartime RAMC training manuals as guides into the ways of a commando medic.

But Doc was not just a soldier and a war hero. He was also Eric Harden: butcher, cyclist, family man, gardener, lover and husband. I hope that this book goes some way towards reflecting the ordinary man who proved himself to be an extraordinary hero on the battlefield. If it does, it is due in no small measure to the willingness of people such as his nieces Josie Elizabeth Haynes (*née* Harden) and Verity Rowbottom (*née* Day) to revisit a vanished era when their Uncle Eric delivered and served meat to the housewives of Northfleet. Their colourful anecdotes and collections of letters and photographs have been of great assistance.

I must also thank Bert Chapman, a former resident of Factory Road, and Joyce Brown, a St John Ambulance Brigade nurse who accompanied Eric on some of his most perilous journeys during the Blitz, for adding to the richness of his story.

However, there are three people without whose support this book could never have been written: my wife Sandra, who has been my guiding light for the past thirty-two years as well as my soulmate and editor *par excellence*, and Julia Wells (*née* Harden) and her husband Bob, whose faith in the project has been as unwavering as their determination to keep the memory of Doc alive.

As the custodian of her father and mother's correspondence Julia has trusted me with her family's greatest treasure. The strength of this book lies in the letters between Eric and Maud. Theirs is a story of love and loss, pain and pride, laid bare in the writings of a quietly courageous citizen-soldier and his stoical wife, caught up in the madness of war. In their humour and heartbreaking sincerity, they represent the authentic voices of an ordinary couple trying to cope in the face of adversity, and this book owes everything to them.

Author's Note

Eric Harden was not a natural writer: his use of grammar was as erratic as his punctuation. However, I have refrained from altering anything other than to add the occasional comma or full stop to make reading the letters easier. Similarly, I have not sought to regularise his spelling of his son's name, which switches at times, and for no apparent reason, from Bobby to Bobbie. The voice you read in the letters is that of Eric 'Doc' Harden VC.

Introduction

Every odyssey has a beginning. Mine had three, though one was more of a false start and another scarcely qualified as a beginning at all. In their own way, each had played their part in propelling me, one winter's night, on a circuitous journey into the rural heart of Norfolk for a meeting that I hoped would give my faltering quest renewed momentum.

Looking back on that serpentine drive along dark and twisty country lanes, it is easy to see a simple metaphor for my own meandering journey in search of the almost ethereal figure of a man I had first encountered forty-five years earlier as a child of 6. 'Doc' Harden, or Lance Corporal H.E. Harden as he was rather formally described, was, quite literally, a comic-strip hero. His exploits leapt from the pages of *The Victor*, a 'boys' picture paper' that prided itself on its rip-roaring tales of 'war, sport and adventure'. Above the masthead, straplines set the scene for a saga of selfless bravery that seemed to defy belief even in the fantastical world of comics: 'The red cross on his arm band was no protection against German bullets but the medical orderly did not hesitate to risk life on a mission of mercy!' I was hooked. What young boy growing up in the 1960s wouldn't have been? It scarcely mattered that the images bore little resemblance to reality or that the backdrop was wrong, the uniforms were wrong and even the manner of his death was wrong. Nor did it matter that the title, 'Harden of No-Man's Land', and the fanciful representation of non-existent trenches were more redolent of the First World War on the Somme than the snow-covered flatlands of south-eastern Holland during the Second World War. What mattered was the impression that those comic-strip images made on me. It was an impression real enough to fire an enduring fascination, for the Victoria Cross in general, and men like Eric 'Doc' Harden in particular.

Fast forward thirty-three years and those same childhood images were swirling around in my head as I motored into Suffolk for a meeting with a man who would introduce me, for the first time, to the reality behind the comic-strip 'fiction'. By then, I was working as a journalist, gathering material for a special publication marking the fiftieth anniversary of VE Day. Among a small army of veterans to be interviewed was a former Royal Marine officer who had settled into retirement near the picture-postcard village of Yoxford.

Bobby Cory had good cause to remember Doc Harden. Almost half a century earlier, on a bitterly cold winter's day, the 32-year-old medical orderly, a married man with two young children, had braved a hail of fire to save his life at the cost of his own. In the course of a couple of hours, Bobby relived every last harrowing detail of that terrible day. There was an air of incredulity in the manner of his telling, as though even after so much time he was still trying to make sense of the seemingly incomprehensible. At times he had to pause as his emotions threatened to get the better of him. By rights, he knew he should have died on that January day in 1945. That he didn't and that he had been able to enjoy a long and successful life was due to Doc Harden.

What he had to say that day struck a chord with me. More than ever, I wanted to know what it was that had made Doc risk his life, not just once but time and time again, in broad daylight, in the face of galling fire and in defiance of orders. In the weeks and months that followed I tracked down as many of the survivors of that hard-fought encounter as I could find. In corresponding and speaking with them, a picture began to emerge of a gentle, generous-spirited man, much older than most of the men he served with, who had nevertheless earned the respect of his younger comrades through his compassion, humour and devotion to duty. I learned much about him as a civilian soldier who was proud of having earned the commando's green beret, but of his life out of uniform, as a father and husband, I knew next to nothing. It was as though his life had been telescoped into a few hours of almost superhuman bravery.

That was how it remained for more than twelve years. It seemed as if I'd reached the limits of my research and come up tantalisingly short. I considered publishing what I'd discovered as a fragment of a broader work exploring courage on the battlefield, but other projects took over and Doc slipped back into the shadows. Then, one day, a friend's chance encounter at a Remembrance Day service in Norfolk raised the

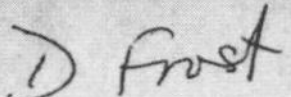

THE RED CROSS ON HIS ARM-BAND WAS NO PROTECTION AGAINST GERMAN BULLETS BUT THE MEDICAL ORDERLY DID NOT HESITATE TO RISK HIS LIFE ON A MISSION OF MERCY!

No. 86
OCT. 13th
1962

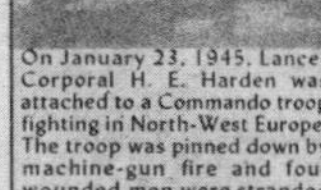

My first encounter with Eric Harden as a comic-strip hero. (Author's collection)

32
THE VICTOR
October 13, 1962.
CONTINUED FROM FRONT PAGE
LOOK AFTER HIM! I'M GOING OUT AFTER THE OTHERS.
NO, HARDEN! YOU'VE DONE ENOUGH. THE TANKS WILL RESCUE THEM.
THAT BATTERY OF ANTI-TANK GUNS IS TOO MUCH FOR US. WE'LL HAVE TO TURN BACK!
LAY DOWN A SMOKE SCREEN, MEN. WE'LL RESCUE THEM UNDER COVER OF THE SMOKE.
THE ENGLANDERS ARE UP TO SOMETHING. FIRE!
HOLD IT, SERGEANT! STOP THE SMOKE. IT'S ATTRACTING TOO MUCH FIRE. WE'LL SIMPLY GET THOSE POOR CHAPS KILLED!
THERE'S ONLY ONE WAY LEFT. I HAVE A VOLUNTEER STRETCHER PARTY HERE—
GOOD LUCK, LADS!
WE'RE NEARLY THERE, LADS!
TAKE IT EASY! WE'LL SOON HAVE YOU BACK AT THE REGIMENTAL AID POST.
WELL DONE, HARDEN! BUT GIVE IT A REST. IT'S SUICIDE TO GO BACK!
WE HAVE TO, SIR. WE CAN'T LEAVE THESE POOR BLOKES OUT THERE.
Harden returned to bring in more of the wounded. While carrying back a wounded officer, Harden was killed when a mortar bomb exploded near him. For his bravery, he was awarded the Victoria Cross.
NEXT WEEK—" The Midnight Raiders "—the thrilling story of a daring attack by the Royal Marines!

possibility of resurrecting the story that had for so long eluded me. He had photographed a woman wearing an impressive row of medals headed by a Victoria Cross. Her name was Julia Wells (*née* Harden) and, with her husband Bob, she had recently retired to a small village in the middle of Norfolk, barely 20 miles from where I lived.

A fitful, faltering quest, born of youthful enthusiasm more than forty years earlier, had taken a surprising twist that led me, that winter's night, to a bungalow on the edge of Reymerston. Waiting for me inside was Julia and a treasure trove of letters and photographs that would enable me, at last, to tell the full and remarkable story of commando medic Eric 'Doc' Harden, VC.

Thorpe St Andrew, Norwich,
July 2012

Prologue

It is January 1945 on the Dutch-German border near the village of Brachterbeek. The ground is frozen solid beneath a crust of snow, which spreads like a giant tablecloth as far as the eye can see to the point where it melts into an ice-blue sky. It is the sixth winter of a bitter, scarring war that has turned the natural order on its head. Potato fields have become battlefields, ploughed by bombs and raked by bullets. A railway station is transformed into a mini fortress, spitting fire. A farmhouse masquerades as a first-aid station, a windmill as a machine-gun nest.

Out in the flatlands, a vicious hailstorm of shot and shell has driven almost everyone to shelter, some into buildings, others into ditches or behind straw-shrouded mounds of potatoes. The only exceptions are three figures in the middle of a bare field utterly devoid of cover. Khaki and green against a sheet of white, they are clearly visible crouching beside the prostrate form of another man. He is lying helpless in snow that is stained red with his blood.

One of the men has a white armband with a red cross emblazoned on it, but this makes no difference. The fire is intense, turning their movements into a frantic blur. In seconds, a stretcher is slid beneath the raised body, straps are tightened and they are up and running, one at the front, two at the back, boots crunching patterns in the snow, every lung-bursting breath revealed in a wispy trail of misted vapour. Bullets crack around them, stitching the snow with powdery fountains. Still they run. Panting. Gasping. Hearts pounding. Pulses racing. Ahead, in their line of sight, bouncing with every desperate footfall, is sanctuary, in the shape of a solitary farm building.

Mortar bombs are falling. Bullets are kicking and flicking the snow around them. But somehow they are unscathed. Against all the odds, they are halfway there, halfway home...

No matter how hard she tried, sleep wouldn't come to her. Night after night, Maud Harden shivered as she lay awake in her freezing home, worrying about her children, a house bearing the scars of war and, most of all, her husband, Eric, soldiering once more on the front line.

In almost three years, she hadn't been able to fully come to terms with their enforced separation. She doubted whether she ever would. Now, in the depths of one of the coldest winters she could recall, she couldn't stop thinking about him and what he was having to endure. The water pipes in the house were choked with ice. Snow was seeping through blast-damage cracks in the walls. But if it was cold enough to freeze a bowl of water inside her kitchen in daytime, what must it be like at night out in the open?

With the streets of Northfleet clogged with fresh falls of snow, Maud imagined Eric trying to sleep in a frozen slit trench somewhere in Holland. If she had it bad, how much worse was it for him? She worried if he had enough blankets, if he needed thicker vests or Balaclava helmets. It seemed strange, 'silly' even, to be worrying about Eric, of all people, not being able to sleep. Back home, he could sleep anywhere, at virtually any time. They used to laugh about it. This irony wasn't lost on Maud as, in vain, she sought comfort beneath two eiderdowns and with her 7-year-old son snuggled up beside her. 'I've got the chance to sleep and can't,' she wrote, 'and you haven't got the chance but could…'[1]

The news from the Low Countries did little to raise spirits. The German offensive in the Ardennes had, at last, been stayed, but forward progress was slow. All along the Reich's western border the Allies were meeting dogged resistance. The best hope for a quick end to the war appeared to Maud to lie with the Russians who were 'running away with it again' on the Eastern Front. 'Perhaps it won't be long now after all before we meet,' she wrote.[2] That was provided the army didn't then whip Eric off to Burma. If they did, she would go crazy, she knew she would. She tried to make light of it. 'Did you say I've not got far to go, dear? No, maybe not but that's this war's fault,' she wrote.[3]

As January drew to its icy conclusion, Maud was gripped by a depression so black she couldn't even trust what she was writing to him:

> Last night I wrote to you but I was feeling miserable so in case the letter was the same I never posted it this morning. I think I had the stay-in-blues and for some silly reason I wanted to go to a dance or something but instead went to bed and froze and couldn't sleep at all. If I was as cold as that, what were you boys there like… Well dear, it's bed time now so I'll close and go up and freeze again…[4]

Your Very Own Eric

It was almost midnight in Factory Road. Everyone in the tiny two-up, two-down terraced house was in bed except for Eric Harden. He was poring over a letter to the girl who had come to mean everything to him. But, as usual, he was fumbling around for the words to match his feelings. They'd been going steady for three years. They had been the best three years of his life, and it was all down to her. But how to get it across? He knew he was no wordsmith, but there were times when he felt that his letters made no sense at all. Once, in exasperation at his own incoherence, he had scribbled: 'I'll bet you read them two or three times before you know what I have written and then I'll bet sometimes you give it up as a bad job.'[1] That hadn't stopped him trying, however. If anyone could understand what he was trying to say, or could read the true meaning behind the awkward lines, it was surely his darling Maud. She knew him better than anyone. So, fondly recalling his last trip to see her, he wrote clumsily:

> I must thank you very, very much for looking after me, and, please dearest, keep it up if you can, no matter what I say or do because whatever it is that I say or do I don't mean any of it really. You are a darling to me and, gee, I love you for it. I hope you get this letter alright, dear, because I will have to wait until tomorrow to post it because I haven't a stamp. That's just like me, isn't it. I wonder you don't get fed up with me what with one thing and another. You have a lot to put up with from me don't you dear?[2]

Before turning out the light and heading up to bed, he closed the letter, as he always did, with three kisses from 'Your Very Own Eric'.

Romance and Factory Road. It wasn't something you would normally associate with the uninspiring and singularly unremarkable red-brick terraced street that branched off like a rib from the spinal column of

Northfleet's flourishing High Street. There was nothing at all romantic about Factory Road. No ornament. No architectural flourishes. It was humble, plain and utilitarian, a working-class street in a workaday town. A century or more earlier it had been very different. Upper Northfleet, as it was known then, was a Kentish pastoral haven noted for its yields of watercress and fruit. It was a place of cherry orchards and grand houses where green and pleasant parklands rolled down to meet the Thames Estuary. Once upon a time, it was the very evocation of 'the garden of England', but not any more. The pastures where mansions like The Hive once stood in splendid isolation were now a hive of industry and pinched terraces dominated by soaring chimney stacks that belched smoke into a smog-clouded sky. The invention of Portland cement had transformed Upper Northfleet's fortunes along with its rural appearance. With its bountiful chalk hills and its proximity to the Thames, the village was ideally situated, not only for the production of cement but for its easy transportation. So the great houses were demolished and the fields and orchards were despoiled with chalk workings to fill the ravenous maw of cement manufacture.

By the 1930s, William Aspdin's experimental enterprise had expanded into the noisy, vast and perpetually dust-shrouded Bevan's Works, one of the largest and most productive cement factories in Europe, with a yearly output of nearly half a million tons. Recognising the strategic value of the town's Thames-side location, more factories took root along the river. Chief among them was the new Northfleet paper mill, Bowater's, which kept the national press supplied with newsprint, and Henley's Cable and Telegraph Works. With industry came jobs and an explosion in house building. A web of streets linking the chalk-rich, riverside escarpment to the new High Street provided homes for hundreds of factory workers and their families. In this way, Upper Northfleet became the thriving heart of a conjoined Northfleet with its own cinema, community hall, playing fields, school and swimming pool.

It was a close-knit community. Bert Chapman, whose family lived next door to the Hardens in Factory Road, likened life in the terrace to *Coronation Street*. 'Everybody knew everybody,' he said.[3] Children played in the streets or roamed the disused and overgrown chalk workings. Known as The Main, this area was a childhood paradise where youngsters 'could climb trees, swing on ropes and build camps and dens and generally have a great time in their own little world of adventures'.[4]

This was the world that Eric Harden grew up in, the world in which he lived and worked. It was the only world he had ever known.

He was born just a few doors away, in the same unimaginatively styled Factory Road, on 23 February 1912, as Captain Scott's ill-starred party were plodding to their doom across the South Polar icecap. The third son and seventh child to William (Bill) Thomas Harden and his wife, Fanny Maria (*née* Seager), he was christened Henry Eric, although he never used his first name, which he hated. Young Eric, with his green eyes and shock of curly brown hair, joined an already crowded household that would be swollen three years later by the addition of an eighth and final child. Hilda (b. 1915) joined Ethel (b. 1895), Ann (b. 1897), Bill (b. 1901), Joe (b. 1903), Mabel (b. 1905), Maude (b. 1909)[5] and Eric at number 44. Conditions were cramped. Downstairs consisted of a small living room and a larger but rarely used 'parlour' that housed the family piano and looked out onto the street. In common with most such terraces at that time, there was no bathroom, just an outdoor toilet with a tiny scullery tacked onto the back of the house. Beyond a curtain in the living room, a narrow staircase led up to the two bedrooms, which were unevenly shared: the three brothers and father in one and five sisters and mother in the other. It was a tight squeeze, which must have strained the family harmony, not to mention the family budget, to the limit.

Though not poor by the standard of the times, the family was far from being comfortably off. Eric's father made a living on the barges that traded along the Thames and Medway. As such, he was following in a long family tradition of river work. Oliver Smith had his own barge in the nineteenth century and his daughter married into the family of David Harden, who was described as a shipwright. Bill Harden learned his trade aboard his father's barge and progressed to become skipper of his own craft, ferrying cargoes, mainly of bricks, into London. Unfortunately, his boat-handling skills were matched by his fondness for the 'demon' drink. It proved to be his downfall. According to family legend, he lost his captain's licence after being caught drunk in charge of his barge. It didn't stop him working on the boats, but it did significantly reduce his income.[6]

As soon as he was old enough, Eric followed his siblings to Lawn Road School, otherwise known as Northfleet Primary School. Just round the corner from Factory Road, when it was opened in 1886 it was the first board school to be built in the town and was distinguished by a grand clock tower that was added seven years later. Eric's own school career was less spectacular. A solid rather than remarkable student, his boyhood interests lay elsewhere: in music, sport and all manner of outdoor pursuits.

The Hardens were a musical family. Eric was a gifted violinist and his brother Joe played the banjo. As well as performing, usually at family gatherings, Eric was also an enthusiastic concertgoer. He grew to love classical as well as popular music and his favourite work was said to be Mendelssohn's 'Violin Concerto'. The advent of the wireless was a boon that allowed him to expand his musical knowledge and over time he acquired his own collection of records that he enjoyed playing. His passion for music stayed with him for the rest of his life and during his subsequent wartime army postings he would seize any opportunity to attend concerts or shows.

Eric's other abiding passion was keeping fit. Of medium height, slim and with an athletically built, he was an enthusiastic cricketer, footballer and tennis player. He even tried his hand at bodybuilding, until an accident with his chest expander resulted in him consigning the contraption to a drawer, never to be seen again! But his greatest and most enduring love was swimming. His eldest sister, Ethel, had been a champion swimmer as a schoolgirl and a talent for water sports clearly ran through the family, encouraged by Bill Harden senior, who had his own somewhat unorthodox teaching methods. Eric's niece, Josie Haynes (*née* Harden), recalled:

> There was a swimming pool in Gravesend and a little one in Northfleet, but Eric and my father [Joe] learned to swim in the Thames. Their father used to take them out on his barge. He would put them into a cradle that was strapped to the side of the barge and he'd lower them over the side and dangle them in the water, so that they learned to swim that way. The Thames was a lot cleaner then. People used to swim in the river a lot in those days. And it certainly worked for them. They both became very good swimmers, just like aunty Ethel.[7]

By the mid-1920s, however, Eric's focus was less on recreation and more on work. Having left school, he might have been expected to follow his father and other generations of Hardens onto the Thames, or, at least, into the closed-shop world of the docks where his eldest brother Bill worked. His father, who held a prized stevedore's ticket, offered one to Eric, just as he did to Joe, but both turned the offer down. Instead, Eric chose to work for his sister Ethel's husband in the High Street butcher's shop that he owned. Fred Treadwell was a notable figure in Northfleet business circles. A self-made man, he had started

Happy days at Dymchurch. Young Eric (centre) displays his athleticism with a group of friends, *c.* 1935. Maud is on the left. (J. Wells)

out as a butcher's boy before buying out his original employers the year Eric was born. After serving as an artilleryman during the First World War, he re-opened his shop and, despite suffering the legacy of gas poisoning, turned it into one of the most successful butcher's in Northfleet. As a Freemason and leading member of the local master butchers' association, Fred was well liked and well connected. In spite of the age gap between them – Fred was more than twenty years older than Eric – they got on well together, sharing a mutual interest in the fortunes of Northfleet Football Club for whom Fred had played before becoming a vice-president.

Yet, for all his close family ties, Eric was not given an easy ride. He started out, just as Fred had done, as butcher's boy, labouring in the shop and the slaughterhouse at the back and delivering orders of meat to customers all around the town. His rounds, originally covered on a bicycle and later in a van, made him a familiar figure around Northfleet's fast-expanding housing estates. With his boyish good looks and cheery charm, he brought to the job all the high-spirited exuberance of youth. Among his regular customers were members of his family, and his niece Josie recalled watching at the window with her brother John for the arrival of their favourite uncle:

> We were very fond of him. He was always full of life and used to run and dash about. He was very fit and agile. We were living in a flat over Halls' paper shop in Rosherville and he used to call out and come running upstairs. Mum always had a cup of tea ready for him...[8]

Sometimes, his enthusiasm and desire to do everything at breakneck speed landed him in trouble, as Josie remembered:

> He liked to drive fast. I remember he helped us to move to our new house in Waterdales. I was sitting in the back and I recall mum asking him to slow up. Then, there was the time he delivered meat to his mum, my gran, in Factory Road. He could be a bit of a mad devil at times and on this occasion, he swept round outside the house doing three-point turns on the brakes until they squealed. I think he did it just to annoy her. If he did, it worked, because she came out with a copper stick and shook at him, saying: 'I'll give you a whack with this if you don't stop!'[9]

Perhaps it was just a case of letting off steam. The hours were long and the work hard under Fred's expert tutelage. As well as days spent toiling in the shop and on the rounds, Eric learned from his brother-in-law the skills of butchery and the techniques of slaughtering livestock. They would stand him in good stead, as in time, Eric would qualify as a licensed butcher and slaughterman. The relentless routine allowed for few breaks, however. Holidays were short and what spare time he had was usually spent with a group of friends whose favourite summer pastime was cycle excursions to the shores of the Medway, where they'd camp and swim. Their most popular destination was the remote seaside village of Allhallows, which, by the start of the 1930s, was being touted as a future holiday resort to rival Blackpool. Although a railway link was being built, the ambitious plans designed to cater for millions of tourists from the capital were little more than a pipedream. However, even without the envisaged amusements and gargantuan pool, there was much to recommend Allhallows. It offered sand, sea and plenty of space to pitch a tent or two, though for Eric the biggest attraction was a lithe, brown-haired, blue-eyed girl with a dazzling smile and a zest for life to match his own.

Maud Pullen was 17. She worked in a seamstress shop in London's Oxford Street and lived with her parents in Crayford, on the other side of Dartford. She was the fourth of five children to Armine (Bob)

Pullen, a regular soldier turned tea warehouse foreman, and his wife Fanny, known as Ollie (*née* Dugay).[10] More importantly, her best friend was being courted by one of Eric's cycling pals. Eric and Maud first met at Allhallows in 1931 when she was invited to join the seaside fun. According to Maud, it was 'love at first sight'.[11] They started dating and the romance quickly blossomed into a full-blown courtship.

But the relationship that began in a tearing rush was destined to take the long road to the altar. As their daughter Julia put it: 'They spent five years courting and saving and camping and planning for the future.[12] For once in his life, Eric was determined to do things properly and ensure that their marriage began on solid foundations. But it didn't come easy to him. The marriage of Prince George, the future Duke of Kent, to Princess Marina of Greece and Denmark in November 1934 was greeted with a mixture of envy and pragmatism. Wondering if Maud had managed to join the crowds outside Westminster Abbey, he wrote to her:

> By the time we marry we will have been going it with one another about four or five years and those two have only been together, well, less than a year. Gee, but aren't they lucky... but then again, I wouldn't like to be them, would you? I would like the wedding part, but after that I would like to be left alone with just you, but they will have to be here, there and everywhere, won't they...[13]

Separated by their work during the week, they lived for the weekends and filled the gaps with letters, a few of which survive to provide a glimpse into their early lives together: their enthusiasms, their tiffs and their makings-up. Like all couples, they had their fallings out, as evidenced in Eric's apologies for forgetting Maud's birthday and for applying double standards to their relationship. 'I ask you to take no notice of the things I do wrong,' he wrote pleadingly on one occasion, 'and yet as soon as you do something that just doesn't please me I am a bit like that. Well dear, there it is, but I think that once we are away together things will be alright, don't you? xxx'.[14] So they were. Most of the letters are concerned with looking back or looking forward to the hours and days they spent and would spend with each other. Typical of these is one written ahead of a camping holiday at Dymchurch, another favourite seaside haunt:

> I'll bet Cecil and May[15] wouldn't come to camp with us August, would they dear? It would be nice if they did, wouldn't it? ... There will be

> that long weekend, and then a week after... so that ought to be good, didn't it? And it will be much better with the big tent too, won't it... There's one thing about that place, we shall have plenty of places to go in the evening, won't we. So, hurry up holidays...[16]

Most weekends were spent in and around their homes in Crayford or Northfleet, with occasional outings to the coast. Allhallows and Minster, across the Swale on the Isle of Sheppey, were the usual settings for camping expeditions. To reach them, they would cycle together on a custom-built tandem that was Eric's pride and joy. He was forever tinkering with it, making improvements and adding pieces of equipment. 'I did some more to it last night,' he wrote ahead of a journey over to Crayford. 'I turned those rubbers round on the pedals. I think they will be alright now until I get some new ones.'[17] Another time, he tested out a new headlamp. 'It's jolly good too, not so good as the other one tho', but nearly... We went down all the hills and up them ... and I believe I put the wind up Harry once.'[18]

The bike proved something of a novelty in Northfleet and was 'quite a hit' in his brother Joe's road. 'All the kids loved to see it,' recalled his niece Josie. 'Nobody else had one.'[19] As well as local trips, when they might be accompanied by Maud's brothers and sister or Eric's younger sister Hilda and an assortment of boyfriends and girlfriends, they occasionally indulged in longer journeys, most memorably a marathon ride to Lulworth Cove in Dorset. Eric was at his happiest on these expeditions. It was as though all his cares and worries were forgotten the moment he pedalled out onto the open road. Sometimes, just thinking about it was enough to raise his spirits. 'When I saw the bike Monday, Maud, I had a better temper...'[20]

Soon, though, he hoped there would be more than bike rides and holidays to look forward to. After five years of saving and waiting, he felt the time was almost right for them to take the plunge:

> Maud dear, please tell me now, do you think we can do it on £100? By going ever so steady I think I would have that in about four months time. Well, look here Maud, you have a talk with your mother or May and see what they say about it. If they think it isn't enough, we will wait until I have got enough. And also Maud, I think I would like you to have a ring, that is, if it is going to be this year, not unless... Oh and Maud, if your mother says it isn't enough, without beating about the bush, please don't try to get

Inseparable. Eric and Maud aboard the tandem that became his pride and joy, *c.* 1934

> round her, but take that as an answer... When we do get married I want everybody on your side to agree that we are doing the right thing. As for me, my mother would like to see you as my wife and so would I, very, very much indeed...[21]

There were no objections and no need to beat about the bush, though Maud rejected the idea of an engagement ring along with a honeymoon as unnecessary expenses. So, a date was set, the money was saved and house hunting began in earnest. Their choice was a semi-detached house still in the process of being built on a new estate on the other side of Wombwell Park from where his brother Joe lived. The road was named Colyer Road in honour of Thomas Riversdale Colyer-Fergusson, scion of a wealthy landowning family. He had lost his life to a German sniper's bullet almost twenty years earlier in an action that resulted in him being posthumously awarded the Victoria Cross.

Lost Peace

Eric and Maud were married at St Paulinus' church in Crayford on 18 October 1936. As they were walking down the aisle, a little more than 100 miles away 200 unemployed workers from a Tyneside shipyard were making their way through the Midlands, bound for London. If the Jarrow Crusaders symbolised the depressed North and the old, failing industries that had reduced thousands of families to destitution, then the Kentish newlyweds were, in their own modest way, exemplars of a growing affluence in a 'New England' where aspirations and living standards were on the up.

By the mid-1930s the worldwide slump had given way to a recovery fuelled by low prices, increasing consumption and rising productivity. Nowhere was the increasing prosperity more apparent than in the south-east. It was a brave new world that J.B. Priestley had discovered during his journey round the country, an England of:

> ... filling stations and factories that look like exhibition buildings, of giant cinemas and dance-halls and cafes, bungalows with tiny garages, cocktail bars, Woolworths, motor-coaches, wireless, hiking, factory girls looking like actresses, greyhound racing and dirt tracks, swimming pools, and everything given away for cigarette coupons.[1]

Part and parcel of this 'New England' was a growing suburbia and an insatiable desire to leave the older parts of town for the new estates that were spilling into the countryside.

Eric and Maud were part of that trend. A housing boom coupled with low interest loans and extended terms of repayment had brought home ownership within reach of many more thousands of people. The year 1936 saw house building in England and Wales peak at 346,000 and, through dint of working hard and saving hard, Eric and Maud were able to live out their part of that dream. A £50 deposit was enough to purchase a share of suburbia, complete with the 'creosoted gate' and 'privet hedge' of George Orwell's vision of semi-detached England.[2] But the newlyweds had to wait a while to move into 195 Colyer Road. The house was still unfinished that October, so they began married life in rented accommodation in nearby Preston Road.

However, by the following December, when their first child Robert (Bobby) was born, they were established in their new house, just a bike ride away from the High Street but a world away from the grimy riverside and the cramped terraces where Eric had grown up. With £60 of their savings, Maud was able to completely furnish the house, while Eric directed his attention towards the garden, which soon replaced his tandem bicycle as the main object of his affection. Gardening had taken root as a hobby in Factory Road, and visiting Maud's parents' house in Crayford had served to further fuel his enthusiasm. 'Your mum's garden looks jolly nice and fresh doesn't it,' he wrote admiringly in a letter to Maud a few months before they were married. 'I would like a garden like that...'[3] Now, at last, he had one to call his own, one that he could design and develop to his own pattern. In no time, with the help of his brother Joe, he had constructed a trellis that was soon entangled with a climbing rose that drew admiration from Maud's mother. It was the beginning of a passion, and roses became his gardening obsession. Behind the castellated privet hedge, his garden took shape, with manicured lawns neatly cut into concentric diamonds set off with a flowering cherry, a Kanzan, to celebrate Bobby's birth. However, the jewels in his horticultural crown were undoubtedly the roses, which he tended with a rare devotion.

Eric's skill and understanding of this most English of all flowers extended beyond his own garden. According to his niece, Josie Haynes (*née* Harden), his butcher's round began to involve offering gardening tips and even, on occasions, a spot of practical help:

> Mrs Shelton across the road from us had roses in her front garden. So, when he took her meat he told her that he would prune her roses for her. But not long after, she came over to my mum. She was nearly in tears. Her beloved rose bushes had been reduced to a few tiny twigs. Mum told her not to worry and that her roses would be all right. And so they were. By June, they were a picture and she was absolutely overjoyed. But that was typical of Uncle Eric.[4]

Just like his garden, business was flourishing. The rash of new houses close to home brought Eric a steady flow of fresh customers. Eric's work took a dramatic turn in 1938, however. The sudden death of his brother-in-law, boss and mentor Fred Treadwell was a tragic blow that changed his life. After years under Fred's wing, he took on the job of managing the business with his sister Ethel, but with this unexpected promotion came added responsibility, even-longer hours and sporadic clashes with Ethel over the direction the business should take. On top of all that, there would be repercussions that he could not have imagined as events far away from Northfleet came to overshadow the parochial concerns of daily life in and around Colyer Road.

Eric and Maud's married life had been played out against a backdrop of worsening international relations and rising tensions. It was a darkening scene that saw the nations of Europe lurch from crisis to crisis as they stumbled ever closer to a war many in Britain were

Eric and Maud are married at St Paulinus' Church, Crayford, 18 October 1936. (V. Rowbottom)

desperate to avoid. Just months before their wedding, Hitler had defied the League of Nations by sending troops into the demilitarised zone in the Rhineland, Mussolini's Italian legions had completed their conquest of Abyssinia and a Spanish army officer called Franco had begun his long march to victory in a brutal civil war that pitted democrats against fascists. By 1938, Europe was teetering on the brink of war. Across Kent, as with the rest of Britain, gas masks were being handed out in their thousands, trenches were being dug and preparations made to face the feared all-out air assault that commentators and politicians alike had predicted would bring ruin from the skies.

As Prime Minister Neville Chamberlain returned from signing away a chunk of Czechoslovakia in return for 'peace in our time', Eric was among thousands of volunteers working overtime in the national interest. He was part of a new citizens' army, the so-called 'Fourth Arm', otherwise known as Civil Defence. As well as managing a successful butcher's business, he served as a member of the Northfleet Division of the St John Ambulance Brigade. It had been formed in 1935, the same year that the Home Office had begun distributing air-raid precaution (ARP) circulars warning against the dangers of aerial bombardment and gas attack. Although not initially a branch of Civil Defence, by the end of the 1930s the St John's volunteers were incorporated into the wider ARP organisation and their first-aid training was extended to deal with air-raid casualties in the event of war.

Eric had joined St John's before he was married. Early on, the headquarters was established in the Grove Road Drill Hall, not far from where he was living with his parents in Factory Road. The Northfleet Division had its own ambulance and, in those pre-National Health Service days without a countywide ambulance service, the volunteers were kept busy answering emergency calls and moving patients to and from hospital. As well as fulfilling a range of duties at the local cinema and such public events as Brands Hatch race days, fêtes and football matches, a duty rota meant that members could be on call at any time of the day or night.

Gradually, however, as the nation stumbled from fragile peace towards the increasing likelihood of war, the emphasis changed from first aid in the stalls of the Astoria to gas decontamination drills under the aegis of the town's ARP organisation. As a keen and dedicated member, Eric played his full part in the shift to a war footing. The Munich Crisis of September 1938 had led to a rapid expansion in Civil Defence services. A network of air-raid wardens' posts was established and, among many arrangements made, first-aid dressing stations and rest centres were set up to deal with casualties and families bombed out of their homes. There were two first-aid posts in Northfleet. One was based at Colyer Road Boys' School, with the main post established at Lawn Road School. St John's volunteers joined with the local ARP in manning both posts, but Eric was primarily involved with Lawn Road, where the ambulance was based and a first-aid room, communications office and rest rooms were kitted out.

Shameful though it was, the Munich Agreement had bought precious time to prepare for a war that Chamberlain still hoped to avoid. But as spring 1939 approached, that time was fast running out. On 15 March, German troops occupied Prague and Bohemia-Moravia was declared a protectorate of the Third Reich. A betrayed and desperately wounded Czechoslovakia had received its death blow and so too had Chamberlain's policy of appeasement. The following month, for the first time in its history, Britain introduced peacetime conscription, calling up all men aged 20 and 21 for six months' military training. For those, like Eric, engaged in Civil Defence, the gas drills and the air-raid casualty training courses took on an even greater urgency as the gardens of Northfleet began sprouting corrugated-iron air-raid shelters named after their originator, Dr David Anderson.

The outbreak of war in September 1939 put an end to weeks of uncertainty, but did not result in the mass destruction portrayed in so many doom-laden, pre-war predictions. Military conscription was extended to all men aged between 18 and 41, but Eric was among millions who were exempted. Anxious to avoid a repetition of the disruption caused by the impulsive volunteering of so many skilled workers during the First World War, the government had published a schedule of reserved occupations in November 1938. The following January a handbook was delivered to every household cataloguing all the occupations and age groups exempted from military service. As a skilled butcher and slaughterman, Eric, at 27, was considered more valuable managing his part of the food chain than as a member of His Majesty's Armed Forces.

By January 1940 fears of aerial Armageddon had subsided into the Phoney War, but there was nothing phoney about Eric's war effort. When he wasn't spending nights manning the first-aid post at Lawn Road, he was battling against shortages and bureaucracy as he found himself in the front line of the government's new food-rationing initiative. Bacon was among the first items to be rationed – though the

4oz per head limit was quickly doubled – and by mid-March a wider meat ration was imposed that allowed 1*s* 10*d* worth of meat per week for each person above the age of 6. A further complication was the fact that offal was not rationed, rendering those humble organs objects of intense competition. Designed to eke out and create a fairer distribution of the nation's limited food supplies, rationing placed great strains on the retailers whose job it was to ensure that people did not exceed their entitlements. Butchers, like Eric, had little leeway. Supplies were strictly controlled by the Ministry of Food and overseen by local committees empowered to deal with any abuses of the system. Soon enough, however, Eric and his colleagues in Civil Defence would have much more to contend with than a queue of disgruntled housewives.

On 6 June 1940, a few days after the completion of the evacuation of the British Expeditionary Force from the beaches of Dunkirk and a month before the beginning of the Battle of Britain, Northfleet endured its first air attack. In what was thought to be the first incendiary raid on a built-up area in England, more than 1,500 firebombs rained down on the High Street, Lawn Road and Downs Road areas. It was an augury of much worse to come.

By accident or design, Northfleet, not far from the docks of Tilbury and the East End of London and with its industrial works lapping the Thames, frequently found itself in the firing line as the Luftwaffe stepped up its bombing attacks in the summer of 1940. Twenty-nine people died and almost as many were injured when bombers struck the town around midday on 16 August. Part of a wider air strike against targets in London and the Thames Estuary, the raid brought the war to Eric and Maud's door. Sticks of high-explosive bombs straddled Colyer Road Comprehensive School, which was fortunately closed for the summer holidays; the lower end of Waterdales, where Eric's brother Joe lived; Preston Road, close to where Eric and Maud had rented their first house together; Detling Road; London Road; and Bowater's Paper Mill.

Having been dug out of an Anderson shelter at the back of Waterdales, a 9-year-old boy surveyed the scene of devastation all around:

> Most of the slates were off the roofs, windows and doors all blown in, sheds, aviaries flattened, dogs, cats, chickens, rabbits all rushing around and a lot of dead ones. Those that were badly injured were put out of their misery… Out the front, it was even worse. There were dead people at the bottom of Waterdales, a lot [more] in Preston Road, Vale Road and Detling Road. There were a lot of

> confused and bewildered people unable to take in what had just happened. A lot were calling for help to rescue the trapped and injured. People from the surrounding houses were doing what they could... Most of the men were in the gardens, digging out trapped and injured victims... Other people were clearing the roadways so that ambulances could get to the victims...[5]

One of the ambulances may well have been driven by Eric. As transport sergeant, he was one of the small team of St John's volunteers licensed and trained to drive the ambulance based at Lawn Road School as well as to administer first aid. For the first time, all branches of the town's Civil Defence organisation were fully engaged in dealing with the shocking after effects of the raid. Contemporary newspaper reports hailed the 'magnificent spirit' of the people living in the bombed areas. One account paid tribute to the ARP services and singled out the medical teams for particular praise:

Eric (second from the right on back row) among a line-up of St John Ambulance Brigade volunteers to celebrate the delivery of a new ambulance, 1941. Joyce Brown, who accompanied Eric on some of his Blitz calls, is standing, fourth nurse from left. (J. Wells)

> Great credit is due to the Civil Defence Services who dealt with the casualties and the damage efficiently and methodically. In company with squads from the neighbouring Authority, the first-aid and ambulance parties removed all casualties to hospital, where a number of doctors were already waiting to give their services.[6]

For weeks afterwards, there were daily reminders of Northfleet's terrifying ordeal for Eric and Maud. In almost every direction, ruined houses and wrecked school buildings lay close to home, gaping in their disfigurement, mute testimony of a conflict that had placed civilians firmly in the front line. The bombing along the Thames continued throughout the summer and into the autumn, with daylight raids increasingly giving way to night assaults as the year wore on. Neighbouring Gravesend endured eight raids in September and, the following month, bombs again fell on Northfleet High Street, damaging homes and businesses. And so it continued into the spring of 1941.

While Eric spent many a night sleeping at the first-aid post in Lawn Road School ready to answer any emergency calls, Maud and Bobby became accustomed to cold, damp nights in the Anderson shelter, which had become a necessary eyesore in their garden. In Factory Road, Eric's unmarried sister Mabel, his mother and his niece Verity had their own Anderson, but, like many others, they preferred to squeeze into a cupboard beneath the stairs when the sirens sounded. Many more families headed in droves to shelter in the deep, brick-lined tunnels that connected the town's chalk pits to the riverside cement works. Some even moved their beds down there, but the Hardens eschewed Northfleet's subterranean retreat in favour of their homes.

For Civil Defence workers like Eric it was an exhausting time. Working by day at their normal jobs, they were frequently on call or on duty at night. The strain of sleep deprivation became the norm. As the night Blitz on London intensified, fire and ambulance services in surrounding districts faced an increasing burden, providing reinforcements for the capital's over-stretched emergency squads. Detailed records of Eric's services during this hectic period do not exist, but a former St John Ambulance Brigade volunteer has testified to him venturing into London during the Blitz on top of his first-aid duties in Northfleet.

Joyce Brown (*née* Hull) was a St John's nurse at the time and accompanied Eric on a number of his ambulance forays. His energy and selflessness made a deep impression on her. Recalling their time together at the Lawn Road first-aid post, she wrote:

> If the siren went, our Eric used to slip around the corner from his mother's house, always ready for any action, always with a kind word for everyone, whatever the time of day or night.[7]

Joyce also remembered an unusual journey they undertook together, deep into the heart of the blitzed capital at the height of the bombing:

> A request came through from Guys Hospital, asking if we could help to get a young lady home to Northfleet. She was very ill and dying of cancer. She wanted to get home to be with her parents and family. I think the doctors thought it would be kinder to get her out of London and the Blitz. Eric was at hand, with one attendant. I was the nurse on the rota. With a raid on and the blackout [in force] we received our instructions from the hospital. If there were any problems we were to get to the nearest hospital. We did have to stop one time because of the gunfire and bombing. But after a short break, we were able to proceed with the journey. What a nerve-wracking journey it was for driver and attendant, but we arrived back at the patient's home safe and sound. We were all relieved for a safe journey, but that, of course, was so typical of Eric. He was always thinking of other people.[8]

Unbeknown to even those closest to him, he was also thinking, increasingly, about his involvement in the war effort. As a fully trained first-aider and ambulance driver, there was no doubting his value to the Civil Defence services. During the worst of the Blitz, from the autumn of 1940 through to the spring of 1941, he had displayed unswerving loyalty and unstinting dedication to the ARP. Such, indeed, was the respect in which he was held that in 1941 he was selected to take charge of a new St John's ambulance bought by the Northfleet Division. At a special presentation ceremony in Wombwell Park, Eric celebrated the addition to the town's fleet of medical vehicles by giving St John's cadets an impromptu 'joy ride'. As the Luftwaffe threat receded and the manpower requirements of the country's stretched armed forces grew, however, he began to question whether he was doing enough.

He was approaching 30, married with a young son and responsible for running his sister's butcher's business. Everything he cared for and had worked for was tied up in his life in Northfleet, but it was no longer enough to merely help defend and protect his fellow citizens from attack. He wanted to play an active role in defeating the nation's enemies, just as the majority of his contemporaries were doing. His eldest brother Bill was serving in the Royal Navy. His brother-in-law, Ray Gurney, to whom he was very close, had rejoined the army at the outbreak of war, and his sister Hilda's husband, Harry Day, was serving with the Ox and Bucks. Only his brother Joe was not in uniform and he was medically unfit for military service after suffering the effects of peritonitis in childhood.

All of this soul-searching was taking place against a backdrop of governmental concerns about manpower shortages, which culminated, in December 1941, in the scrapping of the old schedule of reserved occupations. From then on, only individual deferments would be accepted, with each case being judged on its own merits. Whether any of this had any bearing on the way Eric was thinking is unclear, but there is no doubt that his frustration at not being in the forces was an increasing source of tension. Maud made her feelings clear and later admitted that although she and Eric 'rarely had cross words, by 1941 and early 1942 they were having "strong arguments" about his wish to enlist'.[9] Eric discussed the matter with his brother Joe, who sided with Maud. Joe's daughter Josie recalled:

> There were ructions, though they never fell out over it because they were too close. But dad told him, he should stay where he was. He said, 'You've got your ambulance work. You've got the butcher's shop. You're helping aunt Ethel. You're doing enough.' But the next thing dad knew was he told him he'd decided to join up, volunteered...[10]

In the end, he had presented them with a *fait accompli*. Without saying a word, he had volunteered for the army and the Royal Artillery. Quite why he chose that branch of the service is uncertain, though it was perhaps no coincidence that his brother-in-law Ray was a sergeant in the artillery while his father-in-law and former mentor Fred Treadwell had both served as gunners during the First World War. Whatever his reasoning, nothing he could say or do would pacify Maud. She was, to put it mildly, 'appalled'.[11] But by then it was all too late. For better or worse, Eric was bound for the army and, despite a month's deferment presumably to tie up loose ends, there would be no turning back.

3

Gunner Harden

The road to war was fraught with domestic tension. The arguments had taken their toll and Eric was still trailing a good deal of emotional baggage as he left all he knew for an uncertain future on the other side of the country. Deep down, he knew he'd made the only decision he could live with, but as a husband and a father it pained him to see the hurt that his actions had inflicted on those closest to him. His parting with Maud had not been a happy one, and it was still troubling him days afterwards.

Maud had planned to see him off in London but something, and it is not clear precisely what, had gone wrong and she hadn't been able to make it. Eric thought it 'damned rotten the way things turned out'. In the circumstances though, he felt it was perhaps just as well. Bad luck continued to dog him as he travelled westwards aboard a crowded train. 'I had to stand up from 10.40 till 3.15 and, gosh, I couldn't half have done with a cup of tea.'[1]

His destination was Paignton, and a harsh initiation into army life. South Devon Camp may have been located close to the English Riviera, but there was nothing remotely holiday-like about the brutal regime that Eric joined as a gunner with no number on April Fool's Day 1942. Initial impressions proved disarmingly deceptive. In his first letter home, he noted: 'The NCO's [*sic*] treat us like fathers.'[2] He'd already palled up with two fellow recruits: both of them married men and one of them a butcher and slaughterman just like himself. Not even the dreary weather – it rained almost relentlessly for days on end, turning the ground into a sea of slimy red mud – appeared to dampen his early enthusiasm. He painted a homely picture of daffodils, primroses and polyanthus in full bloom, a billet with 'a very nice sitting room', plentiful food that 'isn't too bad' and of occasional nights spent at the pictures, even if the films were sometimes 'a daft lot of rot'. Overall, things seemed pretty good. 'Well darling, don't you worry about me,' he wrote in what would become a constant refrain, 'up till now I think I will like it.'[3]

Quite whether or not he was deliberately shielding Maud from the truth by playing down the hardships is not known. What is incontrovertible is that he made a thoroughly brave fist of appearing cheery during the first few days at Paignton. However, it didn't take long for the mask, if that was what it was, to slip. He'd already been warned by fellow recruits that training at South Devon Camp was liable to be hard, but nothing had quite prepared him for the back-breaking, soul-destroying misery to come. Even then, the grim reality took a while to sink in. Writing to Maud after a rare sunny morning spent digging trenches, 13 Troop's newly designated Gunner 11006144 Eric Harden observed:

> Well dear I am getting used to it all right now but the first six or seven days I could have dropped where I stood. Talk about commandos, blimey, they don't come into it, you keep going and going and then keep going. I'm glad I was a fit man when I got here. God, you ought to see some of the poor devils, it's nearly killing them, but for myself, I like it...
>
> The worst of all the training here is doing the slow march. I think Mabel said that she liked to see the RAF or somebody do it. She ought to come here and learn it, it nearly kills you. We do all the drills by numbers, 1, 2, 3, 1, 2, 3, 1, 2, 3 and so you go on, up and down, 1, 2, 3, 1, 2, 3 until we say it in our sleep...[4]

He'd been at Paignton little more than a week, but it already felt like six months, and things were about to get a whole lot worse. Wearying nights spent on guard duty followed by arduous days of drilling and marching combined with a shortage of his favourite Woodbine cigarettes did little to lighten his mood. 'We have lost all sense of time or day or date down here.'[5] He longed for the ordeal of basic training to be over so that he could move on to Plymouth where 'they say it is a holiday ... to what it is here'.[6]

Air-raid warnings were a constant bugbear. On average, there were at least one or two a day, although almost all of them were false alarms. A notable exception was on the night of 23–24 April, when the Germans raided Exeter in an attack that heralded the beginning of the so-called Baedeker Blitz directed against some of England's most historic cities. To Eric it seemed 'just like old times at home, the planes going over one after the other'.[7] Unlike home, however, there was little by way of defensive fire. All he saw were the flashes of bombs going off in the distance.

Of far greater concern than the Luftwaffe was his increasingly fractious relationship with Maud. Things weren't helped by him missing her birthday on 27 April, though he maintained he was blameless, having been unable to leave camp to buy anything. He hardly helped matters by his injudicious references in letters home to dances he attended and to his friendship with two married sisters. Maud was not best pleased and let him know it in no uncertain manner. Tempers were frayed. 'I'm not going through what I am now for the fun,' came the testy response.[8] It wasn't long before a measure of calm was restored, however, and another, more mollifying letter, plopped onto the doormat at Colyer Road as Eric sought to allay Maud's concerns about his new-found friends:

> You asked me in your letter if the husbands were at home where we go. Well, as it happens, they are not. The lady of the house, she is I should say about 42, her husband is in the RAF up in the North of England, the other one who is about 30, her husband is in Africa in the RAF. I have only been down there twice this week and that was Monday night and Thursday night and I dug their kitchen garden up for them... Well, sweetheart, you tell me not to forget to miss you. I think you would be really flattered. It's very nice to have somewhere to go but it's not like home, and for all their kindness I feel sometimes very uncomfortable to take their rations because although they are well off in money they are kept tight with their food rations and I don't like taking it. We had a fine time yesterday afternoon, duck, we had a concert given by the RA string band and, gee, it was lovely, and could they play. And then last night they gave a dance and that was good too although I came away about 10. I was too darned tired to dance.[9]

Like many married couples, Eric and Maud were struggling to come to terms with the strains of separation. They had barely spent a night apart in more than five years and it was clearly going to take a while to find a way of bridging the gap and ensuring that petty grudges didn't grow into disproportionately large grievances. Homesickness, so far as Eric was concerned, was also beginning to take a grip. In a tender letter to Bobby written on 26 April, he gave full vent to his emotions:

> You know I am glad you can't see my eyes now my dear son or you would think you have got a weak daddy, but I can't help it if they run now and again can I? It is at times like this that I wish it was like it was last week, then I was tired and too busy to miss you much but I'm afraid I'm not going thro' this week well...

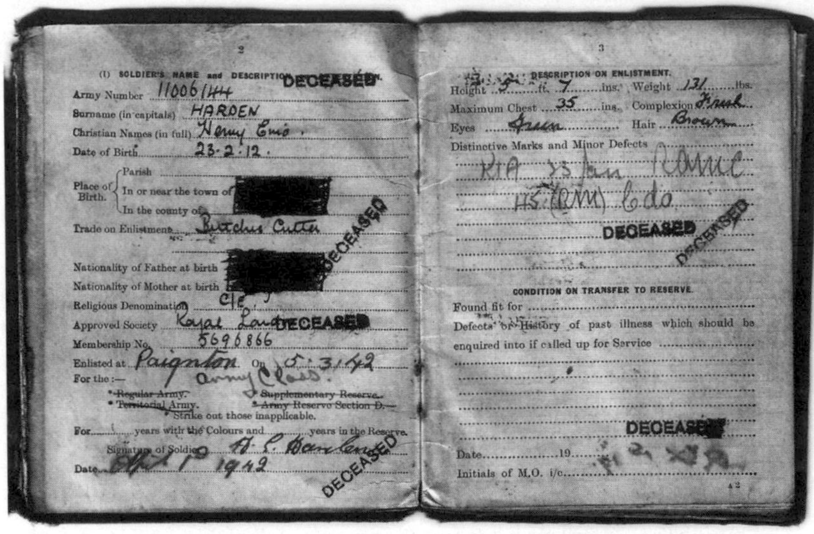

2

(1) SOLDIER'S NAME and DESCRIPTION. DECEASED

Army Number 11006144

Surname (in capitals) HARDEN

Christian Names (in full) Henry Eric.

Date of Birth 23-2-12.

Place of Birth. Parish / In or near the town of / In the county of

Trade on Enlistment Butchers Cutter

Nationality of Father at birth

Nationality of Mother at birth

Religious Denomination C of E

Approved Society Royal London DECEASED

Membership No. 5696866

Enlisted at Paignton On 5-3-42

For the:— Army Class

~~*Regular Army.~~ ~~*Supplementary Reserve.~~
~~*Territorial Army.~~ ~~*Army Reserve Section D.~~
*Strike out those inapplicable.

For ... years with the Colours and ... years in the Reserve.

Signature of Soldier H. E. Harden

Date April 1st 1942

DECEASED DECEASED DECEASED

3

DESCRIPTION ON ENLISTMENT.

Height 5 ft. 7 ins. Weight 131 lbs.

Maximum Chest 35 ins. Complexion Fresh

Eyes Green Hair Brown

Distinctive Marks and Minor Defects

KIA 23 Jan [illegible]

45 (RM) Cdo.

DECEASED DECEASED

CONDITION ON TRANSFER TO RESERVE.

Found fit for

Defects or History of past illness which should be enquired into if called up for Service

DECEASED

Date ... 19...

Initials of M.O. i/c

Eric's paybook. A month's deferment meant he arrived in South Devon Camp on April Fool's Day, 1942. (J. Wells)

Physical weariness may have appeared to offer an escape from the mental pressure Eric was struggling to deal with, but even he was unprepared for what followed. After weeks of stamina-sapping exercises, his spell at Paignton was drawing to a close when a gruelling march went beyond the bounds of toughening up into the realms of tragedy. In a fit of moral outrage, he scribbled a letter to Maud on 5 May, detailing what happened:

> One day here is very much like another, it is the same old stuff every day, they drill you until you drop and then they are satisfied. They killed a man here today, and the devils ought to be done for manslaughter. To get to this camp you have to walk up a hill a lot more steep than Wrotham hill, and just as long. Well, this morning, they marched the chaps down there on to a straight bit of road. There they were drilled for 1½ hours without a break and then they came back. When they were nearly half way up they made them double and it was boiling hot, so you can bet your life what it was like running up it with big boots and so on. When the men got back they nearly dropped and the sweat was running off them. They had 15 minutes break to get into PE kit. That meant no time for a rest and then had to go a mile up to

> Dixons Camp. When they got there they had to run round a football field four times and then do a long jump and then come back again. Well, the second time round this chap dropped down. The NCO would not attend to him and would not let anyone else do so, so the poor fellow just laid down there and died.
>
> That doesn't sound right, does it Maud? But there are fellows going down like that every day here, although, thank God, that is the first to die, but if you drop out here they just leave you like a pig...

Eric was enraged by the injustice and neglect that had resulted in the death of the man who had slept in the next bed to him. Although an extreme case, the incident was not an isolated one, as Eric made plain in a letter home:

> One day, we were drilling out in the road outside the camp and one of the chaps went down. I went to see him and all they would let me do was to put my hat under his head then leave him. There he was lying at the side of the road and we went on with our drill. That chap could have died but if I had stayed with him it would have meant that I went against orders and would have had CB or something...[10]

Training was one thing, but working men to death was something else. Morale slumped to a new low and mutiny was openly discussed. 'We have all made up our minds what we are going to do tomorrow if they try to make us double,' Eric wrote.[11] In the event nothing happened and the threat was never carried out. But none of the recruits from 13 Troop who headed off to Plymouth a few days later were sorry to see the back of South Devon Camp. They left having failed to shine at football or rifle drill and having acquired, as Eric noted with a touch of irony, 'a name that will never be forgotten for the rest of the war'.[12]

After weeks of square-bashing, 'useless' slow marching and exhausting exercises, Plymouth Citadel, where he arrived in the second week of May, was an altogether more agreeable experience. The town itself was a shambles of bombsites and ruins scarring the historic centre: as an important naval base, it had been targeted by some of the heaviest air raids of the war, including several in quick succession during the previous spring. According to Eric, there wasn't much left of 'the best of the town'. By comparison with what he'd seen of London's damage, he considered Plymouth to have suffered far worse destruction. Not that he had much time for sightseeing of any description: the training here was no less rigorous and soon enough he was 'sweating like Hell' on the ramparts above the broad waters of Plymouth Sound. At least the drills served a purpose: for the first time since joining the Royal Artillery, he was beginning to learn what it was to be a gunner.

Along with six other members from the old South Devon 13 Troop, Eric found himself drilling as a member of a nine-strong team on one of the 6-inch guns that formed part of the port's extensive coastal defences. It proved a steep learning curve. 'There is a hell of a lot to learn in this game,' he admitted in his first letter home from Plymouth. Everything, he said, had to be done 'at the double', including lifting and carrying 100lb shells. But he assured Maud that it wasn't as hard as it sounded and was certainly nothing like as bad as life at Paignton. 'I think we have the best Sgt here [and] we have a jolly good officer. He treats us just like a father, and unlike SD [South Devon] he is with us all the time. At SD we never saw one and I think he should be with us.'[13]

Writing on 23 May, he gave Maud some insight into their daily routine:

> We get up at 6.00, clean up our room, which by the way is king to what it was at SD, we polish the floor every morning and everything looks fine when it is done, and then we have breakfast at 7.00, then parade at ten to eight and then all day we do different things, about ½–¾ of an hour on each, and so it goes on all day when we do our gun drill... As soon as we get to the gun shed we have to put on our gym shoes so that we can move on the quick. In each gun team there are nine men and they are posted as follows – Nos 1 2 3 4 5 6 Rocking Bar Layer (7), Auto Site Layer (8) and Setter for Range (9), and at the order 'take post' we all run like mad to our different places, and from then on No 1 takes charge and gives all the orders. Ever since we have been here I have been No 1, but that is only while we are here, because when we get posted to an action post it is a full Sgt that is No 1, and by God, to be a full Sgt you need to know something I can tell you...[14]

Eric and his comrades were learning that there was far more to gunnery than lugging shells and firing guns. Much of the information they were absorbing was coming not in the claustrophobic confines of a 'gun shed', but in the form of a steady stream of lectures. So much so that it seemed at times to Eric as though he was back at school. He assured Maud:

> I'm trying as hard as I can to get on, but you know what a memory I've got and I'm afraid that I won't be able to manage it,

> but we will see... I never would have thought that there could have been so much to it. Every day we get something different and they expect you to know everything they told you the day before.[15]

Yet no matter how hard things got, Eric only had to remind himself of the miserable times at South Devon Camp to lift his spirits. 'After what we had to go through at Paignton, this is a holiday, here we use our heads instead of our feet.'[16] Contrary to his early fears, his habitual forgetfulness was no obstacle to advancement. Diligent and keen, he proved a quick learner. Not only was he made commander of his gun team, a role normally taken by a senior NCO, but he was also selected for specialist training. By June, his letters carried a new unit address. No longer was he in C/70 12 Troop. He was a member of C/70 Specialist Troop and the pride he felt in his rapid progress was evident in his letter home:

> My Darling Maud,
> As you can see I am now among the cream. Every troop of 50 that comes here, the officer picks 10 to take this specialist course, so I am lucky, or at least up to now we think we are, but we haven't started our new job yet. The other chaps went off this morning but 2 of my mates are with me here and one of them is in the same room as me. There are 3 of us in this room and it is on the top floor with polished lino... and there are 5 more on the floor below. We all more or less go about together so we are lucky...[17]

There were additional perks. As well as living in the relative comfort of pre-war married quarters, the specialists were released from the dull routine of fatigues and the boredom of guard duties. More than that, they were rewarded with ten late passes a day between forty-two men, which meant that they could enjoy a night out virtually every fourth day if they wanted. 'It will cost 2/6 to talk to us now,' Eric joked, but on a serious note, the best thing of all about being a specialist was the opportunity for him to be briefly reunited with Maud. 'We can have a weekend if we want it, so what do you think...' he wrote to Maud enthusiastically. 'I wouldn't have been able to get one if I had gone with the others...'[18]

Emotions, once so raw, had softened. As ever, time was proving a healer. A throwaway line from Eric about food shortages had prompted a wave of food parcels and regular supplies of 'fags'. The cigarettes were always welcome, even if the food occasionally missed the mark:

> Maud dear, thanks very much for the parcel, those fags were a godsend, but darling, if you don't mind, don't send anything that is unpacked because it goes bad. That veleta cheese went bad, and all those fruit pies too because we don't get any bread to put the butter on. So, duck, while it is so hot here all you need send is a cake. I would like that very much. I'm very sorry about the other, darling, and I hope you won't be mad at me. Thanks for the tomatoes. They were lovely xxx.[19]

What he wanted more than anything was a new photo of Maud. Letter after letter was punctuated with the same plea. 'It would help a lot just to see it now and again,' he wrote on 27 May, closing with the underlined plea: 'PS, Don't forget the photo please'. He was clearly missing Maud and the comforts of the home they had worked hard to create. 'I am thinking of you all the time,' he wrote in one letter.[20] Then, in another, written a few days later, he added, 'Gee, I wish I could see you even if only for a short while, but we will have to wait a little while yet and then!!!'[21]

Mixed in with the longing were pangs of guilt at having left his wife to shoulder the burden of holding down a job while at the same time running the house and looking after Bobby. Maud was working at a 'secret factory', established in a disused sandpit on Dartford Heath, where aircraft guns and signal-flare pistols were manufactured. Initially, her routine involved leaving Bobby with his aunt and uncle in Waterdales while she caught two buses to get to work. When that became too much, she switched to spending weekdays at her parents' house in Crayford while Bobby attended a nearby nursery, and returning home to Northfleet at weekends.[22] Eric worried that it was too much for her and would make her ill. 'I shall be glad when it is all over so that we can all come home again,' he wrote on 3 June. 'It doesn't seem right that mothers should go to work and come home to more…' Again, a few days later, he continued along the same lines, 'It doesn't seem right that we should be having a fairly easy time of it and the wives should suffer.'[23]

That was the crux of it. Aside from worrying about Maud and Bobby and neighbours' dogs digging up his precious garden, Eric had little to complain about. In fact, on balance, a recruit's life didn't seem at all bad. Even in blitzed Plymouth there were dances and shows to attend. Best of all though, were the excursions across the bay to Whitsand in Cornwall, which stirred happy memories of pre-war seaside jaunts:

> Well dear, when we got off the ferry we had to walk for about three quarters of an hour and the walk was through some of the best country

> I have ever seen. I have heard a lot about Cornwall, but you have to see it to believe it. We got off the ferry at a place called Millbank and then walked to a little place called Whitsand Bay and it is impossible to tell you in a letter what it is like. From the little village you walk up a steep hill for 2 miles and then you are 300 feet above the sea, and as you look down the people look like peas. To get down on to the beach there is a pathway cut in the cliff and it zig-zags for about 2 miles before you come to the beach. And the beach is ... like it is at Dymchurch, and all over the place there are great big rocks, some as big as 3 or 4 of our gardens at home put together; and the sea was coming in when we got there and the breakers were rolling in just as they do at Dymchurch, but I think I can say that it is the best place I have ever seen in my life... I wish you were here with me duck, you would have liked it. After the war we shall have to see if we can't get there...[24]

As well as the diversions, Eric was also enjoying basking in his own success. His increasing proficiency and growing prowess as a gunner had earned him praise and recognition. His gun crew had already been proclaimed the 'cream of 12 Troop' and he was proud to be listed among an elite cadre of recruits assigned for more specialist training, even if the work, which he felt was akin to night school, left him wondering 'if I'm on my head or my heels'.[25] The truth was that he was doing well and climbing the ladder. Just before joining the new course, he had passed his semaphore test and, despite being one of the older recruits, had sailed through all of the fitness tests but one – the mile run – which he attributed to 'too much smoking'.[26] Every minute of every working day seemed to be consumed with acquiring new skills. It was as though he had been eating, drinking and sleeping guns and gunnery for a solid month, but soon it would be over. As long as he passed his exams, he could look forward to an active service posting that would at last represent the fulfilment of his mission to be gainfully employed in the nation's military war effort.

His brain fairly fizzed with possibilities. 'I wonder where?' he wrote. For a brief moment he allowed himself the luxury of daydreaming about where he might end up: perhaps Scotland or somewhere else along the south coast, maybe Wales or places on the other side of the world, such as Australia or India. In fact, it would turn out to be none of those places. His next posting was to a place altogether different from anywhere he could have imagined, for an assignment where all his training, all those relentless drills and taxing lectures, counted for absolutely nothing.

Fate, it seemed, had something else in store for Gunner Harden.

4

Medical Matters

On 17 June 1942 Gunner Harden was suddenly a gunner no more. His past, it seems, had caught up with him as he found himself posted not to a war zone, not even to a gun battery, but to No. 1 Depot of the Royal Army Medical Corps (RAMC).

None of his surviving correspondence gives any clue as how this came about, but it is clear from his letters that the transfer from the Royal Artillery was not of his doing and certainly not what he wanted. The most probable explanation for this sudden and unexpected turn of events was that the slow, grinding wheels of military bureaucracy had belatedly recognised that his first-aid qualifications gained as a long-standing member of the St John Ambulance Brigade rendered him rather more valuable as a medic than an artilleryman, particularly at a time when trained medical personnel were in such short supply. Whatever the truth, there was no hiding his disappointment as he reverted back to Private Harden and headed north to the hutted encampment known as Boyce Barracks at Crookham in Hampshire.

'I wish I was in the RAs,' he lamented in a letter written a few hours after arriving, 'you get used to what you start in, and get proud of your unit and don't like leaving it.'[1] Harder still to bear, after so many personal sacrifices and so much hard work, was the depressing prospect of starting from scratch again in a strange environment.

The camp itself was huge, with 5,000 mostly new recruits crowded into the 'spider' block barracks. Built in 1938, the barracks had been taken over by the RAMC as a replacement for the Haig Lines, an antiquated First World War vintage camp 1½ miles away. Covered corridors linked the prefabricated single-storey quarters to central administration offices and dotted around the camp was a cinema, a gymnasium and shooting ranges. A large and pristine parade ground helped make for an intimidating introduction. 'Boy, what a camp it is,' Eric observed. 'It spreads as far as the eye can see, and clean! I've never seen anything like it. I couldn't begin to tell what it's like here. You have to see it to believe it and bull-shit, blimey, there's tons of it here. I thought we were strict at the citadel but this beats it hollow.'[2]

Fed-up and bored by the idle monotony of another training camp with its petty disciplines, he found it hard to find anything positive to say about Boyce. 'It's not much of a place,' he told Maud. 'It's right out in the country and there's nowhere to go and nothing to do and nobody to do.'[3] Worse still, there wasn't anywhere to indulge his passion for swimming, and all of that at a time when he learned his old friends in the specialist troop back in Plymouth were going down to the pool 'every day for PT'. So wretched did he feel that he even grew nostalgic about his days at South Devon Camp: 'I'd ten times rather be back at Paignton than here.'[4]

His mood wasn't helped by nagging doubts about his performance in an exam he'd taken shortly after arriving. Having sailed through the first test, he thought he'd done enough in the second to gain the pass he needed to become what was known as a nursing orderly 3. Success would mean not only an extra 9*d* a day in his pay, but a posting to a hospital or field ambulance unit within a month or so. The consequences of failure, however, didn't bear thinking about. The longer he went without hearing anything the more agitated he became. 'The worst of it is, if I did fail I shall have to stay in this god-damned place for about two months more. If that's the case, I will ask Bill to get me in the Navy. I can't get back in the RA now.[5]

As in Plymouth, however, his pessimism proved unfounded and by mid-July he was preparing to leave Boyce and pitying the 'poor buggers' who were just arriving. Any sense of joy, however, was tempered by the belief that he was being posted to a hospital near his old stamping ground in Paignton, which was just about the furthest possible place from Northfleet he could have been sent. Meanwhile, his cack-handed attempts to make light of the situation backfired badly. Feeling compelled to explain himself, he wrote:

> Maud dear, you say in your letter that I don't mind going back, you are wrong there, sweetheart. Although it may seem that I don't mind, believe me I feel like crying just as much as you, but what good would it do. I would still have to go... I haven't met the chap yet who wants to go back. It's just I suppose that we try to make out that we don't mind.[6]

It was not the first time he had put his foot in it and not the first time he had got things hopelessly wrong. In fact, his luck was about to change for the better. Instead of going to Paignton, he was instead posted to the Royal Herbert Hospital in Woolwich. Sited on Shooters Hill, the imposing array of six parallel ward blocks was a monument to Florence Nightingale. Designed by her nephew, they were opened nine years after the Crimean War in which she had highlighted the plight of sick and injured servicemen. Unfortunately, while medicine had moved on, the buildings had scarcely changed at all. More than seventy-five years after they were opened, they retained a grim Victorian air that can hardly have been conducive to a sense of wellbeing.

Little is known of Eric's work there between July and September 1942 as only one letter from this period has survived. In it, he wrote of being employed as a nursing orderly on the wards. He did not specify which wards or what his work entailed; however, his duties certainly held little appeal. 'I shan't like it at all,' he admitted to Maud. 'Not many of the chaps here like the wards, but I shall have to put up with it, for a time at least.'[7] Quite what he disliked about the work is unclear. His letter gave no clue, though as a St John Ambulance man with experience of dealing with Blitz casualties it is difficult to imagine his objections were the result of any squeamishness on his part. More likely, given his past comments, his grouse had something to do with the dull routine, which was broken only by the occasional air raid. Either way, the compensation of being a short train ride from home more than made up for any discomfiture at work.

Having seen Maud only once in three and a half months, he was now able to make regular visits to Northfleet, even if it meant having to 'run like mad' to catch the train back to Woolwich. 'It's nice to be able to pop home now and again... isn't it duck?' he mused, already looking forward to the next visit. 'If I can get home next Monday, duck, I think I'll come down even if I only walk to work with you... Expect me when you see me from now on.[8] After so many weeks away, he couldn't get enough of home. But it couldn't last, and it didn't.

On 12 September he received his marching orders to proceed to 12 Holding Depot in Leeds. Typically, he missed his train – 'you know what I'm like when it comes to trains, don't you dear?' – and reached his temporary base just in time to fill a mattress cover with straw before settling down for the night. He woke to find himself in a terrace of tiny 'two-up, two-down' houses that had been requisitioned by the army for billeting RAMC troops waiting to be drafted to units.

Conditions in Harehills Lane were primitive. According to Ted Finch, a former boy recruit who followed Eric north from Boyce Barracks to Leeds, the houses offered little by way of home comforts. 'It was a ghastly place,' he recalled:

> The main problem was lack of heating. There was never sufficient fuel provided by the army. The result was, if anything was made of wood we nicked it and put on the fire. That meant there were no banisters left, a fair number of floorboards were missing along with the odd step on the staircase so that you had to take the stairs two at a time.[9]

Eric found the freezing weather and the more or less constant rain dispiriting. So much so, that the decision to allow them a pail full of coal a day was cause for special celebration. 'That only means a fire in one room,' he pointed out, 'but it is better than nothing.'[10]

Meals were taken in a nearby hall, where an inscription taken from Dante's *Inferno* offered an unusual but not entirely inappropriate greeting: 'All hope abandon, ye who enter'. There, they paraded each morning before being parcelled off to parts of the city on fatigues, filling boxes of food and cleaning buildings or to take part in route marches. Given a choice, Eric preferred the marching. It gave him a chance to see the countryside, and 'lovely' countryside it was too. One morning, after pitching some tents, he and about eighty others clattered out of town, walking and running for about 6 miles in PT vests, shorts and army boots: 'You should have heard the row we made.'[11] Another time, he was able to explore further afield as he accompanied a sergeant to Farley Bridge to escort a prisoner out of detention. The landscape with its plunging valleys and soaring hills flecked with autumn-tinted woods made a deep impression. Struggling to find words to do the scenery justice, he wrote to Maud: 'You have to see it to appreciate it ... but really, dear, I think it was as good as anything I've seen in Kent.'[12]

Such brief escapes were cherished. With no prospect of leave until he was drafted and no idea of when that might be, it was hard to remain cheerful. 'One chap ... has been here 18 weeks ... and lots of chaps have been here from 10 to 15 weeks,' he wrote.[13] As the waiting dragged on, the discipline appeared ever more draconian. 'I'm not in the army now,' he wrote home, 'this is the RAMC... They are ten times more strict ... than they were in the RA.' By way of example, he cited the case of a 'chap [who] got seven days last week for not saluting an officer in the park'.[14]

Carmarthen, winter 1942. 'From what I can gather, they do everything bar kill you here...' (Royal Marines Museum)

Before long, however, he had other troubles to contend with, troubles that were entirely of his own making. It all began with a letter to Maud in which he described a Sunday night out at the local Toc H (a charity-run social club for servicemen). After a concert and singsong, he told her that he and his mate had taken two sisters home. 'The one I was with is married and her husband is in India,' he added.

> When we got to their house, she asked us in to supper and, a funny thing dear, her father (she lives with her mother) has a butcher's shop and they are jolly nice people too, and Con, that's the married one's name, is a jolly nice girl; and, of course, as soon as I knew he was a butcher we were well away, nobody else got a look in. We sat there talking butchers till about 11.30...[15]

Then, having clearly not heeded the lessons of South Devon, he proceeded to dig an even bigger hole for himself. 'If we can manage to get you up here you will have to meet Con,' he added in another letter. 'She is nice and she is just like you, willing and would do anything for anybody and I think myself very lucky that out of all the chaps up here, and who got into Toc H feasting their eyes on her, that she picked me to see her sometimes.'[16] With breathtaking naivety, he not only continued to meet up with Con, but carried on telling Maud all about it. The repercussions were as distressing as they were predictable and they rumbled on even after he left Leeds at the end of October and headed off to join 222 Field Ambulance at Pen-y-Coed, near St Clears in a remote corner of Carmarthenshire.

For several days the correspondence was as intemperate as the weather in the 'wilds' of Wales. In answer to one particularly vexed letter, Eric responded with a display of defiance: 'I was more than sorry to leave Leeds ... and Con as well. She was a nice girl. She was very much like you sweetheart in every way. I think that's why I liked her. We went about together a lot the last fortnight and I kissed her once...'[17] Maud was incandescent. She wrote, making her feelings plain, prompting a chastened Eric to reply:

> I have just received your letter, I won't say nice letter, but I suppose it did seem a bit thick to you. But you know, darling, that you are all wrong, don't you? Say you do, duck, because we don't want to start being nasty, not just now anyway, because it may be a very long time before we see each other again... I'll try and make this letter one to tell you how very wrong you were to write me that letter. I know, darling, it is rotten for the wives to be left and to slog their guts out for us in the army, but believe me, sweetheart, we don't have it a bed of rose, not by a long chalk. At Leeds, just for a short time, I did have a nice time but you don't begrudge me that do you, darling xxx because, believe me, there was nothing in it. But by your letter it seemed as if you thought there was... Even now I can't think what I wrote to upset you, but anyway we will let it sweat... I wish you could be here with me dear, there are some lovely walks around here, and [we] couldn't help but be nice to one another. But there I go again, writing a love letter and it's ten to one you'll find something fishy in it, so I'd better keep off that line, eh?[18]

He closed with 'wishing, oh so much, that I could be with you and Bobby again' and signed it 'Eric, who loves you so much but you don't seem to know it somehow'.

After that things quietened down a little, until, that is, he put his foot in it again. Writing home in November he mentioned, in passing, that he'd received two letters from Con, in one of which she'd enclosed a 'little white elephant' as a keepsake. 'She wants something from me,' he added. 'Do you think it would be all right if I did send something? One of those silver football medals, or something like that, but, please, darling, if you don't want me to just say the word.'[19] It was tantamount to lighting the blue touch paper. Another explosive exchange ensued in which old wounds were reopened before Eric tried to make amends. 'I do feel a bit sorry now,' he wrote, 'but more sorry to think that you don't trust me. Do you really think I'd carry on like they do at work, Maud? Hasn't it struck you, duck, that the girl and I were just friends? She was married and lived up to it. I was married and did the same. We could do no more could we? She saw all our photos and I saw hers. But enough of this...'[20]

If not entirely forgotten, the matter was, at least, set to one side. What had seemed to Eric an innocent friendship, a means of escaping the loneliness of another posting far from home, had, he felt, been blown out of all proportion. He may have been thoughtless, but he hadn't misbehaved. Everything had been, as he put it, 'above board'. It was a storm in a teacup, pure and simple, and, in any case, he had plenty of distractions to keep him from dwelling too long on what he considered Maud's silly jealousy.

Roughing it with 222 Field Ambulance in the rain-swept hills of Carmarthenshire represented a considerable step up in the hardening process for a unit being prepared for the harsh realities of war. Eric was billeted amid a mud-swill of a pig farm, 5 miles from the coast and half an hour's walk from the nearest village, with an animal pen for his sleeping quarters. 'I could say a lot about this place but it wouldn't be nice, so I won't say it,' was his first, less than enthusiastic reaction. 'From what I can gather, they do everything bar kill you here. 30 or 40 mile rout [*sic*] march [in] full pack ... and sometimes a stretcher with patient as well.'[21] However, as he pointed out to Maud, he was prepared to put up with all of that for the simple reason that they were gearing up for active service. 'Very soon, we (that is 222) are going on a big job,' he said, 'that's as much as I can tell you now.'[22] Whether he knew more is uncertain, but after almost seven months of inaction he was buoyed by the very thought of it. 'I think I might enjoy this life, duck, now that I'm really going to start to do something,' he wrote. 'Up to now I have only been messed about from one place to another.[23]

Rumour had it that they would be training in Wales for a month, followed by a spell in Scotland. The more intense the preparations were, the more Eric seemed to enjoy it. In fact, he was feeling 'as right as rain'.

He even changed his opinion about his new surroundings. 'We are nice and comfortable in these sties, duck,' he wrote. 'We sleep much better than we did at Leeds and the food is a lot better and more of it.'[24] Writing to Maud, he made light of camp life, with baths in iron bins normally used for cooking pig food and church services in barn lofts. 'Well duck, we're not too bad in Piggie-Willie,' he joked. 'We have a grunt at Pork Bros next door now and again, but the piggie babs up yonder are not too bad. In fact, everybody takes it pretty well. I suppose it's because things are so bad here that we all make a joke of everything.'[25] In another letter to Maud, he made a fist of trying to explain his feelings about living in the 'mud and splosh' of the back of beyond.

> Not only me, but chaps who have been in it for three years say that this is the worst place they have been in or have seen. And because it is so bad, no one gives a damn what happens and we all more or less enjoy it because we know that we are having it worse than anybody else. But that doesn't mean that you have to worry over me, dear. I haven't got to that stage yet ... really, dear, I like it here. It makes you tough.[26]

As winter came on, temperatures plummeted. Most mornings the ground was coated with a hoar frost that looked 'just like snow'. Some days it was so cold that the pipes froze and on one occasion they had to filch half a bowl of water from the boiler to wash in, but no matter how bad the weather was, there was no letup in the punishing training schedule. In one of their final fitness tests, the medics slogged across 18 miles of rough countryside at night. The moon was up and frost had just started to form a sparkling shroud across the hills as they headed off, squelching through mud up to the tops of their boots. 'Gee, did we go some,' wrote Eric.

> There were six sections went. We were the fourth to start and our Sgt was a big chap, about 6ft 6ins I should think, and he took long strides. Well, anyway, we were the first home and was I ready to drop too. But I enjoyed it, hard as it was. And anyway, we shall have worse next week I expect. But I don't mind it a bit as long as I know that I'm doing some good and not wasting time.[27]

It was, indeed, the ideal preparation for Scotland, where they headed in the last week of November. They were bound for a fortnight's special training at Castle Camp, Inveraray on the shores of Loch Fyne in Argyll. Armed with a cake baked by Maud, Eric bade farewell to Wales with a brief letter written in haste, in which he sought, once and for all, to close the unhappy chapter sparked by his friendship with Con. 'Let's forget all about it and say no more,' he suggested to Maud, 'because I really do love you, sweetheart, and I don't like these tiffs any more than you xxx.'[28] A few days earlier, following news of the 8th Army's stunning victory at El Alamein, he had wistfully pondered the future. 'Wouldn't it be lovely if it were all over,' he wrote, 'and I could be home by the time the roses are out next year.'[29]

For now, such thoughts would have to wait. Everything was on hold. Domestic affairs, personal happiness, even life itself seemed secondary to the greater cause. Right now, Eric thought, it was simply a case of having to knuckle down and 'get on with the job'.[30]

With the Marines

The news came as a bolt from the blue. The first inkling Maud had that Eric was somehow involved with the Royal Marines (RM) was in a throwaway line buried towards the end of a letter describing his experiences training in Scotland.

Written on 8 December from Bucklands Camp in Lymington, Hampshire, where 222 Field Ambulance had concentrated in the aftermath of its Celtic adventures, it began straightforwardly enough. There were the usual pleasantries about post and the hope of a reunion sooner rather than later before he began relating a few stories of his 'tuff time ... up yonder'.

The first one concerned a landing-craft exercise.

> When we were at Inveraray one morning, about 3.00 it was, the boat beached, but, instead of it being right inshore, it beached on a bit of a bank, about 25 yards out. But as it was dark the coxswain thought it was all right and he let the door [ramp] down. The chaps jumped out, but instead of landing on land it was up to our shoulders in water. Four of the chaps got the wind up and refused to jump and they got 14 days CB...

Then there was the day they had to climb up 'a bit of a mountain'. 'It was 900 feet up and in some places it was almost sheer and we had to carry patients down,' he said. 'It's all in a day's work...'

That was when he dropped in his little bombshell. 'We think of going in the marines for a rest cure,' he commented. 'They think they are tuff but when they saw what we had to do they changed their minds. I don't think I have told you up to now, duck, but we are attached to the marines. What they do, we do; where they go, we go also.' With that, he signed off, 'Goodnight Sweetheart and God Bless'.[1]

By luck rather than judgment, Eric had found his way into the Royal Marines Division. The formation, mainly consisting of under-strength infantry-trained battalions filled with 'hostilities only' recruits, had been training in the Black Mountains of South Wales initially in the hope of being employed in the Anglo-American invasion of North Africa. However, Operation Torch in November 1942 joined a long list of the division's abandoned and aborted missions. Since 1940, these had included an assault on the north German coast, an ill-starred expedition to Dakar in French West Africa, a scheme to counter a German invasion in Ireland and plans to seize the Azores and the Cape Verde Islands. More recently, the catalogue of disappointments had continued with the invasion of Vichy-controlled Madagascar in the spring of 1942, in which an independent infantry brigade and an Army Commando unit were used in its place, much to the chagrin of senior RM officers. Part of the problem, however, was of their own making.

The RM Division was an unconventional force with an unusual antecedent. It had grown out of a brigade earmarked as an amphibious strike force capable of seizing a beachhead, either for projected landings or evacuations. Administered by the Admiralty and marine officers who jealously guarded its independence from army control, its direct operational command was, uniquely, in the hands of the chiefs of staff. A by-product of its peculiarity was that it didn't fit easily into any military plan, not least because, unlike army divisions, it lacked a 'tail': those artillery, engineer and medical units that were an essential support to the main force.

It was this shortcoming that the War Office sought to rectify in September 1942 when it agreed in principle to provide the division with army transport and field ambulances. The intention was to mobilise the Marines as reserves for Operation Torch, but it was all to no avail. The supporting units available were insufficient and the offer of American artillery was not enough to make a difference. So the Marines remained unemployed, though with the addition of a field ambulance, among whose number was a certain Private Eric Harden.

Eric's letters home during this period betray only a little of the frustration that was widely felt at such prolonged inaction. Rumours were rife that they were being hardened for the Middle Eastern theatre. The 'big job' Eric mentioned to Maud was almost certainly the invasion of French North Africa, but it had come to nothing, at least so far as the Marines were concerned. Since then, unbeknown to Eric, more ventures were mooted: operations to liberate the Channel Islands and to isolate the Cotentin Peninsula and the port of Cherbourg. All went the same way as all the other failed schemes. In the absence of anything remotely resembling active service, Lymington was a welcome change from the privations of a pig shed in the Black Hills or a freezing loch in Scotland. It offered diversions in the form of a cinema, dancehalls and, above all, the opportunity for more frequent home leaves.

Nine blissful days spent back in Colyer Road with Maud and Bobby over Christmas set the trend, but every joyful reunion brought with it the wrench of parting. 'I'd give anything in the world to make it different,' he wrote after leaving Northfleet shortly before New Year's Eve:

> I feel it as much, if not more than you, but I try and make the best of it. And, darling, I know that Bobby and me and our home is your whole life, and, duck, believe me when I say that you, Bobby, the garden and our home is all that I want although it may seem to you sometimes that that isn't so. I really mean it, dearest, and it does hurt when I have to leave you ... but, darling, if we both try to smile for a while longer it will come out right, won't it?[2]

The constant flow of letters, even when there was little to write about, must have eased the pain. Though not a natural writer, Eric kept up a regular, sometimes even daily, correspondence with Maud and always strove to ensure that there was a letter waiting on the mat when she arrived home from Crayford at the weekend. Mostly, he focused on the light-hearted moments of camp life, but his letters were also a necessary safety valve – a means of letting off steam. The majority of his complaints were concerned with the frustration of inaction and what he saw as the injustices and petty disciplines of military life. Usually short-lived, they sometimes arose out of misinformation and misunderstanding and were invariably accompanied by an insistent plea 'not to worry about me'. Self-pity only rarely intruded into his letters, which were fundamentally good-humoured and full of concern for Maud and Bobby in their daily travails.

Wife and son apart, however, his main preoccupation was his garden, in particular, his beloved roses. 'Did you do anything in the garden?' became a constant refrain. 'I shall have to tell the CO that I want to go home in March to cut my rose trees,' he would quip.[3] Another time, he wrote of bringing bulbs home to plant in the garden and of tending the rose bush he had transplanted while on leave. 'All the flowers and blossoms are out nice here, duck,' he wrote in the first week of March, 'makes me wish I was home in the garden...'[4] Wherever he was and whatever he was doing, flowers and gardens were a constant reminder of home. He rejoiced at spring's arrival, scented with the aroma of different blossoms: 'As soon as you pass one lovely smell another one comes and hits you.'[5] And when a rose bush beneath his barrack room window flushed fresh blooms, thoughts inevitably turned to Colyer Road: 'I hope there will be a few out when I get home.'[6] In their own peculiarly English way, flowers and gardens became metaphors for the peace that he was fighting for, a world secure from the mad ambitions of despots and dictators in which his family could be reunited.

For her part, Maud simply longed for Eric's safe return. She never ceased to worry about him, the more so given his thirst for action and reluctance to accept a 'safe billet'. She learned to tolerate his playfulness and sometimes awkward attempts at saucy humour. A typical example was his tale from the dance floor: 'One of the girls had her foot mixed up with another girl's and tore a lump out of her stocking and the strap off her shoe, no she didn't need first aid (worse luck).'[7] Maud even let pass the unwelcome revelation that he was still hearing – 'twice a week as a rule' – from Connie. As Eric's letters make clear, she had other things on her mind.

'So you would like a daughter, eh? Naughty girl,' he scribbled in January.[8] Then, sounding a note of caution, he added: 'Really dear, if we are going in for another one, and I suppose you will have it, you always win in the end, don't you think it better to wait till this lot's over...'[9] His resistance, however, was half-hearted at best. In the face of Maud's gentle persuasion, he replied: 'Gee, I can see I'm going to have a good time (hold me back somebody), I'm beginning to like the idea, darling.'[10] Even then, he couldn't help wondering if it wasn't more sensible to delay until after the war. 'If you wait sweetheart I promise I'll make you one of the best girls that walked on this earth bar none xxx. I'm pretty good you know, just look at Bobby. That's proof isn't it. I did that I did.'[11] But in all truth, he knew when he was beaten. 'Yes, darling,' he wrote, admitting defeat, 'you have got this idea into my head and as always you win.'[12]

Banter, gossip and family planning aside, Eric had plenty to keep him busy. Attractive though Lymington was, especially in comparison with the wilds of Wales and Scotland, it was certainly no sinecure. Attachment to the RM Division ensured there was no letup in training. The medics of 222 were put through their paces on an assault course that Eric dubbed the 'Grand National'. 'Boy, is it a course too,' he wrote.

'They have thought of everything in it.'[13] With snow blanketing the South Coast, they were also kept on their toes by a round of parades and inspections. Endless hours were spent in 'spit and polish' as Eric grew convinced that his commanding officer was out to make an impression. If so, his efforts paid off. A letter from the GOC congratulated 222 Field Ambulance on its turnout and performance during three months' rigorous training. 'With that the old man got what he wanted,' Eric told Maud on 11 January. 'We are considered the crack field ambulance now and we hope to put the new Combined Operations badge up soon.' Four days earlier, he had noted that 'the Marines are classed as Commandos now'. However, he was a little premature. In fact, there would be several months' more uncertainty before the transformation was complete, during which time Eric's expectations would rise and fall like the proverbial yo-yo.

It was a difficult time, fraught with change that wasn't always to his liking. He didn't mind trying his hand at being a 'spare' driver, but he baulked at the prospect of becoming a store man even if it did come with a lance-corporal's stripe and a few extra bob a week. His army career appeared to have reached its nadir in late January 1943. Following

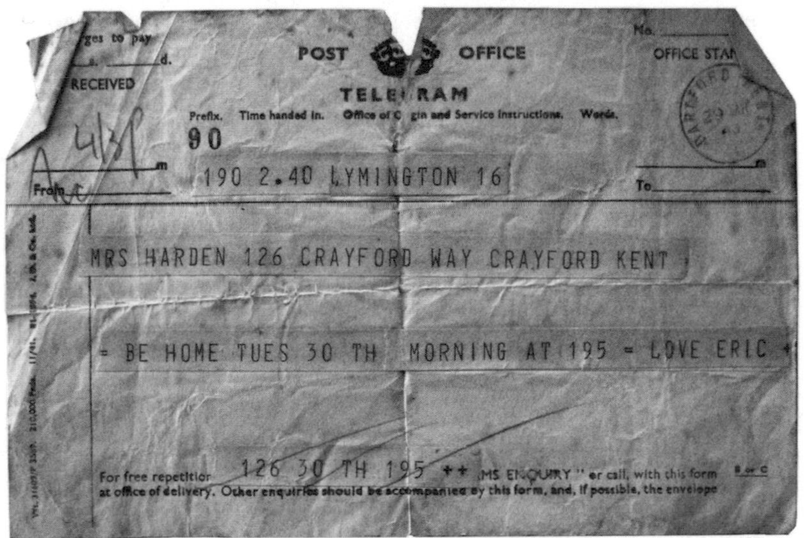

POST OFFICE
TELE RAM
RECEIVED
Prefix. Time handed in. Office of O gin and Service Instructions. Words.
90
190 2.40 LYMINGTON 16
MRS HARDEN 126 CRAYFORD WAY CRAYFORD KENT
= BE HOME TUES 30 TH MORNING AT 195 = LOVE ERIC +
126 30 TH 195 ++
For free repetition ... MS ENQUIRY" or call, with this form at office of delivery. Other enquiries should be accompanied by this form, and, if possible, the envelope

Home leave awaits, 1943. 'We are considered a crack field ambulance now...' Eric wrote from Lymington. (J. Wells)

a weekend spent with Maud, he returned to find himself posted to a medical inspection office in Poole. He had wrongly assumed that he was joining another man as aides to an army doctor. Instead, he discovered he was the only assistant. Moreover, he was expected to administer injections as well as carrying out a range of clerical duties. For all his medical training, the responsibility weighed heavy. 'I have been worried stiff in case I give somebody the wrong stuff or do something wrong,' he wrote to Maud on 29 January. 'The MO is a very nice chap and helps me all he can, but tomorrow I'm going to tell him I can't stand it and to send me back... I wish I could manage the job but it's getting me down and I feel rotten. It's funny how worry gets you down so quick... This is the first time a job has got me down like this.' In fact, he stuck it for a few more weeks during which time his confidence grew, but he never felt comfortable in the role. He missed his mates, the row they made and the feeling of being part of a team.

Maud, of course, saw things differently. All she ever wanted for him was peace and security and a medical inspection office struck her as just about the safest job she could have imagined. What did it matter that it entailed him dealing with a bunch of 'leg swingers'? Eric was having none of it, however. He quickly dispelled the notion that he had landed a 'cushy number'. 'Darling,' he wrote, 'you've got the wrong idea about me staying here. If, by any chance, I do stay with this mob I expect we shall be some of the first to go over when it does start and if I do go back to the 222 I shall still be in the Marines, so, darling, I'm sorry to put you off it but there it is.'[14] Disingenuous or not, he was certainly stretching credulity, but his mind was made up. After a weekend with Maud in Poole, he was glad to return to Lymington:

> Well sweetheart, I've been settling down all right ... this afternoon we had a competition on the assault course. There were about ten sections in it and it was a bit of fun too, I'll tell you. Our section was HQ2. We came in third. Well, duck, it's nice to be back again with all the lads...[15]

After the lonely burdens of the medical inspection office, even the prospect of night exercises and 25-mile route marches seemed oddly appealing, though they weren't without their share of pain. 'Boy, did I have to pay for the easy time I had at Bournemouth,' he wrote to Maud after completing his first 25-mile hike since returning to Lymington.

> When we were about 9 miles from camp blisters began to start. That's the first time I've had blisters. I can feel sorry for the chaps who have them now. I had 4 altogether, three on the left and one on the right foot and one that burst on the way home. And when I got back I had to do two hours' guard... I went to the MI room and cut them all but one and I had to go sick with that one this morning and was excused boots for today.[16]

Blisters healed and bucked up by more regular leave – 48 hours every month and ten days every three months – he was revelling in the physical challenges of training. One night, having lost their way, they spent 5 hours trekking through the New Forest. Another time, they were out all day, marching 25 miles, five of them across rough terrain. During one exercise they were joined by a small dog, which was quickly adopted as a mascot:

> When we had done about 20 miles we took it in turns to carry him because he was just about all in, and if we put him down he would lay there till someone picked him up again. It was funny to watch him, the artful little devil. And yesterday when we were on parade, when the Sgt wasn't looking, we sat him in the front rank. You should have seen him sitting up there, duck. It was funny. The Sgt tried to get him to move but he wasn't having any. Every time he took him out of the line, he would sneak back again...[17]

Amusements apart, they were growing fitter by the day. As he neared his first anniversary of joining up, Eric and his fellow medics were puffing and blowing to complete 11 miles in full battle order in a little over 2 hours. For the first time since Scotland, Eric found himself roughing it for days on end, as gales and rain blew in off the sea:

> There were 13 of us all told with the Cpt and we had to live rough and sleep in the hedges or under a tree or wherever we could make it most comfortable. We cooked all our own food and we were miles from anywhere... Sat, Sun and Mon were lovely and hot. We did a bit of sunbathing in between, and Sun three of us went for a swim... But Tues it changed and it rained for the rest of the week until we were just leaving... I enjoyed the whole week ... and altho' we only had two blankets, gas cape and ground sheet each, I slept like a bug in a rug every night. Sat and Sun night I slept in a ditch (dry) that

> went round a field – we were only about 50yds from the beach – but that had got too wet on Mon night so I moved to another place which was all right until Wed night. I was washed out again, so Thurs I made myself a bit of a tent on some flat ground with trees and all sorts and that was just right...[18]

It hadn't been 'all honey', Eric assured Maud, although he had found time, between 4-hour shifts, to do a spot of 'nesting' and bird watching. One wren in particular caught his attention as it tended its nest full of eggs perched in an overhanging tree barely 15ft above his head. 'Just before it got right dark, the wren used to steal from one branch to another over my head to get to her nest.'[19] The wretched medical inspection office now seemed a distant memory. He was in his element again, warning Maud on 28 April that his spell out in the 'open' had 'put the life of ten men in me'. It was just as well. In the same letter, he gave his first hint of the transformation that would alter the course of his life. When he wrote, cryptically, 'we are going to have a hell-of-a-change in our unit very soon' he could never have imagined to what extent his life would be affected, still less that it would mark a significant sea-change in the role of the Royal Marines as the corps embarked on the next stage of its evolutionary progress towards commando status.

The first signs of change were evident in yet more intensive exercise. Further 'stunts' were accompanied by increasing emphasis on PT. 'The run round the "grand national" each morning was getting too easy for us, so we have to go round twice now,' he wrote, 'and on top of that, now we have a 30ft swinging ladder to climb up and then down...'[20] Though he didn't know it, it was all part of a 'weeding out' process. 'A lot of chaps are being posted to Leeds from our unit in about a fortnight's time,' he wrote on 3 May, 'but it's all right, duck xxx, I'm not one of them xxx.'

The pace was hotting up. One night, Eric found himself part of a force that marched out to a wood freckled with anthills that was to double as their 'landing ground'. He was part of a seventeen-strong headquarters advance party led by a sergeant. They were known as the 'light section', though quite why it was called that was a mystery to Eric given that 'the stuff we have to carry isn't very light':

> We were kept busy all day and Wed night we slept in a field and, believe me or not, duck, although I slept in my short pants with only one blanket, my great-coat, ground-sheet (which was underneath)

> and my gas cape (which I always put right over me when I get into bed), I slept warm and comfortable as anything, even tho' my gas cape was white and stiff with the frost.[21]

Much to his amusement, given his culinary and organisational skills, Eric was cast in the role of clerk and cook till the Friday when they moved to a 'mock' dressing station. There, they tried to snatch some sleep before going on duty at midnight:

> Well, as I said, duck, I always sleep in my short pants and my boots off, the chaps think I'm mad ... but I was one of the few out of the whole unit that had a sound sleep. All the others were frozen stiff. When I make the bed I put the ground-sheet down, sleep on one half of the blanket, pull the other half over me, put my great coat over that, my jacket over my feet, and fold my trousers up and lay them across my great-coat. Over the lot I lay my gas cape. Well, I went off to sleep and remembered nothing until the Sgt called me at midnight. And just after I had dropped off to sleep the wind got up more and it started to rain cats and dogs... I was on the edge of a field and when I sat up the gas cape had been blown away and my trousers were wet through, as were my jacket and trousers. And I had to put them on. So you can bet your life what it was like and was it cold too. I had to bend nearly double to walk against the wind and rain, and it was pitch black too. But, darling, don't go and get put out over all this because I don't mind it a bit... This morning ... we went for a 1½ mile run and did it rain. Next week we have what the CO likes to call a 'sweat-and-rest' week, that is we march 100 miles in 3 days (that is the sweat) and then for 3 days we can do what we like (that is the rest), and I have an idea we shall sleep those three days.[22]

Early-morning runs apart, the next few weeks offered a brief reprieve from the relentless exercise programme as Eric struggled to master Morse code. Every afternoon for a fortnight he racked his brain in an attempt to differentiate his dots from his dashes. It proved an uphill task and he was happy to escape the classroom for an evening dip in the sea or a coastal walk to the accompaniment of nightingales. The recent rains had turned country lanes into a blaze of colour. Everything was growing like 'wild-fire', though even in the midst of such beguiling beauty the shadows of war cast a threatening pall. 'They had a bad raid at Bournemouth on Sat, dear,' he noted. 'Two enemy planes were brought down in the middle of the town besides the bombs that were dropped. I hope they hurry up and start this war wherever it's going to be so that we can get it finished and all come home again.'[23]

Frustration vied with excitement at the prospect of action to come. 'We haven't started on our new way of working yet, duck,' he wrote home on 24 May, 'but when our new stuff is complete I expect we shall be all go.' Eric would have to wait a while yet, however. June brought with it plenty of action, though not the kind he craved. The marching season resumed with a vengeance. An 11-mile trek was completed in 2 hours dead. 'Believe me,' he told Maud, 'it was the worst thing I've had since I've been in the army.'[24] They ran and marched all the way without a break, in shirt sleeves and battle order, through driving rain. 'We were glad of that,' he added, 'even tho' we looked like a load of drowned rats. And, by god, we felt like it too by the time we had finished.'[25] The next day the CO took another party out in an effort to beat their time, but failed, prompting Eric to write: 'It will be a long time before anybody beats that ... but they can keep these records for my part.'[26]

Later that month, Eric volunteered as a medic to accompany a detachment of marines on a ten-day route march. He did so on the basis of a rumour that they might be headed for Chatham, just a short hike from home. As so often, the 222 grapevine proved less than reliable – the destination turned out to be Plymouth! Eric was responsible for ministering to the health needs of thirty-six marines. 'I march at the rear ... about 15 paces behind in case anybody drops out,' he wrote to Maud at the end of the first day's march. 'I don't suppose they have thought of who looks after me if I drop out, but I can have a good look all round and there's some lovely country around here.'[27] It took them more than 7½ hours to cover the 26 miles to Ringwood and another 3 hours for Eric to finish treating their aching feet. 'These marines don't march as quick as us,' he crowed. But, all in all, he reckoned they weren't a bad lot of chaps. 'They treat us like tin-gods when they need us,' he wrote. 'It's times like this that we count as somebody.'[28]

The next day saw a repeat performance. Despite a soothing foot bath in an ice-cold stream at the end of a 28-mile march, Eric faced another 3-hour 'surgery', leading him to comment: 'I hope after tomorrow their feet get a bit better.'[29] His devotion, however, didn't go unnoticed. Four days later, having passed through Bere Regis and Lyme Regis, they had reached the halfway mark and, even with another 100 miles to go, Eric still had a spring in his step. 'I have had a jolly good time,' he wrote to

Maud. 'All the chaps can't do enough for me, you would be surprised, duck. On Wed... the lads went round with the hat. If I had known I wouldn't have let them, but I didn't know until the Cpl gave me 11/6 and said all the chaps thanked me very much for the aid I gave them.'[30]

For his part, and much to the astonishment of his marine charges, he came through the entire march unscathed. Only once had he felt footsore and that was at the end of a particularly hard 40-mile stint, in baking sun, on the penultimate leg of the great trek. 'Gee, my feet are burning with the hot tarred roads,' he wrote. But there were others who were worse off. 'I felt sorry for some of the chaps,' he added. 'They were in bad shape but they stuck it out and unless somebody drops out on the next 6 miles this will be the only lot out of four that have finished without anybody dropping out.'[31]

By the time they reached Plymouth they had covered 190 miles of southern England in seven and a half days of marching, interspersed with two and a half days of rest. 'Not bad,' thought Eric. 'If anyone had told me a year ago that I would have to march nearly 200 miles to get back here I wouldn't have believed [them].' He had never felt fitter. 'I shall be like a Samson,' he told Maud. 'You won't be able to hold me back.' During the course of the march, he had even managed to put on 5lbs. 'Don't ask me how.'[32]

Physique apart, he was also enjoying the company of his new-found comrades. A few days spent relaxing in Plymouth, revisiting old haunts, helped strengthen bonds forged on the march. He found them 'a fine lot' and the feeling was evidently mutual. 'I think the officer wants to try and get me in the marines,' he wrote to Maud. 'He told his batman that I should have been a sergeant long ago. He should tell our CO that, I'll bet he would go mad, eh.'[33]

Eric made no bones about his ambitions to make the grade as a marine commando. He was out to make an impression and he had succeeded. Maud's reaction was predictable. It was bad enough that he had joined the army when he hadn't needed to do so, but to volunteer for the commandos meant deliberately placing himself in harm's way. To Maud, it must have appeared positively reckless and a short leave spent together in July turned frosty. Old tensions resurfaced and priorities were questioned. Back in Lymington, Eric pleaded: 'Darling, will I never be able to convince you that you, Bobby, our home and garden is all that I want. I know that sometimes I upset you but really, sweetheart, it isn't because I mean to, it's just that you take me wrong somehow...'[34] So far as the commandos were concerned, however, there would be no compromising. He had come this far and he wasn't about to duck out now.

Another gruelling 'all day stunt' was followed by a further long-distance march. This time the marines traversed 110 miles across Salisbury Plain, sleeping rough along the way. Eric spent the first night under a hayrick, the next sheltering in a wood and another cushioned by ferns. The sun was 'as hot as hell'. Nevertheless they still managed to clock up 39 miles in full battle order in a single day's march. 'Just as we stopped,' he told Maud, 'a bread van went past so some of us got a small loaf and, believe me, duck, I had dry bread till our dinner was ready. That's about the first time in my life I have been hungry enough to eat dry bread.'[35]

Months of training were reaching a climax. After another day-long exercise, word went round that their fate would soon be decided by a GOC's inspection. There was to be no 'spit and polish' on this test. 'We are to show them what we can or can't do,' wrote Eric.[36] The big day arrived on 12 August. Eric gave no details of what took place, merely noting, 'as far as we know it all went off all right'. He couldn't be sure, of course, but he felt reasonably confident that they had passed muster:

> After today's do, I suppose we will soon be commandos. That's what it was for really, to see if we were good enough for them, altho' we are commandos in everything but name now.[37]

But things weren't quite as clear-cut as he imagined. The next four weeks were unsettling for Eric as well as for Maud as he endured the torture of waiting. Impatient for news of his posting, his mood oscillated between hope and despair. At one point, he grew so frustrated that he put his name down for the Airborne Division. 'What would you say if I became a paratrooper?' he asked Maud, neglecting to tell her that he had already volunteered.[38] The response was entirely predictable, as Eric's reply made clear:

> I have just read your letter you wrote on Sat and, sweetheart, you have put me on the spot this time all right. I thought that you wouldn't mind my being a paratrooper. I didn't expect you to like the idea, nobody does, more so your own wife. It's rotten for all you wives at home, I know darling, and that's what worries most of us who are married, but, you see, sweetheart, I hoped you wouldn't grumble at me and our names have already gone in xxx.

> As I have always said, duck, if our names are on it to go under, we will get it whether we are as we are now with the marines, with the paratroops, or sitting at home by the fire, and so, darling, I didn't think about it twice... I think I was among the first to put my name down, but, please, darling, don't go and worry yourself about it. As far as I can see now we will do 6 weeks hard training, then if we are lucky we get 14 days leave. And, of course, we have to get in them first...[39]

In a telling reference to his status as a member of the RAMC, he concluded with what must have appeared to Maud a less than convincing argument. 'It's easy for people to say "take no notice about being in this mob", but they don't have to put up with snubs that we have to.'[40] The uncertainty about his future was gnawing away at his morale. 'Believe me,' he told Maud, 'we are all walking about like a lot of lost sheep. Don't know whether we are coming or going...'[41]

As it was, his flirtation with the Airborne came to nothing. Writing home on 28 August, he began: 'Well, sweetheart ... you will be glad to hear that the paratroop idea has fallen through after all. There were not enough names sent in...' A few days later he learned that, being over 30, his age would have precluded him anyway. 'I'm rather sorry really because I was just getting used to the idea and I believe I would have liked it all right.'[42] It was not a sorrow that was shared by Maud.

So the waiting went on. 'What will happen now we don't know,' said Eric, probably grateful for the distractions provided by the rough and tumble of river crossing exercises and the physical exertion of cross-country running. More footslogging, night 'stunts' and inspections were interrupted by the 'smashing news' that Italy had surrendered, though even that provoked a degree of frustration. 'If it goes on at this rate, we won't see any action at all in this unit, will we?' he observed, before adding a further question that required no answer: 'That would suit you, sweetheart, wouldn't it?'[43]

In the days that followed, confusion added to the irritation of not knowing what was going on. One moment they seemed about to get their marching orders from Lymington, the next their commanding officer was telling them they were staying put for the foreseeable future. 'We just don't take any notice of anything that's said,' grumbled Eric. 'There is something different every day.'[44] The only certainty, according to the CO, was that 'we are out of the marines'. Disconcerting though it was, Eric barely had time to digest this baffling and thoroughly depressing news when he found himself suddenly on the move with the remnants of 222. 'In a hell of a rush', they pitched up on 15 September at Victoria College, Westbury, a holding depot in Wiltshire. It was a dispiriting place. Eric called it a 'dump'. 'The town is worse than Lymington with no dance hall and only one small picture house.[45]

After a year attached to the Marines, it seemed as though they were, to use his words, 'nobody's baby'. The outlook appeared bleak for 222 Field Ambulance, but not for Eric. In much the same display of nonchalance with which he announced his presence in the Royal Marine Division, he closed his brief letter to Maud with the possibility that 'ten of us might go to Scotland soon as commandos'.[46]

And that was it, aside from the usual 'Goodnight Sweetheart Goodnight…'

The Green Beret

Eric was fighting to stay awake. On the other side of a fireplace, festooned with wet clothes, a sergeant lay in crumpled sleep. He was dog-tired from another long-distance hike in what seemed an interminable sequence of speed marches. This time they'd covered 22 miles in 4½ blistering hours with just a single 40-minute break. The next few days offered more of the same, at a yet faster pace. 'It will be like this right up till we get our leave… that's if I last as long as that,' he wrote to Maud. But there were no regrets. 'I still wouldn't leave this lot of my own free will. They would have to chuck me out. I hope it doesn't come down to that tho'… I like this life. It just suits me.'[1]

He was writing on Armistice Day 1943, from the 'auld' Clyde coast resort of Ayr and a room he shared with another marine. It was a quirk and an enviable perk of being a commando, even one not yet fully fledged, to be accommodated not in some dreary, soulless barrack block but in private houses with ordinary families. That said, billeting arrangements were a matter of chance, and some digs were more welcoming than others. But at 7 Charlotte Street, Eric struck it lucky. His elderly landlady, Mrs Shields, reminded him of his mother and he was happy to be spoiled by her, even if she did serve porridge made with salt instead of sugar. 'She looks after us like sons,' he wrote to Maud. 'She gets us tea after dinner and supper when we get in at night, how's that duck.'[2] In fact in no time at all, it began almost to feel like a home from home, though he was careful not to labour the point. 'I said almost,' and, just to reinforce the point, he added, 'It doesn't matter where you go, it isn't like home is it. And nobody could look after me and make a fuss of me as you do.[3]

Just a short walk away from the seaside esplanade, the lodgings were part of a once-grand Georgian terrace. In more genteel times, his downstairs room would have probably served as a drawing room, but now its generous proportions were cramped by a couple of single beds. As houses go, it may have seen better days, but compared with the dumps he had been in lately it seemed positively palatial. And for 30 bob a week all-in, it represented a comfortable and comforting retreat from the relentlessly exhausting rigours of commando training.

During two stays there in the autumn and winter of 1943 he quick-marched his way ever nearer to the coveted green beret that marked out the men of Britain's elite striking force. His first visit during early October set the trend for the next three months. With rain squalls blowing in off the sea, he completed a 7-mile speed march with rifle and full pack in 65 minutes, trailing in half a minute behind the main body. 'It's the worst thing I've ever done up to now,' he told Maud. 'I was fit to drop when we finished... Three of our RAMC chaps and about 6 marines fell out, so I didn't do too bad.' But he was under no illusions. He knew that first march was just by way of a warm-up exercise. 'Believe me, duck,' he said, 'it is really and truly tuff, no two ways about it.' For the first time he felt glad of the hard training he'd undergone with 'the old 222'. 'We wouldn't be able to stick it if we hadn't had all that,' he reckoned.[4] Even then, there were few certainties beyond the ignominy of being 'RTUed' or 'Returned to Unit', the fate endured by those who failed to make the grade.

Having survived his first stint in Ayr, Eric headed back to the South Coast wearing the lance-corporal's stripe he had scorned as a store man. His destination, after a brief stop at Lewes in Sussex, was the small Hampshire village of Warsash on the shores of Southampton Water and the next stage of his commando training. There, the emphasis would shift from marching to scaling 350ft cliffs and amphibious operations. However, before reaching Warsash, there was a significant milestone in his army career: his initial contact with the unit with which he would be forever associated and with whom he would achieve undying fame. His first mention of any link with 45 Royal Marine Commando was contained in a short letter to Maud announcing his arrival in Lewes in October, but beyond identifying the unit in his address, he gave little else away. In fact, his reticence bordered on the mysterious, with a hint of the cloak and dagger about it. 'There is only one thing I can tell you,' he wrote to Maud, 'this is a very SS job we are on... Please tell the others just to watch what they write, if they write...'[5] Quite what Maud made of it all is unknown, but, for the time being at least, no explanation was offered.

In reality, little about Eric's circumstances had altered. His attachment to 'Four Five', as the commando unit was more familiarly known, merely placed him as a lowly member of No. 1 Special Service Brigade, hence the 'SS'. The unit was a new one, little more than three months old, and its very existence was highly classified. Every move and training programme was marked 'secret', which accounts for Eric's unusually 'hush hush' stricture. Four Five was also still very much in the process of finding its feet and extracting the grain from the chaff.

Born out of the dissolution of the Royal Marine Division, it consisted largely of 'hostilities only' men from the now defunct 5th RM Battalion. As with all the other Marine Commando units formed at this time under Lord Louis Mountbatten's direction, their transformation was not without a degree of animosity from their army counterparts. Since being created out of the 'Independent Companies' raised to fight in Norway in 1940, the commandos had gained a reputation for daring almost unequalled in the wartime British Army. In a period of retreats and defeats, they had staged a series of morale-raising raids against targets along the coast of Occupied France, Norway and North Africa, which had confirmed their status as an elite fighting force. All who served in the Army Commando units were volunteers. That was the main source of early friction between the original army commandos and the new marine commandos. Not only were the overwhelming majority of marines untested in combat, but they were almost entirely 'hostilities only' men who had yet to undergo the rigour of full commando training. Understandably, among the battle-hardened army units that made up the bulk of 1st SS Brigade, there was resentment at the dilution of the brigade's fighting quality.[6] The distinguished commando leader John Durnford-Slater was among those who believed that 'units of conscripted marines could not be expected to maintain the high standard of shock troops'. In short, he was 'dead against the idea' and he was not alone. Lord Lovat, the celebrated commander of No. 4 Commando who took charge of 1st SS Brigade, found the marines 'stiffer and more hide-bound'. He also found their 'old pro' attitude insufferably patronising given that they hadn't the vaguest clue 'what close fighting was about'. Not surprisingly such disquiet filtered down the ranks of the army units who quickly dubbed the marines the 'virgin soldiers'.

Formed at Burley in the New Forest, Four Five was commanded by Lt-Col Charles Ries, a regular marine of 'smart military appearance'. In September, following a short spell at Hilsea Barracks, Portsmouth, the unit headed north to Ayr to continue its preparations for undertaking the full-scale commando course. Originally 450-strong, it boasted five fighting troops, numbered A, B, C, D and E, each with three officers and sixty-two other ranks. A sixth troop, F, contained supporting 'heavy weapons' such as 3-inch mortars and medium machine guns, while H, or Headquarters, Troop was the command and control hub, responsible for administration, intelligence and signals. The medical section, which would eventually grow to contain a medical officer, a sergeant and two privates for admin duties and six troop medical orderlies, were all recruited from the RAMC.

Eric was posted as medic to A Troop and, writing home in November, he told Maud that his job was 'to look after them like we did when we marched to Plymouth that time'.[7] Like the rest in Four Five, marines as well as army medics, he was still on trial. As autumn turned to winter, nobody was guaranteed a permanent berth. Many had already fallen by the wayside and more would follow before Four Five was deemed fit for action. At that early stage, when their future was uncertain and training was fraught with the possibility of failure, it was plain to everyone that they would have their work cut out to stay the course.

Back in Charlotte Street in Ayr, under Mrs Shields' motherly eye, Eric felt he had more reason than most to doubt his chances of making the grade: 'It is every bit as stiff as my mate said it would be, but it's not that, that I worry about,' he told Maud. 'It's if I can stick it at all. Today I had to drop out of a speed march. I'm beginning to think I'm too old for this job after all. All the other chaps are young, between 19–25, and it's getting a bit too hot for me now...'[8]

At 31, he was ten years older than the majority of marines and starting to feel his age. In Warsash the age gap had seemed less obvious. Landing craft in rough seas affected young and old alike. On one occasion the 'boat' did everything but turn over, leaving him feeling rotten with seasickness, but he took comfort from the knowledge that he was not alone. 'A lot of the lads were ill,' he told Maud.[9] Even when things went awry, as they did on one exercise when the landing craft carrying his squad disgorged them into deep water, he was able to hold his own. 'We had to jump for it to get ashore... and, blow me, if the tide didn't go out and we had to swim for the boats to get to the big boat.'[10] Swimming was one thing, but running was an entirely different matter, especially in full kit on ground covered in snow and roads turned to sheets of ice. From 7-mile speed marches to 10-mile cross-country runs and wind-buffeted beach exercises, the challenges came thick and fast. Exchanging rifles for revolvers, at least so far as the medics were concerned, made a slight difference, but not enough for one of them who was sent back to 222 Field Ambulance as 'unsuitable'.

The Commando Memorial at Spean Bridge, a 'speed march' away from the main training centre. 'It will be the worst 18 days of my life,' forecast Eric. (Author's collection)

Tough though it was, Eric knew it was no more than the 'lull before the storm'. Looming ahead of him was the dreaded 'Castle Commando' finishing school with its gruelling assault course set amid the wintry Scottish Highlands. Achnacarry promised almost three weeks of purgatory that would make or break his dream of becoming a commando and wearing the prestigious green beret. 'It will be the worst 18 days of my life,' he forecast. Just thinking about it was enough to make his 'knees knock.[11]

However, the training was not the only thing weighing heavy on his mind. The longer autumn nights had signalled a resumption in the bombing raids on London and the dockside towns along the Thames, bringing renewed anxiety for loved ones back home. Once again Northfleet and Gravesend were in the firing line. In October, bombs laid waste to a row of houses in Dover Road East, killing three people and injuring another eighteen. Bobby's school, Dover Road Primary, had its windows blown out. A few nights later, another deluge of high explosive and incendiaries spread destruction across Gravesend. In Ayr, Eric read the news with growing alarm. 'It sounds as if you have had some bad raids, sweetheart. Gee, I wish it was all over...'[12]

By then, Eric had more reason than usual to worry about his family's safety. In early November, Maud told him she thought she was pregnant. Confirmation followed a few days later. What with the raids and concerns about the family budget, it was hardly the best timing, but Eric was reassuring. Having already convinced himself that the unborn baby would be the daughter Maud desired, he wrote: 'Are you glad, really glad I mean. You are, aren't you? xxx Well, as long as she grows to be [of] a good-hearted lovely nature as you I won't mind a bit.'[13] In any case, he thought 'she ought to be proud of herself when she grows up and knows that she was a commando's baby'.[14] His only worry was that a second child might limit their chances to travel after the war. 'I did intend that we would get about after this lot was over, just to make it up to you.'[15] He was sure they would be all right, money-wise. Since joining the commandos, he'd managed to save almost £5 and he was adamant that Maud shouldn't return to work. 'Cheer up duck and don't worry about a thing except your own little self and look after yourself and take things easy,' he urged.[16]

That was one thing he was not able to do. On 26 November, the 500 or so men of Four Five travelled by train to Spean Bridge, near Fort William, in readiness for their ultimate commando test. Before leaving, Eric was filled with a sense of foreboding. 'I feel fed up with worry if I can do it,' he admitted to Maud.

> I suppose you get a bit fed up with me writing about speed marches, don't you, duck, but do you know what they want the 7 miles in up there? Well, they want it finished in 58 minutes and, gee, you wouldn't believe the difference 2 minutes makes. And 5 miles in 45 minutes. Gosh, the more I think of it the worse I feel about it. And it will break my heart if I'm posted out.[17]

His anxieties were well founded, as Achnacarry's reputation as the toughest and most realistic of battle schools was fully justified. Under the fearsome tutelage of the legendary Lt-Col Charles Vaughan, an officer of exacting standards and former second-in-command of No. 4 Commando, there would be no mercy shown. Based around the baronial seat of the Chief of the Clan Cameron, 'Castle Commando' was every bit as forbidding as its reputation suggested. Living conditions were spartan and the training was harsher still. From leaking bell tents, the would-be commandos were chased and harried across an inhospitable Highland terrain. What seemed a sustained test of endurance began the moment they stepped off the train and speed-marched the last 7 miles to camp through flurries of snow. The march, almost half of it completed at the double, set the tone for the rest of their stay. Ahead of them lay a tree canopy assault course known as Tarzan's Paradise, which featured rope bridges, a 'cat crawl' and a 'death slide', as well as courses in unarmed combat and an expedition onto the wintry moors designed to instil in them skills of survival. Then, just to cap it all off, there were the set-piece 'opposed' landings in the face of thunder-crack explosions, smoke grenades and Bren guns firing live ammunition. Given all of that, there was, understandably, little time for letter writing. What letters Eric did manage to write convey a graphic picture of the demanding regime:

> Well, darling, tonight sees the back of the 5th day, but, gee, the time does go slow up here. We start at 9.15 and finish at 6.45 with an hour off for dinner. The first day we were here everything was frozen solid, including us, but since then it has been rain all the time. I just about managed the speed march yesterday. We have three more of those to do yet and two cross-country ones. They are 25 and 30 [miles] I think. All the other things we try not to think about until we have to do them.
>
> I keep fairly warm in the tent. It's a bit muddy, but we are too tired of a night to notice that, which is just as well really...[18]

The going was tough and getting tougher. Three days later, he updated Maud on his painful progress:

> Well, duck, that's a week of it finished, thank god... We had a day off yesterday, that's the only day we get up here and most of that was spent in camp cleaning, blanco, brasses and the like.[19] We did another speed march today in 62 minutes, the next two have to be done in 58 mins or under. I finished today but had to be dragged in. I don't know yet whether I shall pass this course. As long as we finish with the rest, dragged in or not, it's all right, I think, but a whole lot of the marines were sent back today. Gee, I hope I can do the other two. Just think, duck, another week here and it's just that two hours [that] worries me. Two hours. Mind you, it sounds so easy, doesn't it?
>
> We have to pass out on nearly everything you can think of here. The cliff-climb isn't so good either. Then we have a thirty-mile treck [*sic*] over the mountains and a hundred-and-one other things... If by a miracle I do pass out here some of us stand a chance of going to London. The others will go further north to do the training we did down south. So I hope more than ever now that I pass, Eh sweetheart... Gee, I wish I was at home again. The time goes so slow up here, but it will be worse for the next lot. They will be here for Christmas and they don't get Christmas day off either. That's rotten luck, isn't it, duck. You would think they could let up for just one day wouldn't you, but, no, they are just mad up here and you have to be made of iron. But if it weren't for the speed marches I'd enjoy it. I got a top score with the Tommy-gun the other day out of our troop...[20]

His next letter was sent on 15 December from 7 Charlotte Street:

> Well, it is all over now, duck, thank god. We arrived back home 6.30 this morning. We left camp to march to Spean Bridge at 8.00 last night and caught the 11.15 train. I think I have passed, duck, but I don't know for sure. But if I have I shall be on the 3.25 train from here on Fri and should be home for breakfast Saturday morning xxx Yes, sweetheart, breakfast in bed, Eh? It will be a special train because everybody will be on leave. It was a bit tough the last three days we were there, duck. Everything was frozen stiff, inside the tent was as frosty as outside.

We did our last thirty-mile over the mountains last Thurs, I think it was. We went up and over the next highest peak to Ben Nevis and, gee, it was cold up there too, but the view ... was lovely. You could see for miles and miles all round. I think it is about 2,700ft high and, of course, once up you have to come down again and that was nearly as bad as going up. It shook every bone in your body. One chap in my tent broke a bone in his foot and is still in hospital at Spean Bridge.[21]

Now it is over and we can look back on it. It wasn't so bad really, not much! ... The last three mornings we had to thaw our boots over four candles before we could put them on. They were right stiff. It was funny to see us all with our boots over the candles like that, although we didn't think it was funny at the time. By the way, duck, A2 (our troop was in two sections, A1 and A2. I was in A1) broke the record for speed marching up there. They did it in 53½ mins. That's going isn't it, duck. We and a lot of other sec[tion]s did it in 56 mins...[22]

When we arrived here this morning Mrs Shields got up and lit the fire for us and made us a pot of tea and then made the breakfast. Gee, it was lovely to just sit round the fire with a cup of tea. That's one thing about going out on these stunts, you appreciate a fire and a cup of tea ... all the more when you get back. But, darling, I wish it had been my own home and wife. Gosh, how much better it would have been, Eh? I do hope I come home Fri...

Eric had, indeed, passed. His only regret was that he hadn't been able to write to Bobby for his birthday. 'Believe me, duck, we were too darned cold and tired.'[23] But at least he could now look forward to a Christmas to remember. As he headed south for a festive family reunion he could look forward to the best present of all, an ambition realised in the shape of a commando's green beret.

On the Eastbourne Front

The new year opened with Eric in a buoyant mood. He was taking nothing for granted, but passing the final commando test when so many other candidates had failed was a considerable achievement and a great fillip after all the corrosive disappointments that had marred his short army career. In spite of his misgivings about his age and stamina, he had proved the equal of marines far younger than himself and fully merited his hard-earned place in Four Five. Even the training, as relentless and hard as ever, held fewer fears. Writing home ahead of another round of exercises, he imagined the mud and the drenching to come, but ended on a positive note. 'Take it all round, I don't mind this sort of training. At least it keeps us in tip-top form.'[1]

After a brief stopover in Ayr, on 2 January Four Five decamped to the Argyll coast. Travelling west, beyond the impossibly hilly country around Achnacarry, they braved narrow, twisting roads to pitch up on a rugged, wind-blown peninsula above the Isle of Mull and looking out towards the Inner Hebrides. Life at Acharacle, or 'Ackle Rackle' as it was better known, promised to be every bit as tough as at Achnacarry. There was no NAAFI and little in the way of entertainment beyond an occasional dance accompanied by someone on a dodgy piano and a doddery concertina player, but at least the men were in huts rather than tents. 'The worst part of it,' wrote Eric, 'is it is so out-of-the-way and you can't go anywhere at night.'[2]

Officially styled Dorlin Combined Training Centre, Acharacle was a battle school designed to help commando units to polish and perfect skills in amphibious warfare. Advanced assault training in LCAs (Landing Craft Assault) and LSIs (Landing Ships Infantry) took place on Loch Sunart and Loch Moidart and off the Point of Ardnamurchan, where the peninsula jabs a gnarled finger into the icy waters of the Atlantic. For almost three weeks they faced long hours in tempestuous seas, whipped by winter gales and live ammunition, to practise beach landings in Kentra Bay. Between 3 and 22 January, the marines of Four Five toiled with little break. They took part in four full-scale landing exercises, were instructed in landing craft drill and were lectured on the subject of 'hardening for war'. In charge of proceedings was the chief instructor, Maj. Nicol Gray. Fierce and uncompromising, Gray did little to endear himself to officers or men at Acharacle, but over the course of the next few months the men of Four Five would come to appreciate not just the hard lessons learned on the Scottish coast, but the particular strengths of the man in charge of their training, who would soon exert a far greater influence over their fate than they could ever have imagined.

On a personal level, Eric arrived at Acharacle prepared for the worst and was not disappointed. His sea legs were shaky at the best of times, and winter promised only greater agony. In anticipation of spending 'days and nights on end' at sea and the likely recurrence of the sickness he'd suffered off the South Coast, he asked Maud for a supply of small apples. Someone had evidently told him that an apple a day might keep seasickness at bay.[3] Whether they did the trick, or indeed whether they even arrived in time, is not clear, but he would have need of something stronger than a few apples to settle his stomach on a voyage that few who endured it would ever forget.

Having completed the Acharacle course, the plan was to transport the unit to Southampton by sea, aboard the shallow-draught Belgian ferry *Prince Baudouin*, en route to its new base at Eastbourne. In normal circumstances, it should have been an uneventful passage, but there was nothing normal about the ghastly voyage of the *Prince Baudouin*. Indeed, it was the only time in Four Five's often hazardous history that the entire unit was in serious danger of being lost in one fell swoop. Sadly, Eric left no account of the journey that would be remembered by many as one of the most terrifying ordeals of their commando careers.[4] Others, however, recall a wretched trip that cured many of the notion of ever becoming sailors.

The ferry hit trouble in the Irish Sea when it ran into a severe gale, with winds gusting up to 70mph. In no time, the *Prince Baudouin*, top-heavy with davits strung with landing craft in place of lifeboats, was 'tossing about like a cork in a mill race'. One moment the ship appeared to be in a deep valley of black water, with waves towering above it on either side, the next it was riding high with a bird's-eye view of the wild tumbling waters. Men who had been manning Bren guns as defence against enemy aircraft were ordered below, onto troop decks rank with the smell of fuel oil and vomit. Among the many rendered temporarily *hors de combat* were the colonel and a duty officer who suffered a broken leg after nearly being swept overboard.

So bad were conditions that an effort was made to ride out the storm by diverting into Milford Haven, but the gale made it impossible for the *Prince Baudouin* to make fast to its allocated buoy. After several failed attempts and a near collision with a minesweeper, she was forced to retreat to Liverpool. By then, the winds were gusting at Force 10 or 12 and in the inky blackness the ferry almost blundered into a minefield. In a desperate attempt to avert catastrophe, the captain almost caused another as the ship came close to capsizing under the strain of its sudden change of course. To one marine, it seemed as though the vessel was 'sailing on its side'. Another swore he saw the bridge-mounted Oerlikon guns touch the sea. One of Eric's pals in A Troop, Fred Harris, recalled:

> The ship was now standing on its ends at times. It was literally like a cork. Not too many of the lads were in any fit shape. The heads were full of 'green' men, rank had no meaning at all... Back on the mess decks it was sheer purgatory. There were heaps of bodies, all groaning, some actually asleep, and a few NCOs trying to put on a brave face. I, like most others, just wanted to die...[5]

In all likelihood, given his own record for seasickness, Eric was one among the army of suffering. The torture continued all the way into Liverpool, where Four Five's wretched voyage was cut short. Around 400 relieved commandos trooped ashore, some of them almost collapsing the moment they set foot on *terra firma*. 'My legs felt six feet long and I sort of rolled along rather than walked,' Fred Harris recalled.[6] After a few hours' shore leave, the marines marched from the docks to Lime Street station. Many were half drunk and singing the usual barrack room songs with more than the usual gusto. They were greeted at the station by a withering broadside from the unit's second-in-command, which ended with the immortal line: 'I now leave 45 Commando and I leave them with a nasty taste in my mouth!'[7]

Eastbourne, the next stop on Four Five's infernal and seemingly eternal training itinerary, was a refreshing change after the dubious charms of Achnacarry, Acharacle and the storm-tossed Irish Sea. The war had cast its shadow over this once-busy seaside resort: the 4-mile sweep of shingle beach that curved beneath Beachy Head was largely deserted and the town itself bore the disfiguring scars of its 'front-line' status. Bomb sites and ruins testified to Eastbourne's ordeal as south-eastern England's most raided town. By the time Four Five showed up, it had already endured eighty air attacks with more to follow, but for all that, there was a faded elegance about the place, not to mention some welcome compensations. Leave, though sometimes erratic, became more frequent. There were cinemas, pubs and a NAAFI. There were concerts and dances at the seafront Winter Garden, even if they were occasionally disrupted by the wail of air-raid sirens. More than anything, and for the first time in a long while, they felt settled. For the next few months Eastbourne would be home.

After Bucklands, his time in Eastbourne was the longest time that Eric spent anywhere during his military career, and as it would for many others in Four Five, Eastbourne would leave him with fond memories. Firstly though, he had to find a billet. Some marines, having been told that there were no billets available, took up temporary residence in the Commercial Hotel. The CO, together with his new second-in-command, Nicol Gray of Acharacle fame, and adjutant, Brian White, wound up in the Latham House Hotel with fifteen elderly ladies and a harridan of a hotel manager who maintained a strict 11 p.m. curfew. Others, such as Fred Harris and his A Troop pal Don Vinten, found themselves sharing their rations as well as their accommodation with hosts 'as poor as church mice'. It was all rather hit and miss, but once again Eric came up trumps when he pitched up at 46 Woodgate Road, a large, four-bedroomed corner property not far from the seafront.

His landladies were Evelyn and Dorothy Streeter, a sweet-natured pair of spinster sisters. Socially well connected, they were said to have a family association with the local newspaper. Eric shared the billet with another marine from A Troop, Liverpudlian Walter Bigland, who was more than ten years his junior:

> Seeing that Eric was so much older than me, I just let him do all the talking when we arrived. Nothing was too much trouble for him. If ever a bloke had a blister, he'd come and sort it out right away. That was his nature. He always put others first. He had a good way about him and it worked out well for us in Woodgate Road. It was a beautiful house, absolutely massive, and an excellent billet. We couldn't have wished for anything better and the two ladies were marvellous. Although they were elderly spinsters, they weren't in the least bit prudish. They knew all about life and didn't impose any restrictions on us. They treated us wonderfully well.[8]

In fact, the two Misses Streeter, or 'the girls' as Eric affectionately called them, spoiled them rotten. 'They would put us in cotton wool if they had their way,' Eric wrote to Maud after spending a little over a month in Woodgate Road.[9] The mothering extended to fireside chats, copious amounts of tea and sympathy and the luxury of the occasional orange slipped into their packed lunches. Indeed, on one memorable occasion they slipped in a couple of oranges for each of them.[10] As Eric put it, they were 'a good sort' who couldn't do enough for their young 'guests'. Returning from one exercise looking like drowned rats, they stripped off their sodden clothes and enjoyed hot baths while Evelyn and Dorothy went into action. By the time they re-emerged 'the two girls had made a pot of tea, made up the fire, pulled the two armchairs up ... and made sure they shut the door each time they came in so that we couldn't get cold'.[11] After that they served them a hot supper and later, with their marine charges tucked up in bed, got to work washing and drying their clothes ready for the morning.

Theirs was, indeed, a devotion above and beyond the call of duty. Eric repaid their kindness by helping out with chores about the house. He was happiest toiling in their rambling garden, 'a lovely garden gone all to pot'.[12] It became his project and his sanctuary. Whenever he had time, which wasn't often enough, he busied himself in his surrogate garden, mowing, pruning, tidying and mending fences.

Back home, Maud could have done with a spot of Streeter-style tender loving care herself. The stressful air raids of late 1943 had continued into 1944. Bombs were still falling on Northfleet. One, on 11 February, had demolished a house in Factory Road. The blast had blown doors off their hinges and brought ceilings down in the house where Eric had grown up. His mother, sisters Mabel and Hilda and niece Verity, who all had a lucky escape, were forced to evacuate until repairs lasting months were carried out.[13] During all of this, Maud was trying to hold down a job (she had refused to give it up) as well as looking after Bobby and the house, not to mention the garden. Just to make matters worse, she was experiencing a far from easy pregnancy.

'Gee, sweetheart, you are having a rotten time of it ... aren't you?' wrote Eric. 'Poor old duck, you girls have to put up with something, don't you. How you put up with it I don't know, and you still have long time to go too, haven't you?'[14] Another time, he urged: 'You will be careful when you lift young Bob before and after a raid won't you,' he urged. 'I know it's rotten sweetheart but you mustn't strain yourself

Eastbourne, May 1944. A Troop, 45 Royal Marine Commando, ready for action. Eric was away on a course and missed the photo call which features almost all his closest friends.

Front row (left to right): Cpl Reed, Cpl Doswell, Sgt Shaw, Sgt Gray, TSM Falconer, Lt 'Tommy' Thomas (later MC), Capt. Eric 'Buzz' Grewcock, Lt Armstrong, Sgt Lawrie, Sgt Sweet, Sgt Atkinson, Cpl Porter. *2nd front row*: Cpl Carrie, N. Patrick (later MM), L.J. Lee, J. Barclay, L/Cpl Boniface, Cpl Lee, L/Cpl Stallwood, F. Cramp, L/Cpl Akers, Cpl Bidmead, A. Mitchell, E. Morris. *Middle row*: J. Coulter, (Ginger) Young, N. Brown, A. Allan, F. Cheesmur, D. Vinten, J. Wort, T. Kilkie, F. Harris, T. Lovett, L/Cpl Dryburg, (Dinger) Bell. *2nd back row:* W. Reid, J. Watson, S. Cairns, S. Mundy, J. Haville (later MinD), J. Tew, L/Cpl Findley, Cpl Cook, G. Timmins, W. Barclay, C. Stratton. *Back row*: Cpl Horan, (Taff) Thomas, D. Huggins, A. Mullhall, (Jock) Mair, R. Davis, (Taff) Whitney, P. Cartner, J. Croxon, T. Dawson. (F. Harris)

now. I know it's easy for me to talk, duck. There's not much else you can do, but you will be careful, won't you?'[15]

His letters were laced with concern, sympathy and guilt at not being able to help. April found him in a particularly melancholy mood as he contemplated Maud's 30th birthday, the third birthday in a row they had spent apart:

> As I write this, the sun is out and it is as warm as any mid-summer day. When the weather is like this it makes you think of all the good times we are missing, doesn't it? No more going for swims or tennis or getting the car out and going down to Minster or Dymchurch or some such place, at least not until this lot is over.[16]

He couldn't help feeling his letter 'a very poor way of wishing you a happy birthday', but it would have to do until after the war. 'And then we shall make up for it, eh?'

Next year, he hoped, would be a different story. Next year, he thought and hoped 'most of us will be home and finished with this life for good... If only it were next year now, eh duck.'[17]

If he was feeling homesick it didn't last. It wasn't that he didn't care, he simply had no time to dwell on anything much beyond the daily grind of training geared towards a single overriding objective: the Allied invasion of Western Europe. As the weeks turned to months, everyone, Eric included, knew something big was in the offing. It was not a question of if, but when and where their war would begin. Night patrols and beach landings were rehearsed with increasing regularity, and any gaps in the schedule were filled with yet more marching. Speed marching, long-distance marching – just about every variation on the theme was tried and tried again. By the last week of March the frenzy of activity reached fever pitch. 'If we have many more stunts,' Eric told Maud, 'we will be fit to drop instead of fight.'[18]

At sea and on land, Four Five were pushed to the limit. Officially described as 'advanced invasion training', the focus was on fostering unit élan through teamwork. Mutual trust, understanding and initiative were the watchwords as troops and sections prepared for all eventualities and all manner of combat scenarios. In an indication of what their likely role might be, particular emphasis was placed on contested river crossings. Eric had scarcely set foot in Eastbourne when he found himself slogging through snow on an all-day stunt that culminated in a cross-country hike to a river that they reached around 8.30 p.m.:

> There was no bridge or any other way of going across. We had to swim and it was 10 or 15ft deep in the middle and, gee, was it cold too. It was about 50yds wide. We took a life-line across first for those who couldn't swim. They blew up their Mae-Wests and pulled themselves across. We went on for another two miles and then the trucks picked us up and took us straight to our billets...[19]

When they weren't getting soaked trying to cross rivers, they were getting soaked coming ashore from landing craft that heaved and wallowed as they scuttled across the wintry waters of the English Channel. 'Gee, was it cold … this morning,' Eric wrote of one such chilling exercise in February. 'It was a very flat beach and low tide so we had to walk 2–300yds in water up to our waists and march across country for 5 or 6 miles.'[20] So intense and so relentless was the training that he almost forgot his own birthday. 'We had marched about 7 miles inland and another chap and myself were waiting behind a wall and it suddenly came to me, but it didn't feel much like a birthday then tho'.'

Just as it was in Scotland, Eric's correspondence was curtailed by the endless round of exercises. When he wasn't being tossed around a pitching landing craft or striding out across some field in the middle of Sussex, he was often too weary to put pen to paper. What letters he did manage to write were usually in the form of snatched notes, brief and to the point, scribbled off at the end of arduous days with the deadening prospect of more gruelling challenges to come. Even so, they gave enough of an insight into the back-breaking routine. March was a particularly taxing month: during a six-day period, he took part in an all-day stunt followed by an all-night stunt, an 8½-hour exercise that kicked off before dawn and another river crossing. That same month he also completed at least two 25-mile cross-country marches, one of which ended with his troop having to dig in as though preparing for an enemy counter-attack. 'It is all stunts with us these days, darling,' he told Maud without exaggeration.[21] There was more to come. Much to his evident discomfort, the month drew to a close with a succession of seaborne assault practices. In the midst of one of these, Eric noted sardonically: 'We had a dry landing for a change. We didn't know what to make of it.'[22]

As well as being exhausting, such potentially hazardous drills were not without mishap. Casualties were not uncommon. Most injuries were minor, with medics such as Eric required to treat myriad blisters and strains, but occasionally they were more serious. Writing to Maud on 2 March, Eric referred to one amphibious landing exercise that went awry. 'We nearly lost four of the lads today,' he noted matter-of-factly, 'three of them got ashore alright but the other one is in a bad way.' Exercises involving live ammunition were another source of casualties. A practice attack on a ruined farm above Birling Gap involving covering Bren-gun fire, 2-inch mortars and a smokescreen, dissolved into chaos when a gust of wind blew in. By the time it cleared, eight men had been wounded. In a separate incident, two marines suffered shrapnel injuries when a mortar misfired during a demonstration in a quarry on the outskirts of Eastbourne.

Inside the town, Four Five's training grew ever more realistic, sometimes incongruously so. Around the blitzed homes in Bourne Street, Four Five marines honed their skills in house-to-house fighting with some of them taking the part of Germans. Four Five sniper Eddie 'Tommy' Treacher was one of those recruited to the role of ersatz Nazi. He recalled marching through Eastbourne in full German uniform without anyone raising an eyebrow:

> We went to this housing estate where they were doing this exercise and of course we had to hide ourselves as the enemy and B Troop come in and had to find us, shoot us of course. And, of course, it's all dummy ammunition type of thing, blanks, a lot of noise, and we had to fall down dead. You can't win against the British. So there we was laying in the middle of the road, dead.[23]

From time to time the mock battles and make-believe invasions were interrupted by troops heading off for specialist training. At various times, B, C and D troops departed Eastbourne for spells at the Commando Mountain Warfare Centre in Cornwall to practise cliff climbing and amphibious landings on a rocky shoreline. E Troop meanwhile, spent three weeks of March qualifying as parachutists at the Parachute Training School at Ringway, Manchester. Still smarting from his failure to join the paratroopers the previous summer, Eric tried to wangle a place with them. Once again he missed out, though, as he told Maud, 'it wasn't for the want of trying...'[24]

April saw Four Five reunited as a commando unit. From section and troop training the focus switched to larger-scale exercises, but within the broader framework more specific roles continued to be rehearsed. While prepared for any eventuality, each troop was allotted its own assault task. All seemed to involve carrying heavy loads of equipment. Around 100lbs per man was the average, which seemed strangely at odds with their role as shock troops trained to travel fast and light, deep into enemy territory. Even more incongruous was the thought of having to carry so much gear while negotiating narrow landing-craft ramps and wading through fire-swept water onto an enemy-defended beach. But, like generations of British soldiers before and since, theirs was not to reason why. They merely shrugged and did as they were told. For Eric's A Troop, that meant carrying Four Five's consignment of inflatable rubber dinghies, while for others it involved shouldering bicycles and scaling ladders as they discovered what it was to be combat porters.

By late April, an exercise pattern was established. Firing on the range at Beachy Head was invariably accompanied by the overhead roar of British and American aircraft on their way to France. As planning intensified, the CO's disappearances grew more frequent, and the adjutant took to shutting himself in his office for long periods. The tell-tale signs of impending operations were reinforced by a tightening of security and the peremptory imposition of censorship.

The first of Eric's letters to carry the censor's stamp was dated 27 April. Thereafter, his correspondence was necessarily brief, with the focus on family affairs and such non-contentious matters as gardening and visits to the cinema. Studiously avoiding any mention of the subject that was uppermost in his mind, he wrote instead of seeing Laurence Olivier's *Jane Eyre* ('I think you said you didn't like it, didn't you, duck. I thought it was very good') and about the chances of his brother-in-law Harry returning home from Italy (where he had just been wounded for a third time). Perhaps fearing that Maud might be wary or anxious at his lack of news, he indulged in unsophisticated subterfuge. 'There isn't much to write about these days, is there?' he lied in a letter written on 11 May.

With the likelihood of action only weeks, possibly days, away, Eric turned his thoughts to Maud and their unborn child. He wished that he could be home to keep a careful eye on her, but he knew that that was out of the question now. 'I hope you are still free from raids and getting a good night's sleep,' he wrote. 'Well, sweetheart, you have only another two months to go and I bet you will be real glad, won't you? You are looking after yourself, aren't you dear? Don't go and do things that will mess you up...'[25]

The training had begun to slacken off. In glorious May sunshine, Eric and his mates counted down in a flurry of sporting activity. At football and athletics, it was the green beret *vs.* the red beret as commandos of the 1st SS Brigade competed against paratroopers and glider-borne troops of 6th Airborne Division in a carefully orchestrated programme designed to integrate units that would soon be fighting shoulder to shoulder in France. In between the sports, there were dances, swimming galas and a review of the entire brigade by King George VI. Then, finally, they were off, 'quietly and quickly', on the first leg of an epic journey to war.

They left Eastbourne without fanfare at 4 a.m. on 25 May.[26] Eric spent his last day with friend and fellow commando medic, Sid Gliddon, and a couple of girls they knew. They took a bus ride into the country and whiled away the evening at an ENSA (Entertainments National Service Association) concert before strolling back to their digs to pack. It was an emotional parting. During his four months at 46 Woodgate Road, Eric had come to be treated as the son his doting landladies never had. They fussed over him to the very end, waiting up all night to see him safely off to the station where Four Five assembled for the short train journey along the coast.

The next stop was a vast tented camp near Southampton. It was one of many staging posts along the South Coast where an army of British, Canadian and American troops was gathering in such numbers that it seemed to one marine 'a wonder that the British isles didn't tip up on end'.[27] The 'Stalag', as it was dubbed, was the 'nearest thing to a prison camp' that Fred Harris had ever seen. Security was tight to the point of stifling: military policemen patrolled perimeter fences and every move in and out was carefully monitored. For days on end, the men of Four Five were incarcerated in a 'canvas city' complete with tented library and cinema, playing endless games of cards and watching concert parties strut their stuff. Eric tried to make the best of it. 'It seems to be very comfortable,' he wrote to Maud. 'This life is alright until it rains, then it is not so good...'[28] But he knew, just as all the other marines knew, that it was only a matter of time before they would be on their way. 'Well duck, I don't know how long we are to be here but I hope it isn't many days. This is the worst part of the lot I think...'[29]

After two years and two months of training and waiting, those last days must have passed in an agony of knotted nerves. 'I'm longing for the time when we can all go out together,' he wrote on 26 May:

> I wonder if that will be this year. Gee, I hope so. I have just about had enough of army life... I suppose you still hear all sorts of different buzzes about how, when and where all this is going to start and end. If so, you know more than we do here. For all we know, it will start tomorrow or two months' time, but I do say the sooner the better and let's all get home again...

Cooped up with little to do, his thoughts wandered back to Maud and his garden:

> I suppose, like here, it has been very hot and there must be lots of roses out in the garden. Have you kept them watered as I

> said? And the lawn, that I suppose is getting brown by now. I should like to have been home this last two or three days. We could have spent most of the time in the garden, couldn't we? Has Bobby found any more birds' nests lately, duck? And how are you? Don't forget to be very careful will you, my sweet. It isn't much longer and it will be finished with. That won't be too soon for you, eh?[30]

There wasn't much more to say beyond that which he couldn't say. Except, that is, to mention that he'd run out of his precious Woodbines.

So the days passed, in a mixture of tedium and apprehension, waiting for the order that would send them on their way. In all, twelve days were spent incarcerated in the Stalag and, to the very end, Eric remained a model of discretion. His last letter before leaving betrayed no hint of the emotional turmoil he must have been feeling as he prepared to face his baptism of fire.

Written on 3 June, just a couple of days before the off, it read:

> My Darling Sweetheart
> ... Well duck, up to now everything is alright with me, and I hope to god that it will be so with you, now and later on.
>
> But just don't worry about me, sweetheart. I know that will be hard to do but please try, won't you darling. It has been rather dull here today so no sun-bathing and the dust here gets everywhere. It makes you feel very dirty. It's a good job they have showers or I don't know what we would do.
>
> Well sweetheart, all we can do in these letters is just repeat ourselves, so until I have something different to write about I think that will be all. By the way, we have been very comfortable here except for the dust. Well dear, I hope this will find you still fit and well and not worrying too much. I'll close and write again soon, so
>
> Cheerio Sweetheart God Bless
> Your Very Loving Eric xxx
> For Bobbie [*sic*] xxx

With that, Eric, or Doc as he was now universally known throughout A Troop, went off to war.

Preparing to Make History

It is one of the most iconic images of the countdown to D-Day. The caption simply reads: 'Men of 45 (RM) Commando, 1st Special Service Brigade, in high spirits as they prepare to embark for invasion.' It was taken by Capt. Leslie Evans, an official army photographer, barely three days before the landings in Normandy. Although obviously posed, it is nevertheless a striking representation of eve-of-battle euphoria that speaks volumes about the commando men of Four Five who were about to put months of training to the sternest of tests. In the photograph they are a close-knit band of brothers who have found common cause in their shared travails. Hardened by the withering winds of the Welsh uplands, toughened in the wintry wilderness of northern Scotland, they have attained a peak of fitness. But their faces betray them. Behind the raucous élan, the inexperience is almost tangible. The faces are of men who are, for the most part, little more than boys. Few have reached their mid-20s. Some are as young as 19. Stripped of uniforms and weapons they could be a bunch of football fans celebrating a famous cup victory. They are an untried elite made up of conscripts, 'hostilities only' marines, refashioned and retrained as commandos. None have ever ventured onto a real battlefield before. None have even fired a shot in anger. The nearest any of them have come to death or injury is as civilians during the Blitz that brought war to their very doors. With one notable exception, theirs is the swagger of youth. The odd man out in this carefully orchestrated scene is Doc Harden.

Perched on a strange ladder-like contraption designed for laying across barbed-wire beach obstacles, he sits hunched beneath the weight of his heavy invasion pack. In contrast to the enthusiastic cheers of the much-younger marines alongside him, he displays the less effusive smile of a man older, wiser and, possibly, more wary of what fate has in store for them on some distant shore. What thoughts lay behind his smile as the

The iconic photograph of mainly A Troop men was taken at the Southampton 'Stalag' on 3 June 1944, as they prepared for the invasion of Normandy. Doc Harden is seated on the far right. The full line-up is (left to right): Jimmy Tew, L/Cpl William Boniface (kia 12 April 1945), Jimmy Lovett (kia 8 June 1944), L/Cpl Freddie Stallwood (kia 8 June 1944), Ian Kilkie (wounded), Bowen (wounded), John Timmins (kia 28 January 1945), Cpl David Reed (kia 12 June 1944), Neil Brown, Johnny Haville, Leslie 'Nipper' Lee, holding bicycle (kia or dow 9 June 1944), Robert 'Dinger' Bell (kia 6 August 1944), Derrick Cakebread, Jeff 'Taffy' Whitney, (behind Jeff) Sid Mundy, A. N. Other not of A Troop, Cpl Tasker, 'Ginger' Young (lost a leg at Bréville, 12 June 1944), Fred Cheesmur, and (seated) L/Cpl Eric Harden VC (kia 23 January 1945). The marine obscured by 'Nipper' Lee is Jim Barclay. (via F. Harris)

photographer lines up his shot can only be imagined, but if he is feeling any sense of caution, then it would not misplaced. Of the twenty men pictured, five will be dead before the month is out and three more will not live to see the war's end.

Leslie Evans' photograph, one of the most widely published of all pre-invasion pictures, was taken in the Southampton Stalag on 3 June as the marines of Four Five waited with growing impatience for the off. There was no selection process. The photographer, who would shortly be following them down the ramps of landing craft grounded on the sands of Normandy, merely gathered up the group nearest to him. As chance would have it, all of them belonged to A Troop. These were just some of the men Doc had lived and laughed with over the past eight months, ministering to their myriad ailments as they marched across mountains and moors. In that time a mutual trust and respect between medic and marines had developed. He admired their youthful vigour and self-confidence, while they valued his judgment and quiet selflessness, particularly when it came to providing decidedly non-regulation hangover cures. We have already had brief encounters with some of them, but it is time to properly introduce a few of the men Doc would be responsible for in the tough days to come.

Fred Harris was typical of the young marines preparing to go into action for the first time. A 21-year-old Londoner from east Tottenham who had moved out to Ponders End, Enfield, near King George's reservoir, he was known to one and all as 'Cabbie' for the simple reason that a particular sergeant got it in his head that all cockneys were taxi drivers. Fred, who was working in a factory in Edmonton prior to his call-up, didn't bother to disabuse him and the name stuck. Turned down by the RAF, he joined the Royal Marines, did his basic training at Lympstone and was posted to the 5th Battalion. The following year, he married the Chingford girl he'd been courting since 1938 and volunteered for the commandos. A Bren gunner, he palled up with his No. 2, Don Vinten, and the pair of them quickly became inseparable. They billeted together, trained together and now they were ready to fight together, though, as the great day drew steadily closer, the excitement that bordered on exaltation was, by Fred's own admission, tinged with 'apprehension and nervous tension'.

Also in the same support section was another Londoner, Derrick Cakebread, who exulted in the altogether more predictable nickname of 'Cakes'. Another Tottenham boy who had endured the Blitz, Cakes had been going steady with a girl he'd met at a dance more than three years earlier. A few months younger than Fred, he had followed the same path (via Lympstone, Glasgow and the Black Mountains of Wales) to Four Five. It had been touch and go for a while up at Achnacarry: during the 20-mile route march he'd felt a pain in his foot that Doc thought was a broken bone. Fearful of being RTUed, he struggled on to earn his green beret and a place in hospital where Doc's diagnosis proved painfully accurate. An excellent marksman, he was made a troop sniper: 'I never volunteered or nothing like that. One day the quartermaster came and told me to sign a piece of paper and said "you're a sniper". Then, he gave me a sniper's rifle and next thing I knew I was on a course, learning field craft, snap shooting and judging distances.' It was a role he'd grown to enjoy. He appreciated the independence it gave him and he liked being self-reliant. Too young to be scared, he took most things in his stride, but shortly before leaving Eastbourne he was shaken by the news that one of his closest friends had been seriously injured clearing some mines. It was the first really bad knock he'd received, but it would not be the last.

Like his London chums, Walter Bigland knew what it was to be on the receiving end of German bombs, though his experience was hundreds of miles to the north-west, on the banks of the Mersey. 'Scouse' Bigland, as he was inevitably nicknamed, had enjoyed narrow escapes during the Liverpool Blitz of May 1941. Once, while running messages for his local ARP unit, a bomb had burst nearby, wounding a policeman who was with him. A publican's son, he split his time working in the local Co-op by day and as a Civil Defence volunteer by night. Given the opportunity, he would have followed his father's footsteps into the Machine Gun Corps, but the unit had been disbanded and he decided to volunteer for the Marines with three friends instead. Basic training over, he joined 2nd Royal Marine Field Battery and had transferred to 31st Light Battery as a gun layer when it was announced that the Royal Marine Division was disbanding. Having seen marines training to become commandos, he decided to join them, but a lack of fitness after months of nothing but gunnery drills caused him to think again. After a gruelling route march up and down Portsdown Hill left him gasping for breath and embarrassingly adrift of the main party, he asked to be 'returned to unit'. The man who talked him into staying was Capt. Eric Grewcock.

Aged 25, Eric Grewcock had been A Troop commander since its inception in August 1943. A former 5th Battalion officer, he was an enthusiastic and gifted rugby player. Approachable and encouraging, he believed in teamwork and was a man who preferred to lead by example. To the men he commanded, he was 'Buzz' Grewcock, a nickname derived from his constant desire to know the latest troop gossip, or 'buzz' as it was known, and was universally well liked and respected. Beneath him were two section officers, Lt Bob Armstrong, a stolid, straight-talking Yorkshireman, and Lt 'Tommy' Thomas, a formidably fit South African dubbed 'Sabu' on account of his swarthy complexion, whose fearlessness made some of his marines wary of him.

As well as the two subaltern-led sections, the sixty-strong troop was made up of a small headquarters sub-section, presided over by Capt. Grewcock and including TSM (Troop Sergeant Major) Freddie Falconer, a medical officer and a signaller, together with a support section commanded by Sgt Sid 'Sweetie' Sweet. Support consisted of specialists like sniper Derrick Cakebread and a 2-inch mortar team: Johnny Haville and Dickie Mason, a couple of 'old sweats' and the best of mates, who had served together in the 5th Battalion. They were joined by an extra Tommy-gun section and Fred Harris' three-man Bren-gun section, which was ready to provide additional firepower whenever and wherever the need arose. Then there was Doc, medic and honorary marine, who was every bit as much a commando as the rest of them. He would go into action armed with a new revolver, a replacement for one he'd unaccountably mislaid during a training exercise. Not that he ever imagined having to use it, except in dire circumstances or self-defence. After all, it was his job to save lives, not take them.

Doc was one of six troop medical orderlies. He reported to Capt. Hugh Smith, Four Five's medical officer, who was attached to headquarters with a staff of one RAMC sergeant and two private soldiers. In combat, Doc's role was a vital and potentially hazardous one: to give immediate succour to wounded men and ensure their safe and swift evacuation back to an aid post behind the lines. His job was to accompany A Troop, or any of its sections, whenever they faced the prospect of casualties. D-Day promised to be the ultimate challenge. The fighting was bound to be fluid as well as fast and furious. Everything depended on speed. No unnecessary delay could be countenanced and to that end the marines were ordered to desist from stopping to help any man wounded. All casualties were to be left to the medics.

As highly skilled first-aiders with a rudimentary understanding of the human body, the medics were trained to treat the injured as quickly as possible. The priorities, as set out in the RAMC training manual, were: to prevent immediate death by checking for haemorrhages and breathing difficulties, to prevent any worsening of condition by covering wounds and burns with anti-septic impregnated dressings and anti-infection powder, splinting broken bones and treating shock and, most importantly, to prevent further injury or wounds by getting the patient under cover, something that was often easier said than done. All of this was to be done methodically and without haste. The first principle of first aid was to stay calm whatever the circumstance. After that, it was the medic's job to rejoin the main party, wherever it might be.

During the days spent in the Stalag the daunting nature of the mission and its enormous scale was revealed in a series of briefings. Each unit was assigned its own tent, where maps, sand table models and aerial photographs were available to be studied. To the very end, however, there remained an air of mystery. Security, so rigidly adhered to throughout the training, continued to be applied to the plans now unfolding. The men of Four Five knew they were to land on a French beach. They could picture it with all its distinctive seaside villas. They even knew what landmarks lay beyond it, but what they didn't know was precisely where it was or what it was called. In a successful effort to ensure secrecy was maintained to the last, all place names had been methodically cut from the maps.

The defaced charts, however, were sufficient to show that 1st SS Brigade's D-Day objectives were nothing if not ambitious. Landing in the wake of the assault battalions, No. 4 Commando was to capture a coastal battery on the left flank while the rest of the brigade, spearheaded by No. 6 Commando, drove 6 miles inland through enemy lines to join forces with glider-borne troops flown in overnight to capture two parallel bridges straddling a canal and river. In case of failure by the airborne forces, Four Five were to use the rubber dinghies they were carrying to force a crossing. It promised to be quite a dash. Lord Lovat's plan allowed just 3 hours for them to achieve the link-up, and that was just the beginning of the operation. Once across the two waterways, No. 6 had the job of seizing a village on high ground to the east, while No. 3 Commando and Four Five were to infiltrate along the coast. There, the marines were to capture a formidable-looking concrete-shielded gun battery if it had not already fallen to a night assault carried out by paratroopers of 6th Airborne Division. After that, they were to forge ahead and clear a neighbouring seaside resort. The overall goal of commandos and airborne forces was to secure the extreme left flank of the invasion beaches before dark and to hold it, come what may and for as long as necessary, against the inevitable counter-attacks.

Day by day, minor details of the plan were altered as RAF reconnaissance flights revealed the impact of bombing sorties on the bunkers and gun positions that made up Hitler's much-vaunted West Wall. 'You'd hear one thing one day,' recalled Derrick Cakebread, 'and then you'd go back the next day only to be told the RAF have cleared that one out.'[1] Amid the constant flow of instructions, there were also grim warnings about what to expect. Walter Bigland remembered being among a group of commandos told to prepare themselves for a beach strewn with bodies from the assault landing. Always, they reiterated that 'we were not to see to the wounded' and that 'they were to be left to the medical orderlies coming up behind'.[2] From time to time, the monotony of waiting was broken by inspections and parades. Maj. Gen. Robert Laycock, Chief of Combined Operations, and Maj. Gen. Robert Sturges, former commander of the Royal Marine Division and now GOC Commando Group, both made fleeting appearances. Troop-strength marches were the only means of escaping the Stalag, although even these were accompanied by escorts of military policemen in order to prevent contact with the outside world. Sometimes, just for the sheer hell of it, the marines would break into a speed march to make the 'redcaps' sweat.

Finally, on 4 June, orders came through to pack their gear, gather up all the paraphernalia of war they were to carry into action and parade in readiness for departure. Some made it as far as the waiting transport. No sooner had they done so, however, than they were stood down and told to unpack their kit and blankets and return to their tents. The invasion had been temporarily cancelled on account of the unseasonably bad weather.

The next morning the whole process was repeated, only this time it was for real. Though slightly improved, the weather was still cutting up rough in the Channel, but there was a limit to how long the invasion could be delayed. Orders were issued to 'belt up' as transport came grinding in to the Stalag. Live ammunition was issued and camouflage netting to cover steel helmets was passed around. 'Later, we were told to leave the helmets behind,' recorded Derrick Cakebread. 'We would go in wearing our green berets. We guessed the theory was that Jerry would be so scared at the sight of us he would run away!! We had some doubts about this, but orders were orders.'[3]

Before leaving, the army and marine commandos were called together in a rough circle around Lord Lovat. The brigade commander had decided a 'word of encouragement' was in order. His impromptu speech, part of it in colloquial French directed at No. 4 Commando's two troops of Free Frenchmen, lasted little more than 2 minutes and was well judged. 'There was no nonsense, no cheap appeal to patriotism,' wrote John Day, one of Four Five's officers.[4] Lovat's message was plain: touching on past achievements, he congratulated them for being chosen to fight together for the first time as a Commando Brigade. He didn't disguise the difficulties or the dangers that lay ahead, but merely stressed that the advantages of initiative and overwhelming fire support lay in their favour. 'The enemy coastline would be flattened and defences pulverised before we arrived,' he said encouragingly. 'Three "maids of all work" infantry battalions, landing at zero hour, would clear the beach, then find us exits through the minefields above the tide mark – as easy as kiss your hand. It was all laid on a plate.'[5] He forecast a long day ahead in which the brigade 'was going to make history' and he closed with a word of warning: 'If you wish to live to a ripe old age – keep moving tomorrow.' It was, wrote Day, 'truly inspiring' and 'imbued each man with the spirit of this great task'.[6]

The departure, however, was not without a tragic twist. As Doc, Cabbie, Cakes, Scouse and the rest of Four Five were parading ready to board the transport a shot rang out from one of the tents. There was momentary confusion before it was realised that it had been no accident. Inside the tent lay the body of Four Five's chaplain, a revolver by his side. He had held an inter-denominational service in the camp the day before. It had been well attended but his sermon about 'death and destruction' struck a wrong note. Mutterings about the depressing nature of his preaching prompted a meeting with Lt Colonel Reis where, according to Lovat, 'the cleric was suspended and told to return from whence he came'. His death was listed as a 'battle casualty'.[7]

But the padre was not the only man missing from Four Five as the commando convoy rolled out of camp for the short run down to Warsash. Don Vinten, Fred Harris' shadow and No. 2 on his Bren gun, had contracted mumps while in the Stalag. On Doc's instructions, he was immediately quarantined. 'I couldn't even say "cheerio",' recalled Harris. Sentiment apart, he was left with more practical concerns:

> Between us, we carried a Bren, 12 spare magazines, a spare barrel and a hold-all full of cleaning gear. This was on top of the rucksack containing 36 hours' rations, spare clothing, climbing ropes, grenades, mortar shells and anything else the kind officers and NCOs deemed necessary.[8]

His plea for assistance was met with a sympathetic shrug but no more. 'The sergeant major just said, "Do the best you can 'til we get to the 'other side'."'[9]

And so it was, shortly after midday on 5 June, that he clambered awkwardly onto one of the waiting trucks, weighed down by twice his share of ammo and equipment. Fred Harris was headed to France as a lone ranger.

The next few hours at Warsash passed in a fug of wearisome waiting. Eight months earlier, Doc had dismissed the small riverside village as 'a rotten little place'. To Maud, he had bemoaned the lack of entertainment: 'There's nothing there at all,' he had written. Nothing much had changed,

Warsash jetty, eve of D-Day. The men of Four Five board their landing craft. (via F. Harris)

but at least this time he wouldn't be there long enough to worry about it. In any case, there was plenty more to think about as he lay on the crowded banks of a River Hamble crammed with landing craft, with little other than the wail of bagpipes for distraction.

Embarkation so far as Four Five was concerned began around 3 p.m. The entire commando was to be carried aboard five landing craft infantry (small), four from the 201st Flotilla and one from the 200th Flotilla, which were anchored, line abreast, alongside Warsash jetty. Doc's A Troop, heavily laden with packs, weapons and assorted equipment, clambered aboard the second in line, LCI 530. Flat-bottomed, wooden-hulled and with a dearth of deck armour, it offered little by way of protection from incoming fire and even less by way of comfort. Not that that came as any surprise. After months of training in similar craft, they were resigned to a cramped and wretched crossing likely to be made worse by the dirty-looking weather out in the Channel. A freshening wind blowing at 15 knots from the west threatened nothing but misery in the narrow troop spaces below decks. But all of that lay ahead.

As Commander Rupert Curtis RNVR led Convoy S9 down the tree-lined Hamble Estuary, they were followed by the cheers and shrieks of a boat party of Wrens. There was an air of nervous exhilaration that heightened as the column of landing craft curved out into the East Solent and a roadstead teeming with ships and craft of all types and sizes. Curtis recalled:

> To us it presented a thrilling and unforgettable spectacle, as indeed, we must have done to the troops lining the decks of the transports. For here was a long line of 24 infantry landing craft each with its deck crowded with eager commandos wearing the familiar green beret – and from my bridge came the proud skirl of the Scottish pipes. The sight and sound stirred the hearts of the men in the ships and their cheers echoed from shore to shore of the Solent. I suspect that not everyone remained dry-eyed.[10]

As the convoy took up station in Stokes Bay there was a flurry of last-minute preparations. Codes were distributed and maps handed round, only this time with place names and objectives clearly indicated.

At last, the secret was out: Normandy was the distant shore and the beach at La Brèche, codenamed Queen Red, 2 miles west of Ouistreham near the mouth of the River Orne, the commandos' landing point.

By then, the sky was already darkening. The landing craft were beginning to wallow. Commander Curtis wondered how the commandos were faring. 'Not well' was the answer many would have given. The early excitement had faded. From being keyed up and full of ribald banter, Derrick Cakebread noticed that everyone had grown steadily quieter. 'We were advised to try and get some rest, but that was easier said than done.'[11] There were no bunks and men sprawled wherever they could find space. Those who managed to sleep did so fitfully. Walter Bigland was among those who dozed as best they could. Derrick Cakebread didn't sleep at all. He merely sat with his eyes closed, wondering if he would come through the next few hours and how many of his mates would survive. Many more were soon too ill to think of anything. As the landing craft slipped their moorings at 9.30 p.m. and headed out through the Lumps Fort gate and into the Channel, short, steep waves began to pummel the small craft, causing their bows to plunge and pitch heavily. To Fred Harris, it felt 'horrendous' and the sickness tablets with which they had been issued had little effect. 'Most of us were seasick,' he recalled. 'It didn't help that we'd been given self-heating cans of soup which was all we had to eat or drink.'[12] In no time, the swaying hold was slippery with a foul-smelling cocktail of soup and vomit that made the crossing an endurance test all of its own.

While the men of Four Five continued to wretch, the armada of landing craft sailed on, in the comforting company of a naval sloop. Newly laid buoys marked the entrance to a swept channel that stretched to within 8 miles of the French coast. At that point, Commander Curtis gave orders for the flotilla to split into two columns, LCI 530 taking its place in the port rank. Until now, weather apart, the crossing had been uneventful, but in the darkness the boat crews could see flares falling, 'probably over the coast, perhaps indicating that our airborne men were beginning to drop on to their targets'.[13] Still they ploughed on, leaving slower-moving vessels trailing in their wake. Then, all of a sudden, 'long, flickering tongues of flame' stabbed the darkness. It was the guns of the navy's bombarding force ranging on pre-selected targets ashore. Overhead, a thundering mass of Allied aircraft were heading to the coast to strafe the enemy defences. 'Perhaps one ought to have felt sorry for them,' observed Commander Curtis, 'such was the weight of firepower brought against them, but we didn't.'[14]

Nor, in all likelihood, did Doc or any of the other commandos as they waited for their D-Day to begin.

The Longest Day

Eight miles off the Normandy coast, a flickering lamp pricked dawn's grey smother. It came from the commando convoy's solitary escort. Her duty safely discharged, HMS *Stork* signalled a brief farewell: 'Good morning,' the message read, 'and bloody good luck.' Rupert Curtis, commander of the landing-craft flotilla, wracked his brain in vain for a Nelsonian reply, before giving up. 'Thanks,' he responded simply, 'we'll need it!'[1]

Low scudding clouds mingled with the early-morning murk, smeared with smoke thrown up by the crushing bombardment. Somewhere in that eerie smog, waves of small assault craft were bouncing like corks as they sped for the shore, sprayed by shell splashes and spitting machine guns. Troop transports were disgorging hundreds of soldiers into landing craft for the final run-in. More anxious minutes passed as the commando flotilla waited its turn to join the carefully choreographed assault.

Finally, at 7.55 a.m., the moment arrived. Curtis signalled his force to divide into its pre-arranged invasion formation: the first wave of twelve landing craft, under his command, carrying No. 6 Commando, brigade headquarters and 41 Royal Marine Commando, followed, after an interval of 30 minutes, by a second wave of ten LCIs, commanded by Lt Cdr Jack Deslandes, carrying No. 3 Commando and Four. Five minutes later, and 35 minutes after the first minesweeping flail tanks crawled ashore on the eastern edge of Sword Beach, Curtis started on his final approach. Spouts of shell bursts churned the already choppy sea. Then they were gone; wake trails vanishing into the haze. Aboard the second wave, an officer on LCI 530 shouted down to Four Five's A Troop sheltering below deck: 'We're in the news. The landings are in the news.'[2]

For Doc and the sixty or so commandos cooped up in the hold, hours of nervous tension were almost at an end. At 8.30 a.m., in keeping with the landing timetable, the second wave began its 40-minute run-in to Queen Red beach at a steady 12 knots. Between them and a few hundred yards of sand, along a 5-mile stretch of smoke-shrouded coastline, lay thousands of potentially lethal underwater obstructions, tipped with Teller mines and grazenose shells, stretching as far as the low-water mark. Shore batteries, seemingly unaffected by the 'stunning avalanche of bombs and shells', presented more danger, and to make matters worse, a strong easterly flood tide threatened to throw the entire landing off course.

Battling against shelling, hidden defences and a sea far rougher than anticipated, the second wave closed the shoreline abreast: Four Five on the right and No. 3 Commando to the left, nearest Ouistreham. Incredibly, despite weaving to avoid the menacing stakes above and below the surface, Four Five's craft contrived to maintain their stations. LCI 532 rode the right flank with 517 on the far left, with the rest, in right to left order of 528, 530 and 517, sandwiched between them. A mile or so from the beach, orders were passed for the commandos to file up the stairways onto the deck in readiness for landing. Crouching low, they sought whatever shelter they could find. Some risked taking cover behind ammunition lockers near the boats' vulnerable and highly flammable fuel tanks. Most were simply relieved to breathe air untainted by the stench of sweat and vomit.

By now, the noise was deafening and the sights extraordinary. 'You almost forgot to be scared,' recalled Derrick Cakebread. 'It was a sight to behold,' added Fred Harris, 'no two ways about it. There were boats as far as you could see, big ones, little ones, one or two stood up on end in the water. Shell fire and smoke. And God knows what.'[3] On the port bow a tank landing craft was belching flames and smoke. Not far away a destroyer lay stopped, 'her back broken and her bow and stern sticking up out of the sea at a grotesque angle'.[4]

Straight ahead, the shoreline was at last visible through the murk, its landmarks instantly and reassuringly recognisable. Rising from the marram-tufted dunes, the commandos could make out the disfigured outline of La Brèche villa, marking the entrance to exit 25. Just discernible beyond that were the ruins of a holiday camp, a shell-battered house and the turrets of Coleville château. 'It was just like we'd seen on the photographs and sand table models back in England,' said Derrick Cakebread. But just as the beach was revealed, so the ragged line of landing craft hove into the view of the enemy gun positions near Ouistreham. They would have to run a gauntlet of fire on the final run-in.

The gun flashes were plainly visible: it didn't take long for the gunners to find their range. Soon, the sea around the landing craft was a seething cauldron. Two of the landing craft carrying army commandos were hit. Another struck a mine, killing thirty men. Then it was Four Five's turn to suffer: in the final surge for the beach, LCI 517 snagged an obstruction and began taking in water; next, 518 was struck by a shell. Men from A Troop lining the two sides of LCI 530 watched appalled as flames gushed aft, perilously close to the 4,000-gallon non-sealing fuel tank. An explosion then would have almost certainly destroyed both craft in an instant, but thankfully the fire slackened before dying away. Passing the bobbing bows of a half-sunken tank landing craft, LCI 518 continued to the beach where another shell burst on the bows, decapitating the naval ramp party.[5]

As the men on 518 struggled to find a way off, the ramps at the head of 530 fell away steeply towards the rushing surf. Disembarkation began

Four Five landing at La Brèche, Queen Red Beach. A Troop's LCI 530 can be seen in the background. The steepness of the landing ramps is plainly visible. (via F. Harris)

immediately, into an in-coming tide. Progress was painfully slow as the heavily laden men struggled down the narrow, swaying ramps. One moment they hovered above water barely ankle deep, the next they were part-submerged beneath waist-deep waves that sent men flailing. Getting off safely was a lottery. Walter Bigland was lucky: he escaped with a dry landing. Fred Harris, whose experiences on the run-in had been enough to rid him of his seasickness, was less fortunate. When it came to his turn, the ramps were swinging unsteadily. 'There was no time to hang about,' he wrote. 'If you didn't jump off, you either fell off or were thrown off.'[6] Overloaded with extra equipment, he stumbled down the ramp and tripped and fell, head over heels, into deep water. Fortunately, his section leader saw him. Sgt 'Dolly' Gray plunged into the surf and, grabbing the struggling Bren gunner by his collar, dragged him to the water's edge before making off up the beach. Fred was left gasping for breath 'like a tortoise on its back trying to turn over'.[7]

Bringing up the rear, Doc Harden had it even worse. In a letter to Maud written almost a month after the landing, he gave the barest outline of his experience. 'My boat was one of the unlucky ones,' he said. 'Some of the lads got ashore with only their boots wet, but that's the luck of the game. Some of the poor lads didn't even get ashore, so what's a swim against that?'[8] His was a narrow escape. With a backpack weighing up to 80lbs, a bag of medical supplies and a revolver, a lesser swimmer might easily have foundered without ever having set foot on French soil. As it was, his thoroughly wet landing was merely the start of a long and eventful trial that continued on a beach strewn with dead and wounded men. No details exist of his actions that day, but, from the evidence of those who landed with him, it is possible to imagine the harrowing scenes that greeted him on Queen Red beach.

By the time Doc struggled ashore the defences in the immediate vicinity had been largely subdued, but men were still being lost to mortar shells, which were 'falling all around'.[9] The beach was a chaotic jumble of men and equipment. Routes across it were marked by ribbons laid across the sand. Amid the din, a beachmaster was bawling at men to get off the beach. The carnage of the earlier assault was apparent everywhere. Tanks lay abandoned, with acrid smoke spewing out of hatches and slits, while at the water's edge bodies bobbed like flotsam in a surf stained red with blood. More lay in untidy heaps, littering the sand wherever they had fallen.

To Derrick Cakebread, it seemed as if the beach was covered with hundreds of bodies. 'It was a shock to realise that a little while before they had been laughing and joking like ourselves,' he recalled. 'We were young boys really and to see so many dead bodies lying crumpled with terrible wounds, some of them floating in the sea, was dreadful.'[10] One of Four Five's troop commanders likened the grisly mayhem to an 'unruly scrum'. Aware of their orders to stop for no one, the commandos of Four Five pushed on towards a straggle of barbed-wire infested sand dunes, the beachmaster's barked instructions to 'move fast' and 'not to bunch' ringing in their ears.

They needed no urging. Shells were still falling amid the clutter of landing craft, tanks and men clustered along the shoreline. 'It was scary all right,' recalled Cakebread. 'With all the extra stuff we were carrying, it was hard enough to walk let along run, but believe me, we ran that day.'[11] Among those moving as fast as they could away from Queen Red beach were Fred Harris, water pouring from every part of his body and equipment, and Walter Bigland, struggling under the weight of an inflatable dinghy in his rucksack and a bicycle slung over his shoulder. On his way across the beach, Bigland saw medics treating some of the casualties. In defiance of orders, he stopped to help a friend bandage one man's injuries. He had no memory of who the medics were, but thought it possible one of them could have been his own Troop medic, Doc Harden.

Since hitting the beach, medical parties had been busy with a constant flow of casualties. As part of a force whose objectives lay deep inland, the commando medics had been ordered 'not to treat anyone on the beaches, but to press on and leave them to the beach medical teams'.[12] Faced with the sights of wounded men crying for help and floundering in the water, however, medics from all units rendered what assistance they could. Some commando medics were seen plunging into the surf to haul ashore casualties trying to crawl away from the fast-rising tide. Doc may well have been among them, but that must remain a matter of conjecture. Good soldier that he was, it is unlikely that he would have remained on the beach any longer than was necessary. As a commando medic, he was well aware that his primary duty that day lay with his troop, and, as his mates swept across the beach and prepared to strike inland, he knew better than most that their hazardous mission was liable to place even heavier demands on his particular skills.

Lord Lovat had envisaged a rapid push from the beach, avoiding pockets of resistance by infiltrating between strongpoints to reach their ambitious first-day objectives. Yet despite landing on time and in precisely the right spot, the commandos' advance had fallen behind schedule.

Minefields, mortars and snipers combined to cause delay to a plan that over-estimated the speed at which even the best-trained and most highly motivated men could cover ground in combat conditions while weighed down with burdensome loads. Peter Young, CO of No. 3 Commando and a decorated veteran of raids on Dieppe and Norway, described progress that morning as 'maddeningly slow'. The terrain didn't help. Between the beach and their first forming-up position, in a small spinney, lay 1,100yds of marshes cut by slimy, deep-sided ditches. Walking across it would have been difficult in any circumstances, but for men hampered by extra loads of ammunition, bicycles, rations, mortars, anti-tank weapons, inflatable dinghies and, in Doc's case, an extra-heavy medical rucksack, the going was excruciating. From the edge of the wood, the blast of a hunting horn blown by Four Five's adjutant acted as a rallying cry. Not that it was really necessary. The route from the beach, across a road, tramlines and drainage channels, was waymarked by a line of green berets snaking across the squelching bog.

Their floundering progress was interrupted by 'an unearthly, blood-chilling, bellowing noise' that sounded 'like a gigantic cow in agony'.[13] This was their introduction to 'Moaning Minnie', a multi-barrelled mortar known as the Nebelwerfer. In the coming days and weeks, they would come to know that eerie sound all too well. Thankfully, on this occasion, its bark was worse than its bite, as the soft ground deadened the bombs' impact. 'The marsh saved us,' Derrick Cakebread reckoned. 'If it had been hard ground, there'd have been a hell of a lot of casualties.'[14]

By the time they reached the first checkpoint, around 10 a.m., the men of Four Five were thoroughly mixed up. There was a pause while the commandos reorganised. A bedraggled CO issued instructions to his officers. They, in turn, briefed their NCOs. Word had reached them that 5th Parachute Brigade had captured the bridges over the Orne and the neighbouring canal intact. It was imperative to push on and reinforce them. Before they could do so, however, there was a brief scare. 'Suddenly,' Fred Harris recalled, 'a cry went up. There were German tanks coming. For a moment we feared the worst, but, thankfully, they turned out to be our own Sherman tanks.'[15] Eventually, after a renewed flurry of mortar fire and a further delay while No. 6 Commando cleared an enemy strongpoint barring the way, Four Five headed off on a route that took them through the villages of Coleville and St Aubin-d'Arquenay to the Orne river crossing at Benouville, soon to be christened 'Pegasus Bridge' in honour of the airborne force's heroic *coup de main*. Along the way, they saw evidence of No. 6 Commando's fighting advance: 'We passed corpses and wounded men at the side of the tracks we followed and groups of German prisoners began passing back towards the beach-head escorted by walking wounded from 6 Commando.'[16]

Aside from a few stray bullets, sporadic shelling and isolated skirmishes, the march was largely uneventful. Indeed, they appear to have received as much attention from enthusiastic locals as they did from the Germans. Derrick Cakebread remembered a Frenchman offering glasses of wine as they passed by. 'I didn't have any as I wasn't much of a wine drinker then,' he said. 'And we had been warned beforehand to be careful of anything offered as it may have been tampered with by the enemy.'[17] In one of the villages along the way, Walter Bigland and a party of Four Five were surrounded by local people who insisted on serving them Calvados before posing with them for an historic group photograph. 'There we all were, in a semi-circle, drinking a tot while someone took our photo... I never did see that photograph.'[18] According to Four Five's history, they reached the first bridge – on schedule – around midday. The Airborne record has Lovat's piper, Bill Millin,

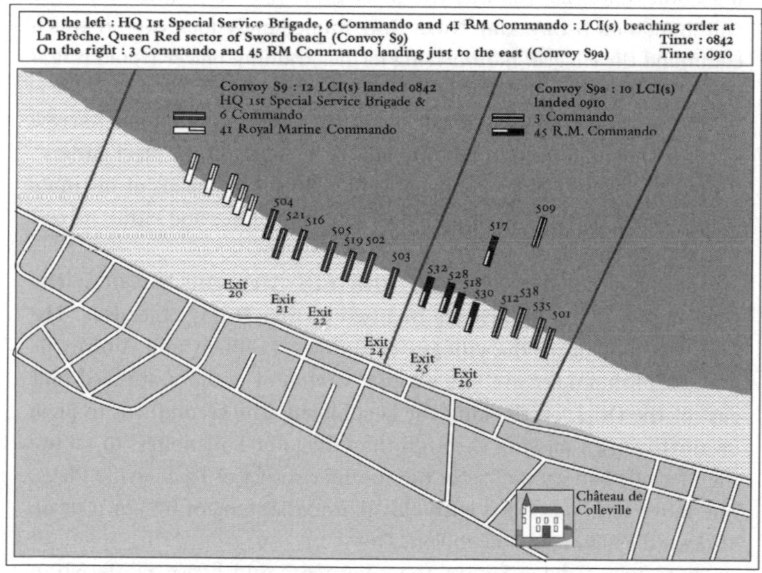

How the Commando Brigade landing craft hit the beach at La Brèche on 6 June 1944. A Troop, 45 RM Commando was carried aboard LCI 530.

playing the commandos into Benouville an hour later. Either way, their arrival was timely. The red berets were exhausted 'and beginning to feel disconcertingly like the settlers in the circled-up wagon train, Indians whooping all around them as they prayed for the cavalry to turn up'.[19] The scene was an extraordinary one. 'There were gliders everywhere you looked in the fields,' wrote Derrick Cakebread. 'It was marvellous so many had managed to land so close.'[20] But the situation was still 'pretty grim'. The bridge was under fire from a château about 500yds away. Oblivious to the shooting that was going on, Walter Bigland offloaded the inflatable dinghy he'd carried all the way from Southampton and, without thinking, prepared to pump it up in accordance with his original orders. At that point, an airborne officer came up and asked him what he was doing. 'He told me, I'd got to run across the bridge, not paddle across the river!'[21] Soon, the riverbank was awash with discarded dinghies as commandos, in groups of five, sprinted over the river and then the canal, with the crack of bullets whistling around them.

Not everyone made it. Among those wounded by one particularly troublesome sniper was Four Five's CO. Charles Ries was hit in the thigh and had to be evacuated to the beachhead, where he was wounded a second time. His loss was the most grievous blow suffered by the commando on D-Day. Maj. Nicol Gray immediately took over. It was a command the rugged, hard-driving former training officer would retain with distinction throughout the rest of the campaign.[22]

Most of those who made it safely over the river and canal had narrow escapes. One man recalled hearing bullets 'pinging off the steel girders'. 'I remember tracer bullets passing right between the heads of my mate and I,' noted Derrick Cakebread. 'Just a second closer and either he or I would have bought it.'[23]

Having effected a junction with 6th Airborne Division, the commandos of 1st SS Brigade had two further D-Day objectives. The first was to capture the villages of Hauger, Le Plein and Amfréville and establish a defensive line along a stretch of orchard-studded hills east of the Orne, overlooking the beachhead. The second was to push on northwards, passing through the village of Sallenelles, to secure the Merville battery and seize the summer resort of Franceville Plage. The latter task, described with classic understatement by Lovat as an 'awkward assignment', fell to Four Five.

There was a delay before the advance could begin while No. 6 Commando cleared the last Germans out of Le Plein. Above them, on the high ground, the marine commandos could hear their army comrades 'flushing the Hun out with flame throwers'.[24] Then, with dusk coming on and time running out, they were off, the cyclists of C Troop leading. They were closely followed by Eric Grewcock's speed-marching A Troop and, a bit further back, the CO's reconnaissance group, followed by the rest of the unit. The coast road was wide open. Despite there being precious little cover, the advance guard was able to make haste through Sallenelles. Next stop was Merville, barely 2,000yds away. Before they got there, however, the plan went awry.

Unseen by the main force, the two leading troops turned up a narrow lane running to Merville, while the rest of the column, with the CO's party now unexpectedly in the van, continued towards Franceville Plage. They hadn't gone more than 200yds when a burst of machine-gun fire stopped them in their tracks. The reconnaissance group scattered and the rest of the column dived for cover. A confused firefight ensued with a pillbox perched on a sand dune. For 20 minutes Gray was pinned down. Finally, he decided to make a dash back to the main column. Chased by machine-gun bullets, he made it unscathed and lost no time in regalvanising the advance. Mortars were quickly brought up, and under their covering fire, Four Five resumed its march on Merville along another route, leaving the reconnaissance group to make their own way.

Led by Gray, the commandos made a flanking move onto open ground north of the battery. Almost immediately, they came under fire from one of the battery positions. In a departure from his original plan, Gray decided to make a full-scale assault on the gun site. Before he could do so, however, he was instructed by brigade HQ to abandon the planned assault on Franceville Plage and to concentrate solely on capturing and holding the nearby village of Merville.

It was to prove no easy task. 'In our original briefing,' Fred Harris recalled, 'we'd been led to believe there were only a few local troops, "bomb happy" engineers and pioneer types, labour battalion people, but the ones we faced were a different class of soldier altogether.'[25] The fighting was grim. Aerial bombing had left the village in ruins, rendering it ideal for defence. A signaller attached to Four Five described it as 'a fortress'. 'There was a lot of house-to-house fighting and sniping,' said Harris.[26] It was not until 7 p.m. that the last Germans were winkled out, leaving Four Five's marines in sole occupancy.

Headquarters was established in two wrecked cottages, while the men, some of them 'a little bit shaky'[27] from their prolonged action, dug in. It took them under an hour to turn the village into a bastion, criss-crossed with slit trenches. A few hours later a self-propelled gun set nerves on edge as it began demolishing a nearby farm. Fears, however, that it might presage an all-out assault proved unfounded, and the rest of D-Day passed with Four Five in lonely isolation, its commandos 'tense and alert'.

For the first time since leaving Warsash they were able to gulp down a brew of tea and in the fading light they were treated to the spectacle of the 6th Airborne's Air Landing Brigade being flown in as much-needed reinforcements. It was a heartening sight to men weary from the strain of a relentless combat initiation. But what would be remembered as 'the longest day' was not over yet.

Around 3 a.m., a signal arrived, telling them to pull back from Merville at first light into defensive positions some 3 miles away on the high ground around Amfréville. 'Just over an hour later the unit prepared to move again,' wrote the unit's intelligence officer. 'In the dim half-light of early morning men rose silently from their trenches to assemble on the line of march, silently buckling on their equipment, and reflectively rubbing the blackened stubble on their chins as they waited for the order to march.'[28]

10

Fighting for Survival

As Doc trudged back towards Amfréville in the pale light of early morning he had much to reflect upon. From the moment they had left Warsash, almost 36 hours earlier, there had been no letup and precious little time for rest. A rough crossing had been followed by a rougher landing amid the shambles left by a bloody assault. After that it had been one long slog, with marches that might have been reminiscent of hard days spent training in Scotland and along the South Coast, were it not for the showers of mortar bombs and the spray of machine-gun fire accompanying their trek along the Orne. No other unit had ventured as far or risked as much on the first day. As well as being physically draining, their bold endeavours had been mentally exhausting. For all their impressive stamina, no amount of training could ever fully prepare men for the shock of combat.

Doc had seen and treated his first battle casualties. Though Four Five had got off relatively lightly, its losses were not insignificant for so small a unit. When time allowed for head counts to be made, they revealed three officers and seventeen men had been killed or wounded on D-Day – some without even stepping ashore – and another twenty-nine men were missing. Doc would have known them all. He would also have seen comrades, deprived of sleep and fatigued by the strain of battle, struggling to overcome the natural fears of men facing action for the first time. No doubt he would have taken comfort not only from his own survival, but also from the realisation that he had withstood his first test without letting either himself or his mates down. If his courage that day had been no more marked than that of many of his comrades, it had, nevertheless, been sufficient to show he could 'take it' and could be relied upon when it mattered most. As for the future, well, only time would tell. He preferred not to think too deeply about it. 'I take everything as it comes,' he told Maud in one of his first letters home from Normandy, 'and it doesn't worry me a great deal.'[1] If true, it was just as well, given the tests to come.

The first of these was at Franceville Plage, the 'fortress' village that had defied capture on the evening of D-Day. Anxious about his brigade's slender hold on the high ground east of the Orne, Lord Lovat ordered Four Five to extend the commando line to the coast around Merville. To assist, he gave them two troops from No. 3 Commando, tasked with the job of recapturing the battery site, which had been reoccupied by the Germans. With the help of a naval bombardment and the support of the brigade's medium machine guns and a solitary 6-pounder anti-tank gun, Four Five were to advance again through Sallenelles, skirting Merville, to launch an assault on the former seaside resort of Franceville Plage.

The operation did not go well. A morning's mortar duel spilled over into the afternoon to disrupt Nicol Gray's final briefing and the approach march began under a hail of mortar bombs that intensified as the commandos neared Sallenelles. The brigade's machine guns replied, but the covering fire was insufficient to prevent the loss of a jeep carrying ammunition and casualties among Four Five's mortar team. Dodging fire from the nearby battery, Gray led on to Merville and the slit trenches his men had dug the previous night. There, he paused to deliver his final instructions while Franceville Plage shook beneath the vicious pounding being delivered by two cruisers and a couple of destroyers.

The men of Four Five were already well acquainted with Franceville. Apart from their brief visit the day before, they had spent hours studying aerial photos and rehearsing their capture of the resort so that every last building was familiar to them. Gray's plan was to advance along the main street, code-named 'Piccadilly', with E Troop on the left leading A Troop and B Troop on the right, ahead of D Troop. All being well, the commandos would reach the beach before splitting up to secure the village and an enemy position further east. Flank protection would be provided by C Troop. The three main objectives were named 'Freeman', 'Hardy' and 'Willis' after the well-known chain of shoe shops. If it was someone's idea of a joke, it was in extremely poor taste. There was nothing remotely funny about the fight for Franceville Plage.

While shells reduced the eastern corner of the resort to brick dust, the commandos darted across the open ground separating Merville from the outskirts of Franceville. So far, so good. The nearest villas were occupied without drawing fire. C Troop immediately swung left, bombing their way through a wood riddled with dugouts and slit trenches. Then, as

A and D Troops took up position in a wood fringing Franceville, E and B Troops set off along opposite sides of the main street. They hadn't gone far, however, before they were fired on from a hidden pillbox. With bullets skipping along the street and ricocheting off walls, the commandos scattered into nearby houses. From that moment on, the assault was in trouble.

An attempt to smash the pillbox using a PIAT (Projector, Infantry, Anti-Tank) gun proved unsuccessful and, as Gray moved forward to discover the cause of the delay, an anti-tank gun burst into life. The first shell landed among Gray's covering party, instantly killing Four Five's regimental sergeant major and a corporal.[2] It was the signal for Franceville to erupt into violent conflict. For a few moments there was pandemonium as men caught in the open scuttled for whatever cover they could find. The struggle that followed was fractured and frenzied and fought at extremely close quarters as parties of men on both sides blundered blindly into one another.

In a night of confused fighting, it appeared for a time that Four Five could be cut off by an enveloping attack. 'The enemy ... seemed to appear from all sides at once, and it became difficult to distinguish friend from foe as fleeting figures slipped from shadow to shadow or rifle shots came from the flanks,' recorded the unit's historian.[3] Gray saw the danger in time and ordered his men to fall back. They retreated, house to house, fighting desperately to escape. Among those trying to evade the German counter-attack was Doc Harden and the men of A Troop, who had pushed on as far as a sandy knoll near the shoreline. Bren gunner Fred Harris recalled the chaotic withdrawal:

> Pulling out we dispersed into the gardens. For a while it seemed like everyone had disappeared. NCOs were calling out orders and leapfrogging from house to house. We gained more ground... Other groups could be heard who were in much the same position as ourselves. There was a sudden lull. Word went round that the Germans had pulled out. In actual fact, a French commando had been ordered to approach them under a flag of truce, suggesting that they surrendered as the whole British army was behind us. The answer was short and sharp, with long bursts of machine-gun fire and mortar bombs. It started up again and they counter-attacked and the commando with the flag was killed.[4] By this time I had set up my bren gun and was bringing fire down on a pill-box from which a machine-gun was firing...[5]

Harris was not alone. At the front of the villa where he'd taken refuge, three commandos, L/Cpl Fred Stallwood and marines 'Nipper' Lee and Tommy Lovett, were having 'a pop' at the pillbox with rifles. At some point, they were joined by Derrick Cakebread. The A Troop sniper had already been busy. During the approach to Franceville, he and another man had been ordered to flush out some Germans that were troubling the advance. Mission accomplished, he followed the sound of guns into the embattled resort, arriving just in time to see the failure of the white flag ruse. 'The next thing we knew was we were getting stonked by everything they could throw at us, grenades, small arms fire, mortars, the lot,' he recalled.

Pinned down in the same garden as his mates from A Troop, he saw a stick grenade arcing through the air to land among them. According to Harris it came from a German who followed up the explosion by bursting through a hedgerow shouting '*Hande hoch*'. Unimpressed by such ungentlemanly conduct, Harris simply rolled over and riddled him with bullets before blasting the hedge just in case there were more lurking behind it. The clash, typical of so many in Franceville that evening, was over in seconds. It was only when the German lay dead that Harris noticed blood dripping down his wrist. Both he and Cakebread had been hit by fragments from the grenade, though, fortunately, their wounds were not serious enough to put either of them out of action.

As they recovered their senses, word reached them via their section sergeant that it was time to leave. With his injured arm beginning to stiffen, Harris went to pass on the news to the three men who had taken up position inside the house:

> German fire was still raking the road which we had to cross. I said if anyone had a smoke grenade to toss it into the road and we'd make a run for it. I gathered my Bren to my chest (it was awkward to carry now). Tommy threw the grenade, but the wrong way round, and we had to run in front of the smoke. Then we were off like greyhounds. I saw one guy (from another section) go down, but he crawled to safety; unfortunately, the three lads were never seen again.[6]

It was a case of 'every man for himself', and in their pell-mell dash they soon became separated. Cakebread cut through some more back gardens to reach a crossroads, where he lay up in a ditch. Harris reached higher ground, though how he got there he was none too certain. Eventually, he found his way to a dressing station, was patched up and later joined a patrol sent back to Franceville to search for stragglers. By then, the commando attack had dissolved into a battle for survival.

With his unit in danger of being overwhelmed from the front and cut off in the rear, Nicol Gray ordered C Troop to clear an escape route. A schoolhouse converted by the Germans into a strongpoint was captured and fierce counter-attacks were beaten off. C Troop's intervention enabled stragglers to be gathered and the wounded to be brought in, but by 11 p.m. it was clear to Gray that they were fighting a losing battle to hang on. Out of contact with brigade and with ammunition running dangerously low, it was time to cut and run.

Such a withdrawal was fraught with hazard, even under cover of darkness. Gray's hastily arranged plan was for two troops, B and E, to fall back to the trenches they had dug the previous night in Merville. Once there, they were to cover the retreat of all those who were capable of leaving. Gray's greatest dilemma was what to do about the large number of wounded men under his command. The thought of abandoning them to the enemy was repugnant, but, given Four Five's plight, he had no option. Those who could walk or be helped were to take their chances; the rest would be left in the care of two of Doc's fellow medics who volunteered to stay with them. Four Five's unit historian later heaped generous praise on L/Cpl Relf, himself slightly wounded, and L/Cpl Dunlop, describing their selfless action as 'typical of the RAMC personnel with the Commando'. The work of the medics was, he added, 'always magnificent' and that was certainly the case at Franceville.

Caught in the middle of the bitter street battle, the medics were seen repeatedly braving the crossfire to rescue and treat wounded men trapped in the open. As one among this gallant company, Doc undoubtedly merited his share of the tribute paid to them. 'Throughout the confused street in Franceville,' the unit historian wrote, 'the medical orderlies, led by Captain H N Smith, RAMC, and Sergeant Curren, RAMC... worked wonders in tending the wounded under fire and bringing them into cover.'[7]

The withdrawal provided more evidence of their devotion. Despite the dangers from an unseen enemy close behind, the medics supported those injured who were able to limp or be lifted and, by 11.45 p.m., all were accounted for inside the 'tight' perimeter established in Merville. In the circumstances, the withdrawal was conducted with remarkable success, though the reoccupation of their old position was not without incident. The men of A Troop had to 'scrap for their former homes'.[8] As Derrick Cakebread succinctly put it: 'The Germans were back in our slit trenches and there was a fight and we got them out.' From then on, it was a matter of holding on with whatever arms and ammunition came to hand. In Cakebread's case, that meant using captured German weapons when his supply of bullets ran out.

Four Five's position was precarious. The commandos were surrounded, almost out of ammunition and with precious few heavy weapons. They had suffered the shock of defeat with heavy casualties. Although precise details would remain unclear for some days yet, Four Five had lost eighteen men killed, thirty-nine wounded and twenty-four missing, most of whom had been left behind in the makeshift dressing station. Those who remained were exhausted after more than 48 hours of unrelenting action. But a new day in Normandy brought with it only the promise of more sacrifice and further struggles to come. Shortly after dawn, a patrol returned from Brigade HQ with a wireless set they had managed to smuggle in through enemy lines. One of the first signals was received around 8.30 a.m. It was a bleak instruction from Brigade HQ telling them that Merville was to be held 'at all costs'.

Within an hour, a bombardment by mortars heralded the beginning of Four Five's next ordeal. What followed was a day of unremitting pressure summed up in a few sentences in the unit's war diary: 'During the morning the position became worse. Two heavy attacks had been driven off. The enemy had also brought up an anti-tank gun and was shelling and mortaring our positions...'

A and C Troops bore the brunt of the attacks, all of which were repulsed with heavy losses. The close-quarter nature of the fighting was illustrated by an astonishing incident involving Four Five's commanding officer. In the midst of the second attack, Nicol Gray was touring his troop positions when he suddenly found himself peering straight at two Germans in the process of setting up a machine gun. The quickest to react, Gray shot one man with his rifle, which promptly jammed, and the second with his automatic pistol.

Despite beating off the attacks, the noose around the defiant but out-gunned commandos of Four Five was gradually tightening. The Germans brought up self-propelled guns to pound their positions. Four Five's PIAT gunners kept them at bay for as long as their ammunition lasted, but it was an unequal contest. The brigade's attempts to relieve them having failed, orders were received to pull back to the position they had originally set out from over 24 hours earlier. Once again, they were to break out after dark, only this time the line of retreat passed through country that was already occupied by the enemy.

In the event, darkness didn't come soon enough. With one end of the village engulfed in flames and heavy guns firing unchecked into his position, Gray issued instructions that flew in the face of all military teachings. His orders were for a withdrawal through 4 miles of enemy-held territory, to be carried out in broad daylight while still in contact with an attacking force! The prospects did not look good. 'We began to wonder where the rest of our army was,' wrote Fred Harris.

Four Five's war diary devotes just a single sentence to a fighting retreat that survivors likened to a nightmare: 'By 2000hrs the Cdo had successfully broken through silencing two MMG posts on the way and capturing one 81mm mortar whilst suffering only two casualties.'

Behind that bland statement of fact lay an agonising journey and a story of miraculous survival in which groups of men, cut off from the main body, desperately struggled to evade capture as they tried to find a way back through fields ripe with wheat and enemy troops.

They slipped out of Merville under cover of a naval bombardment, but they had barely covered a mile before enemy machine guns found them. It was the start of what Fred Harris called 'a running battle' all the way to Sallenelles and beyond. With the way back blocked, Gray detached a portion of E Troop to distract the German machine gunners while the rest of the commando slipped away. His ploy worked brilliantly. Not only did the rearguard succeed in destroying the enemy posts, they managed to escape along with the rest of Four Five. Skirting Sallenelles, most of Gray's men completed the trek to Le Plein without further incident. However, some, having either gone astray or fallen behind during the retreat, faced a tortuous time temporarily marooned in enemy territory. Among those lost commandos searching for a way out was Doc.

Taken by surprise by the sudden turn of events in Merville, he had been forced to leave all his kit behind in the hurried withdrawal:

> We had to get out quick. I lost everything... All I had was what I stood in and my pistol. I was changing my socks at the time and had only changed one, so came away with one dirty and one clean one and one handkerchief...[9]

His troubles, however, soon extended far beyond matters of dress. Separated from the rest of his troop, he found himself in a mixed group of eighteen commandos. In a letter to Maud, he described what followed:

> We were bang in the middle of Jerry land and decided to wait till dark to get out but Jerry opened up on us just before dark, so we had to get out quick. I took five chaps with me and led them back to our lines... We didn't walk... We had to go about 5 miles cross country on our bellies. Gee, I'm glad we learnt all that field craft now. It came in handy. I said there were six of us, but only three of us made it. As strange as it may seem to you, duck, I was the only one to keep awake. You see, very often we had to lay out as flat as we could and as soon as our heads were down we were asleep. I'm sorry to say that three of them fell asleep and we had to leave them there.
>
> When the three of us reached our lines our own men opened up on us and wounded one of the chaps. He is back in England now so two of us out of six came through... Was I scared at the time?[10]

Night was falling when the remnants of Four Five began filing in to Le Plein. They had a wild look about them. Dirty, dishevelled, their eyes red-rimmed with tiredness and their faces bristling with three days' accumulation of stubble, they were almost out on their feet. They had endured what Derrick Cakebread described as a 'living hell'. So many mates had been lost amid scenes of almost indescribable confusion and to what end? The bomb-blasted ruins of Franceville were still securely in German hands and would remain so for weeks to come. Merville, too, had been given up. It seemed as though all their sacrifices had been in vain. Only later would they discover that their stand at Merville had helped deflect a large enemy force away from its main objective of recapturing the positions held by Lovat's brigade. Indeed, given the close-run fight for the high ground, it may even have tipped the balance in favour of the commandos that were retaining their precarious grip on the elevated ground east of the Orne.

Back then, the only comfort lay in a hot meal and much-needed sleep, the first many had enjoyed since leaving Warsash. The church at Le Plein was given over to Four Five. Every available space was taken up with men weary beyond measure. Faced with a nave crammed with snoring soldiery, one late arrival made a bed on the altar table. Exhausted though he was, he couldn't sleep. Somehow, it seemed disrespectful. So he rolled off the table, replaced the altar cloth and candlesticks and folded himself into a sitting position by the wall. He was asleep in seconds.[11]

The next few days saw little letup, but at least they were no longer out on a limb. Terse entries in the unit war diary speak of a struggle still in the balance, of thrust and counter-thrust and increasingly desperate attempts to wrest away control of the high ground from the commandos.

Four Five spent 9 June digging in and getting accustomed to the surroundings that would become all too familiar in the weeks that followed. Having been allotted positions covering the western approaches to Le Plein, they found themselves in a squeezed perimeter that cut through farmyards, straddling hedged gardens and orchards thick with apple trees. They were sandwiched between No. 6 Commando on the left and brigade HQ on the right, with roads dribbling off towards Amfréville a few hundred yards away. Sniping apart, the first day was relatively quiet. It was the calm before another Normandy storm.

'There was slight enemy activity over our positions in the early morning but no bombs were dropped.' So began the war diary entry for 10 June, its clipped, under-stated tone giving little indication of the day's fierce drama:

> Between 0800 and 1100 hrs the enemy began an attack on our lines but was driven off. 45 RM Cdo suffered no casualties but helped to inflict severe casualties on the enemy. By 1100 the enemy had moved round to No 4 Cdo posn. Prisoners taken were identified as of the 3 Bn 858 Regt. A vehicle believed to be a mobile mortar was spotted about 1515 and after F Tp had put down a 10 minute shoot one patrol of A Tp went out and found it was only an ordinary truck.[12]

In fact for much of the morning the fighting around Four Five's forward was intense. Most of the early shelling and mortaring had bracketed the forward edge of an orchard in advance of the slit trenches, presumably in the mistaken belief that it marked the outer limits of the perimeter. If so, it was a fatal mistake. Though they 'pushed hard, swiftly and with great determination',[14] the first wave of attackers were slaughtered as they advanced uncertainly through the pitted orchard. Swerving away from the posts held by No. 6 Commando, the survivors blundered into Four Five's line of fire. Heavy guns added to the cacophony of noise as the enemy's forming up positions around Bréville were pounded by artillery and battleships. In the midst of it all, a second attack came in, only to meet the same fate as the earlier one. More mortaring and machine-gunning then followed before a third and final assault was stopped dead in its tracks.

The attacks had spanned somewhere between 3–4 hours and not until midday did the German effort show signs of weakening. Four Five's intelligence officer recorded: 'Throughout the morning wave after wave of German infantry had flung themselves against No. 6 Commando and ourselves, supported by heavy mortar and machine-gun fire. Each time we had, with difficulty, beaten them off.'[13]

No ground had been given and patrols sent out in the afternoon found only a few dazed and wounded men amid heaps of dead. One patrol from A Troop led by Capt. Buzz Grewcock found a wrecked half-track surrounded by bodies. A few hours later, another patrol sought and found trouble, raiding enemy positions close to the main German base at Bréville. The raiders returned with a captured machine gun, but took a fearful mauling, losing three men killed and four wounded.

The morning of 11 June dawned much as the previous days had, with the shriek of shells and mortar bombs. Four Five's slit trenches were showered with shrapnel that kept the medics busy with more casualties. As they darted backwards and forwards, ferrying injured men to the aid post they shared with No. 6 Commando, the Germans launched another attack. Like all the others, it was repulsed, but the enemy refused to go quietly. For 5 long hours they kept up a sustained bombardment with the unwelcome addition of a self-propelled gun. Eventually, the commandos' mortars forced them back and the fight resolved itself into a series of patrol clashes. Later, a party from A Troop probed as far as the ruins of Sallenelles, returning with a few wounded prisoners and news that more had been evacuated during the night.

The brigade had been living 'cheek by jowl' with the enemy for the better part of six days. On three of them they had withstood attack after attack. The time had come to hit back. An attempt to follow up their successful defence by capturing Bréville on the night of 11 June had failed when an attack mounted by a battalion of the Black Watch was defeated. However, a second assault was immediately ordered for the next night, and was to be carried out by 12 Battalion, the Parachute Regiment, supported by Sherman tanks from the 13/18th Hussars. Once more, Four Five was to be in the thick of it.

During a day punctuated with more shelling, the plan took shape. Derrick Cakebread was in his slit trench when orders came through for A Troop to muster on the village green. They were met by Nicol Gray. 'The colonel just came along and picked the first 20 blokes and told the rest of us to go back to our slit trenches. We still didn't know what it was all about.' Only later, did Cakebread realise how lucky he had been.

The battle for Bréville opened at 9.45 p.m. with a heavy bombardment that was answered by a crushing counter-barrage. Mortar bombs and shells burst among the paras and tanks as they moved up to the start

Wreck of a German self-propelled gun in Bréville, scene of a bloody on the night of 11/12 June 1944. (via D. Cakebread)

line. Thirty-three shells fell in the vicinity of brigade HQ, shrouding the village in smoke and dust. The night sky was lit 'by the flames of burning buildings and the flash of exploding shells'.[14] Tank fire and machine guns added to the unearthly noise and, above the din, the twenty-strong patrol from A Troop heard the unmistakable cries of the paras as they charged into Bréville.

Led by Capt. Buzz Grewcock, the Four Five contingent had left Le Plein a quarter of an hour before the main force, with the intention of capturing some enemy positions along the line of the paras' advance. For a while, they followed behind a tank until it veered off course. Pushing on alone, they approached the buildings that were their objective, but just as they were preparing to attack they were caught by a thunderous burst of shellfire. 'Shells just seemed to rain down,' said Fred Harris. 'An 88mm gun opened up from somewhere. Mortar bombs began falling. We quickly went to ground while the paratroopers got to work. They knocked out Bréville, but our lot copped it badly.'

Capt. Grewcock and Cpl David Reed were among four men killed in the storm of fire. Another man lost a leg, while others suffered shrapnel injuries. Of the twenty men belonging to A Troop, only two, Sgt Sid Sweet and Marine Neil Patrick, succeeded in reaching the objective, a farmhouse and outbuildings, which appeared to be unoccupied. Suddenly, a dark shadow loomed up and in an instant both men opened fire. 'The response was immediate,' wrote Patrick, 'and came in the form of a loud hissing noise and a blanket of evil smelling gas.'[15] The 'victim' was variously reported as being a cow or horse. Either way, it was a poor return for the loss of more good men.

The cost of taking Bréville was appallingly high. The paras alone lost 162 men killed and many more injured. A Troop's patrol suffered 50 per cent casualties. Two more fatalities sustained in the shelling of Le Plein took Four Five's death toll to forty-six officers and men. Ten per cent of the unit had been killed in only a week's fighting with many more injured and missing in action. Of the nineteen cheering men who had lined up with Doc for Four Five's most famous photo call, one fifth were already dead. For Doc it was enough merely to have survived a first week in France that ended as it began, with a life-or-death drama.

In the midst of the night's fearful bombardment, the barn that served as a joint first-aid post for Four Five and No. 6 Commando was struck by two shells. Fire quickly spread, as medics, led by Capt. Tasker, No. 6 Commando's MO, battled to save as many casualties as possible. It was a desperate conclusion to a sometimes desperate week, but, unbeknown to Doc and his mates, the tide had begun to turn.

By the time he felt able to describe something of what he had been through, the whole complexion of the campaign had changed and there was a hint of the seasoned soldier in his attempt to ease Maud's fears for his safety. 'Don't you get worried over this sort of thing,' he wrote of his escape from Merville. 'It goes on nearly every day. We just get used to it...'[16]

11

Vixen, V1s and a 'commando baby'

By the standards of the first two weeks in France, 19 June was a relatively quiet day around Amfréville. Patrols had gone out. A few enemy outposts had been shot up and a prisoner had been taken. In return, the Germans had plopped a few shells inside the Commando perimeter, adding to the indiscriminate damage already inflicted on the wretched Normandy villages whose geographical misfortune it was to be located on one of the most strategically important ridges in the Allied beachhead. Two weeks in the firing line had been sufficient to complete their descent into ugly ruin. But now the early frenzy of destruction had given way to sporadic acts of violence, as the fighting, waged across a patchwork of fields and a tangle of hedgerows, reached an uneasy stalemate with neither side strong enough to defeat the other. It was the beginning of a drawn-out period of deadlock that led to the sector east of the Orne being dubbed the 'phoney front'. Like most generalisations, this was only partially true and reflected neither the strain nor the hazards of living under the threat of daily bombardment. Nevertheless, compared with the sacrifices of the early days it represented the nearest thing to a pause in the fighting the men of Four Five had experienced in a fortnight of intense action. It was a welcome respite that afforded them an opportunity to renew contact with loved ones who had been craving news ever since the landings were announced.

Normally the most diligent of correspondents, Doc had scarcely put pen to paper since leaving the Stalag in England. Indeed, writing of any description had been way down on his list of priorities, well below food, sleep and staying alive. As he explained to his sister Mabel: 'We could not write the first four days we were here because we were far too busy…'[1] Even if he had had the energy, the inclination or the time to write, he hadn't the means to do so, as most of his kit, including his writing pad and field-service envelopes, had been lost in the rush to escape from Merville. For the first eleven days since landing on Queen Red beach, he had neither written nor received any letters. It was as though he had been existing in a vacuum. A few days' rest had given him the breathing space to think beyond the confines of his dressing station and the slit trench he shared with his friend and fellow medic, Sid Gliddon.

In his first letter home, he imagined his garden full of roses but with an overgrown lawn in need of a good mow. He hoped that Bobby was well and that Hitler's new V1 terror weapons, the so-called 'flying bombs', hadn't struck anywhere close to home. Most of all, he wanted his heavily pregnant wife to know that he was praying for her. Constrained by a mixture of official and self-imposed censorship, he skimmed and skirted the realities of a war he thought Maud would find too hard to bear. In time, he would revisit some of his experiences, though always he would take care to tread warily through the jumble of memories to avoid inflicting unnecessary pain. But he had not been ready for that in his opening letter. Instead, he confined himself to a single, oblique reference to the fighting by praising the aerial support they had received. 'The RAF have been doing some good work here,' he wrote, without expanding on it save to say, 'I hope they keep it up.'[2]

Only now, on D-Day plus thirteen, with the under-strength Commando Brigade well-established on the ridge alongside the similarly depleted units of the 6th Airborne Division, was he a little more forthcoming:

> My Darling Sweetheart,
> Just a few more lines, altho' there isn't much to put in them, but it is nice to receive them isn't it? We didn't have any post yesterday so I am expecting a letter today. How are you and Bobbie [*sic*]? I hope you are free from those raids he is sending over there, but I expect he is only sending them to the ports, eh?
>
> Well, dearest, things go on very much the same here. Sometimes we are out on the prowl and sometimes here resting up. Except that it is far more grim, it could be just another stunt. There's no life at this place at all. It's just a small place with hardly anybody here, but, of course, the town is smashed up very badly so can't expect anybody to be here and what people there are, are either very old or young.
>
> How is the garden, sweetheart? Mabel told me that the roses look very nice. Gee, how I would like to see them just now. What is left of the gardens around here are very nice, duck. I should think it was

a lovely place before we started on it. It's a shame to smash lovely places up like this isn't it, duck? Well, my dear, once again, that's about the lot so until tomorrow,

Cheerio My Darling. God Bless,
Ever Your Loving Eric xxx[3]

For a little over ten days, Doc and all that remained of A Troop had been rooted to the dugouts they had prepared during their first full day in Le Plein, near the ruinous fringes of Amfréville. Much had changed in that time. Lord Lovat had gone, evacuated with serious wounds the same night that A Troop mourned the loss of its much-loved leader. Capt. Buzz Grewcock's place had been taken by the adjutant, Brian White, whose skill with a hunting horn had helped rally the unit that first day in the marshes beyond the beach. His arrival coincided with a reorganisation of Four Five made necessary by heavy losses and a shortage of replacements. Unable to maintain five 'fighting troops', the unit was reduced to four, with D Troop broken up to provide reinforcements for the rest. At the same time, the positions on the ridge had been strengthened by the addition of 4th SS Brigade.

However, amid so many adjustments, there remained some constants, not least their location near the shattered remains of Le Plein and Amfréville. For six weeks, without relief, the men of A Troop lived in a mixture of two-man slit trenches and farm buildings. Mortaring and shellfire were a more or less daily feature of their time there. To combat the effects of the bombing, they had burrowed themselves at least 4ft beneath ground level, and turned their trenches into mini shelters, with roofs of timber and scrap that, in the absence of tin helmets, were a godsend against the rain of shrapnel. The makeshift roofs contributed greatly to the fall in the number of casualties in late June and July. Of all the constants, however, the greatest was the frustration of days on end spent in the same holes in the ground, dodging shells and patrolling the same stretch of Norman countryside. Entries in the unit war diary, full of repetitive stock phrases, sum up a grimly tedious time when the days seemed to blur into one another:

June 15: Enemy shelling of our positions continued at intervals through the day...

June 16: Our position was shelled and mortared... C Tp was ordered to send out two patrols...

June 17: An enemy shell fell on B Tp positions, killing two sergeants. The shelling continued for half an hour...
June 18: A patrol from B and E Tps went out with the intention of neutralising three machine guns...
June 19: The patrol went out again... Enemy shells fall in our area intermittently...
June 20: Enemy shells fell all around the area...

So it continued, with the commandos bent on an aggressive policy of patrolling and sniping and the Germans responding with a daily diet of 'hate' served from the barrels of concealed mortars and hidden gun batteries. So routine did it become that Doc was not being entirely disingenuous when he claimed, in what was to become a common refrain, that it was 'a job to know what to put in these letters, duck'. 'For the past two or three days we have more or less been at a standstill. I expect we shall push forward again, tho' all in good time...' he wrote on 22 June, before signing off, 'Well, sweetheart, there's really nothing to write about...'

One commando described this period as 'merely boiling down to a routine and acting out our parts which we had carefully rehearsed in England for many weeks beforehand'.[4] Well-trained though they were, the men of Four Five had never anticipated having to endure such a long spell of static warfare. As shock troops equipped to travel light, they had expected tough assignments, night infiltrations and fights to capture and hold key strategic features until relieved by conventional forces. However, it had always been expected that these missions would be of short duration. Their original brief had envisaged them holding the ridge for a week before being withdrawn to England in readiness for more amphibious operations. But things hadn't worked out like that. The fighting had been much harder than expected and the German defences far more durable. Caen, an ambitious first-day goal, was still in enemy hands. For all the Allies' overwhelming superiority in the air, the ground war had taken on much the same appearance of the First World War, with casualty rates to match.

As the commandos hunkered down in their slit trenches, echoes of that earlier conflict were all around. Officers talked of dominating no man's land and of organising listening posts to guard against sudden surprise attacks. To men trained to carry out spectacular hit-and-run operations, such methods of fighting seemed frustratingly dull. But for all its routines, life on the ridge was far from 'cushy' and nor was it as devoid of incident as Doc would have had Maud believe.

A perfect illustration was the patrol action fought by A Troop in the early hours of 29 June. Operation Vixen, as it was officially styled, was one of the most celebrated and successful of all the small-scale operations mounted by the commandos during their defence of the ridge. It followed days of intense patrol activity and was part of a plan designed to 'pin the Germans back in their own positions ... relentlessly, systematically, but also economically'.[5] It was sanctioned by Derek Mills-Roberts, who had succeeded Lovat in command of the brigade. Four Five were specifically chosen to carry out the sortie in order to sharpen their raiding skills. Since landing in Normandy, Mills-Roberts, who had always had his doubts about the policy of converting Marine battalions into commando units, felt Four Five's lack of combat experience had been reflected in its performance. In his opinion, the unit had not displayed the same steadiness as the brigade's other units. Operation Vixen was a chance, as he put it, 'to show the rest of the Brigade exactly what they could do'.[6]

The plan was an audacious one. The target was an enemy headquarters situated well behind the German lines. To reach it would require stealth and stout hearts with the raiders having to find a way through a strongly defended area on the other side of a road between the lines. 'The plan,' wrote Mills-Roberts, 'was that once they were across the road they would wreak havoc in the rear area and then retire, having inflicted casualties and lowered enemy morale'.[7]

Nicol Gray chose A Troop to make the attack and gave command of the raiding force to Lt Tommy Thomas, the belligerently brave South African section leader. Little was left to chance. The operation called for covering fire from Four Five's mortars and machine guns, supplemented by mortars from two specially loaned units, the firepower of 150 Field Regiment, Royal Artillery and the guns of two destroyers. The idea was to swamp the German positions with a deluge of shells, leaving an open avenue through which the raiders would pass. Along the way, they would drop off an officer and fifteen men from E Troop to establish a 'firm base' followed by a covering party from A Troop to hold the road, which Thomas' twenty-strong strike-force had to pass over. The intention, set out in secret, was uncompromisingly simple: to 'destroy all the enemy in the area...'[8]

By 2.45 a.m. on 29 June everyone was in position. A tense 15-minute pause followed before the crushing bombardment sent the raiders bounding forward, faces blackened and hearts pounding. Doc was among the covering party sprinting beyond the straggle of apple trees to reach the road.

As was the norm on such patrols, he was the only medic in a force of around sixty men. Saddled with a stretcher that hampered his movement, he would be responsible for patching up and evacuating any casualties back to Four Five's aid post. What might have been a difficult proposition had things gone awry, proved in reality to be remarkably straightforward as the mission went off like clockwork.

The moment the barrage lifted, Tommy Thomas had led off. Attacking with bayonets and grenades, the commandos took the Germans completely by surprise. The unit history recorded:

> Having dealt with the enemy's forward positions the raiding party went on to their main objective, two houses which constituted an enemy headquarters. After some hard close-quarter fighting, the houses were set on fire and the occupants disposed of. There was still some time to spare before the party had to withdraw and so Lieutenant Thomas decided to penetrate still further into enemy lines. An enemy strong point was attacked and overcome, all the defenders being killed. By now the Hun had started to counter-attack and it was obviously time to withdraw. In spite of having been wounded by a grenade Lieutenant Thomas withdrew his patrol in good order in the face of an enemy counter-attack and the whole party returned to our lines without any serious casualties.[9]

Back among the covering party and at headquarters there was some anxiety when contact was briefly lost with Thomas' force. For a moment, they feared the worst. But then, a message came through, saying that the raiders were 'proceeding home independently'. It wasn't quite as easy as it sounded. Having had 'a glorious time wandering around the enemy's area, tossing grenades into farm buildings',[10] Thomas had to be alert as the Germans, recovering from the initial shock, attempted to block the raiders' escape route. The young South African proved himself more than equal to the threat. Leading his men out of the trap, he headed back to report a resounding success.

A Troop had stirred up a 'hornet's nest'. Such was the savagery of their attack that the German defences were briefly paralysed and, in the mayhem that followed, at least half a dozen enemy vehicles were set ablaze and buildings were blitzed. At the cost of just three men, including Thomas who was slightly wounded, the raiders had inflicted 'much damage' and a considerable number of casualties. What Gen. Richard Gale, GOC 6th Airborne Division, considered a 'first-class piece of enterprise' helped secure the Commandos' total mastery of no man's land. Never again would the Germans attempt to attack the commando positions, either by day or night. The success was recognised by the award of a Military Cross to Tommy Thomas. The rest had to make do with a commendation and the satisfaction that came with knowing they had helped establish Four Five's reputation as a fighting force.

It is doubtful whether Doc would have had any inkling about the wider ramifications of the raid, still less of history's judgment. Most likely, he was simply grateful to have been under-employed on a night of such high drama and even greater risk. Back inside the perimeter, he dashed off a couple of letters home. As usual, he threw a veil over the most exhilarating few hours he'd spent on the ridge since coming back from Merville.

Sticking to his old familiar story, he wrote to 'Mum and All':

> Things are about the same here. We go out now and again to try and smell Jerry out. Sometimes we find him, sometimes we don't. The same goes for him. It's a funny game isn't it, seeing as we are not much more than about 300yds from each other...[11]

In his letter to Maud, he did his best to keep up the pretence, though not well enough to prevent the censor removing five words that may or may not have related in some way to the previous night's foray:

> Well darling, things go on very much the same here. A patrol here and there [words censored] Quite a lot of stuff flying about, but as time goes on we are getting used to it...[12]

The only references to events in Normandy were an admission to Maud that 'we don't like Jerry's mortar fire' and a desire, expressed to his mother, to see the stalemate broken: 'I shall be glad when we start to push forward again. The sooner we do that, the sooner it will be finished, eh.'

For the time being, he would have to continue to be patient. Operation Vixen may have been a great fillip for morale, but it signalled no change in the Commando Brigade's holding role. What little action there was remained confined to patrols, sniping and 'stonks', with the odd air attack thrown in for good measure.

For much of the time, the men of Four Five were reduced to the roles of observers as the war rumbled on around them. The only comfort in all this inaction was the dramatic drop in the number of casualties. During the eighteen days following the paras' attack on Bréville, Four Five lost only two men killed, both victims of shelling. The curtailment of patrol activity due to an increasing danger from minefields and booby traps further reduced the loss rate to just two fatalities in the whole of July.

The paucity of battle casualties, however, did not render Doc entirely redundant. Accidents and illnesses ensured steady work for medics trained to deal with everything from stomach upsets to gunshot wounds. Among the cases that Doc dealt with was one affecting his former housemate from his Eastbourne days, Walter Bigland.

The young Liverpudlian had been helping to shift crates of ammunition in the orchard occupied by A Troop when one of the boxes split the skin on his left hand. Bigland recalled:

> It didn't bleed, so I just pulled the skin off... Next morning, my hand had blown up, so I went to see Cpl [*sic*] Harden. He asked the sergeant major to pull me out of the position. I went into headquarters for the night and was then sent down to 6th Airborne Division first aid post. They promptly marked me down for evacuation. I couldn't believe it...[13]

Doc's original diagnosis had been spot on. The wound had become infected and blood poisoning had set in. Not all the complaints were as serious, however. Most were merely irritants, and none more so than the insect menace. Mosquitoes competed with the mortars in making men's lives a misery. Around dawn and dusk, they descended in clouds on the fields and orchards to turn an otherwise peaceable 2-hour watch into a veritable torture. 'In spite of putting on two layers of uniform they would bite through the lot, though the face and the hands were the main targets,' wrote Jim Bailey, who was a member of E Troop. Some men even took to wearing thick woollen gloves, but it was all to no avail. 'The bites on me came up like half-crowns and itched like blazes,' wrote Bailey. '[But] one dared not scratch them with dirty finger-nails because they became infected [and] it became a disciplinary offence if this happened.'[14]

There was little anyone could do. Writing to Maud, Doc commented: 'It's a good job you aren't here because there are lots and lots of gnats [*sic*] and things and, gee, wouldn't they have a feast off you... A lot of the chaps here get them [bites] far worse than you... and that's saying something.'[15] Various creams and ointments were tried without much success. Men even tried burning and smoking them out, though their efforts sometimes proved to be more dangerous than the insects themselves. Eventually, and after much grief, men keeping watch were given face veils akin to those used by beekeepers. But, effective though they were, they were found to impair night vision. 'So we scrubbed that,' wrote Bailey, 'and carried on suffering.'[16]

Mosquitoes apart, Doc could think of little else of importance to report without risking incurring the censor's wrath, so he focused on non-contentious matters, seeking, wherever possible, to make light of an increasingly frustrating period. Typical of this was a reply he sent to Maud's enquiry about the fighting she had read so much about in the newspapers but so little in his letters:

> You ask if we have battles in our trenches, duck. Yes, we have had a few but now we go in for bigger things than that. Yesterday one of the lads jumped down in his trench and found a snake in it. We got it out and killed it. It was about three feet long and today they caught another one in the next orchard to this.[17]

Sometimes, presumably when he considered it safe to do so, he harked back to the dramatic days immediately following the landing. Usually, his recollections were in response to Maud's gentle prodding and were invariably innocuous, such as the time he wrote on 2 July: 'Alright and now, my darling, for all the answers,' he began promisingly, before launching into a very selective account of his post-D-Day experiences:

> It was four or five days and nights before we had sleep after we landed. And, altho' we did not have much to eat or drink for that time (and in any case did not have a lot of time for that), after the 5th or 6th day we had fairly good grub. It could be better of course, but it's just enough. And, yes, I look after myself as much as it is possible out here. I have had one stand-up bath since we have been here and then we heated some water up in some big tins and stood in a tub about 2ft across and 1ft deep. Some of the lads had a bath in a rubber dinghy but by the time it was our turn there wasn't enough water, so [we] did with the tub...

There were moments during his enforced idleness when it even seemed to him that life was considerably more dangerous back home than it was in France. For just as the war on the ridge was settling into a somnolent stand-off, so it began to hot up for people living in the south of England, who found themselves on the receiving end of a deadly and terrifying new aerial threat. The German V1 offensive was launched in mid-June and peaked in July when scores of the pilotless flying bombs known as 'doodlebugs' or 'buzz bombs' were fired across the Channel. London was the main target, but Kent, dubbed 'Doodlebug Alley' by the press, was second in a grisly league table of V1 strikes. A total of 1,444 'buzz bombs' fell on the county, bringing with them a fresh wave of destruction that was fully exploited by Nazi propagandists. Leaflets scattered over British positions in Normandy spoke of an incendiary attack 'without precedent' and concluded with the chilling boast: 'No shelter affords protection against the terrific effects of the new German Weapon.'

Understandably, the grim tidings caused great anxiety among men whose loved ones were in the firing line, and Doc was no exception. In his earliest letter home, written on 17 June, he expressed the hope that Northfleet was not under attack from 'those pilotless planes'. His concern about the V1 menace would become a recurring theme of his Normandy correspondence, and with good reason. As paratroopers were completing the capture of Bréville, the first V1, with its 1,000kg warhead, had gouged a massive crater on wasteland in Swanscombe, just a few miles from Colyer Road.

For a while, he clung to the false belief that the Germans' main targets were the Channel ports and the invasion supply line, but by the end of June it was clear that they were hell-bent on inflicting maximum misery and indiscriminate carnage. The buzz-bomb Blitz was uppermost in his mind the day he returned from taking part in Operation Vixen. 'How is everybody at home with these planes all over the place?' he asked his mother. 'As soon as you get used to one sort of thing he sends over, he goes and sends something different, doesn't he?'

He would have urged Maud to move to a safer place if he'd thought for a minute that she would have listened to him. Instead, he contented himself with the conviction that either the powers-that-be would come up with a means of defeating them, or that supplies of the weapon would run out. 'They are wonderful things when you think of it, if they weren't so horrible and deadly,' he wrote grudgingly. 'But he must run out of them sooner or later, eh? Or we hope so anyway.'[18]

The irony of the situation was inescapable. As a commando medic, he had landed in France fully alive to the risks he was willingly facing, little realising that within days his family would be living in even graver peril. Amid the relative peace of an apple orchard in Normandy, he imagined

Eric Harden, aged two. (J. Wells)

Young Eric, athlete and swimmer. (J. Wells)

Cycling was all the rage in the 1920s and '30s. Eric (centre) with a group of friends. (J. Wells)

Eric and his sister, Mabel, in the back garden of 44 Factory Road, August 1935. A watering can is hanging on the side fence; it was here that his passion for gardening was born. (V. Rowbottom)

Eric, the butcher's delivery boy, c. 1930. (J. Wells)

Serious pose for a formal portrait, shortly before his 17th birthday. (J. Wells)

Maud Pullen, a stylish photo taken while she was courting Eric. (J. Wells)

Eric and Maud during one of their trips to the Kent coast. (J. Wells)

Family wedding group (left to right): Mabel Harden, Fred Treadwell, Ollie Pullen (Maud's mother), Eric, Maud, Fanny Harden (Eric's mother), Armine Pullen (Maud's father), May Gurney (Maud's sister). (V. Rowbottom)

Family group. Eric and Maud, in foreground, with son Bobby and niece Verity, sister Ethel and Eric's mother in his beloved garden during the early part of the war. (V. Rowbottom)

Eric (back row, far right) at the formal handover of the new ambulance, 1941. (J. Wells)

Eric as a sergeant in the St John Ambulance Brigade, with cadet and nephew Eric Muir. (J. Wells)

Maud, Bobby and Eric, shortly after he was transferred from the Royal Artillery to the Royal Army Medical Corps. (J. Wells)

War comes to Factory Road. The destruction wrought on 11 February 1944. Eric's mother, sisters and niece had a narrow escape from their home which has its windows boarded and tiles missing from the roof. (V. Rowbottom)

'Doc' and his friend and fellow commando medic Sid Gliddon in May 1944. (J. Wells)

Eric's Troop commander, 'Buzz' Grewcock (right) shakes hands with Maj. Gen. R. E. Laycock during an inspection of the unit at the Southampton 'Stalag' on 31 May 1944. Looking on is, the commanding officer of Four Five, Lt Col Charles Ries, who was wounded and evacuated on D Day. (via J. Wells)

Pre-D-Day parade. Maj., soon to become Lt Col, Nicol Gray is on the far right. (F. Harris)

Waiting to land. Men of C Troop, 45 RM Commando, prepare to beach on the morning of D-Day. (via F. Harris)

Weighed down by bicycles and other equipment, commandos splash ashore on Queen Red Beach. (via J. Wells)

A Troop sniper Derrick 'Cakes' Cakebread. Eric had treated him for a broken foot during training and they served together from D-Day to Brachterbeek. (D. Cakebread)

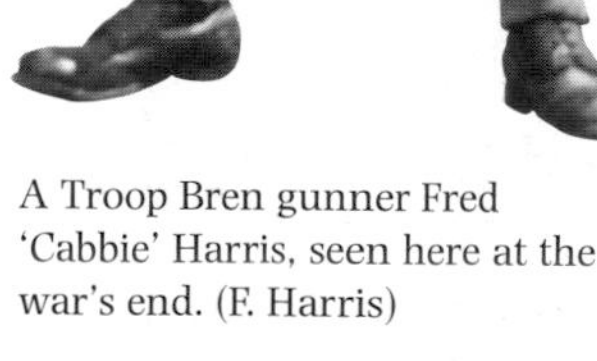

A Troop Bren gunner Fred 'Cabbie' Harris, seen here at the war's end. (F. Harris)

Time for a smoke and a rest in Le Plein. (via D. Cakebread)

The Commando Brigade memorial in Le Plein and a barn that was used as shelter by men of Four Five. (J. Wells)

Around the camp fire. Men of Four Five in Normandy during the summer of 1944. (via F. Harris)

Normandy march past in Le Plein on 14 July 1944 to mark the consecration of the memorial to the men of 1 Commando Brigade who were killed during the defence of the ridge. (via F. Harris)

Family group, with Maud, Bobby and Julia (V. Rowbottom)

An artist's impression of 'Doc' Harden bringing in Marine Wheeler at Brachterbeek. It shows him without his smock and with a helmet instead of the green beret that he actually wore. (via J. Wells)

A smiling Dickie Mason, in the foreground clad in light-coloured airborne smock. Mason was one of the volunteer stretcher bearers. (F. Harris)

Johnny Haville in Germany at the end of the war. He was Mentioned in Despatches for his part in the Brachterbeek rescue mission. (the late J. Haville)

GEMEENTE MAASBRACHT

NR

ONDERWERP

BIJLAGE(N)

MAASBRACHT,

Lt Col N. G. Gray.
45 Royal Marine Commando
BLA.
6 Feb 45.

Dear Mrs Harden.

I write to tell you how very sorry I am that your husband has been killed in action. His death has hit us all very hard for he was trusted, loved & respected by all ranks of the Commando. He lost his life to save lives of our wounded. Three times he went out to bring in casualties, who would have died but for him. On the third time he was bringing in his badly wounded officer, when he was killed instantly.

I am sorry, that I shall always be proud of having had Harden in my unit. He was a very brave & gallant man & his devotion to duty & his comrades was a fine example to us all. I have recommended him for the Victoria Cross & I hope that he will be granted it.

We have buried him peacefully beside some of his comrades.

Let me know if I can help in any way. Again, you have my sympathy.

Yours sincerely

N. G. Gray.

N.G. Gray.

Lt Col Nicol Gray's letter to Maud in which he revealed that Eric had been recommended for the Victoria Cross. (J. Wells)

Maud, Bobby and Julia at home in Colyer Road in February 1945 at the height of the press hiatus. On the mantelpiece is the photograph taken in Eastbourne of Eric and his pal Sid Gliddon. (J. Wells)

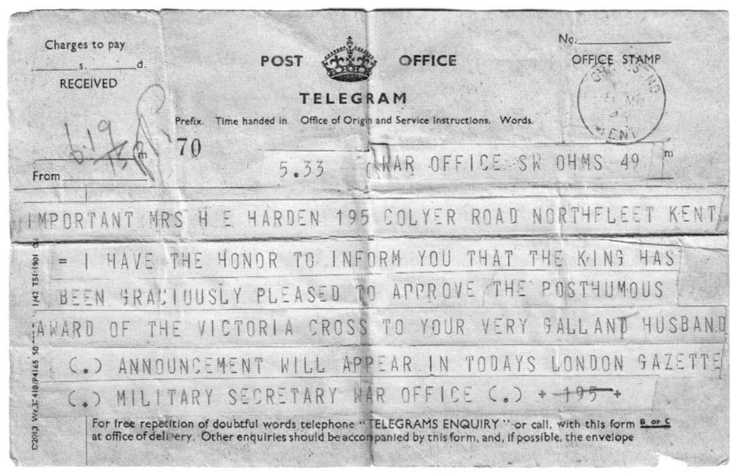

Charges to pay
s. d.
RECEIVED

POST OFFICE
TELEGRAM

No.
OFFICE STAMP

Prefix. Time handed in Office of Origin and Service Instructions. Words.

70

From

5.33 WAR OFFICE SW OHMS 49

IMPORTANT MRS H E HARDEN 195 COLYER ROAD NORTHFLEET KENT

= I HAVE THE HONOR TO INFORM YOU THAT THE KING HAS BEEN GRACIOUSLY PLEASED TO APPROVE THE POSTHUMOUS AWARD OF THE VICTORIA CROSS TO YOUR VERY GALLANT HUSBAND (.) ANNOUNCEMENT WILL APPEAR IN TODAYS LONDON GAZETTE (.) MILITARY SECRETARY WAR OFFICE (.) + 195 +

For free repetition of doubtful words telephone "TELEGRAMS ENQUIRY" or call, with this form at office of delivery. Other enquiries should be accompanied by this form, and, if possible, the envelope

Telegram announcing the posthumous award of the Victoria Cross. (J. Wells)

Eric's grave with its moving inscription in Nederweert War Cemetery. (J. Wells)

Maud and Bobby after the VC investiture at Buckingham Palace in April 1946. Maud asked the King to present the medal to her son. (J. Wells)

The Eric Harden VC Memorial Hall, headquarters of the St John Ambulance Brigade in Northfleet, was officially dedicated in 1952. (V. Rowbottom)

Harden Bridge complete with memorial plaque. The ruined windmill used as an observation and machine-gun post by the Germans is clearly visible. (J. Wells)

his pregnant wife and son taking cover in an air-raid shelter hastily restored to meet the new threat.[19] It hardly seemed right that while his family worried about where the next doodlebug might fall, he only had to contend with a growing sense of boredom.

'Well dear, we have quite a lot of time on our hands now,' he wrote to Maud on 30 June, '... the trouble is there is no life at all here, but then I suppose that sometimes when things go rather quiet we are apt to forget this is war and not a stunt, where we can go out at night instead of stand-to...' Then, as though to underline the contrast, he shifted his focus back to Colyer Road and the threat that was looming large in his mind. 'Well darling, I hope this still finds you safe from Jerry's planes. I hope he hasn't been over too often lately, and you do use the shelter, eh, duck? You will have to look after yourself now you know. It isn't much longer is it...'

Indeed, it was not. With her husband secure in the quietest sector of the Normandy beachhead, Maud entered the final stages of her pregnancy with the sky over Kent 'an almost continuous crazy chaos'[20] of spluttering V1s, screaming fighters and ear-splitting anti-aircraft fire. During the week ending 8 July more than 800 flying bombs were launched against England. On one day alone, 161 made it through the defences and over the coast. As Maud went into labour in the early hours of 7 July, more V1s were heading towards Kent and the nation's printing presses were rolling out newspapers full of Churchillian defiance.

Speaking for the first time about the V1 attacks, the prime minister had told the House of Commons a few hours earlier:

> I don't want any misunderstandings. We shall not allow the battle operations in Normandy, nor the attacks we are making against specific targets in Germany, to suffer. They come first. We must fit in our own domestic arrangements in the general scheme. There is no question of the slightest weakening of the battle. It may be a comfort to some that they are sharing in no small way the burdens of our soldiers overseas.

Comfort or not, by the time the first editions hit the news stands, Maud had given birth to a daughter she called Julia, although it would take another three days for the news to reach Doc and even longer to sink in.

Across in France, overjoyed at the thought of being a father again and at reports that the Germans had finally lost their grip on Caen, Doc's head was spinning with questions:

My Darling Sweetheart xxx
Thanks very much for the letter today. I have just received it and thanks, darling, for Julia xxx. Gee, I'm glad it's all over and so are you, I bet, aren't you, duck? Yes, darling, it does seem as if you did well. I expect you were glad of that weren't you, duck. Did you manage to get to hospital by bus or taxi or did you have to have the ambulance? Well my darling, now that it is all over just you look after yourself when you come out xxx. No going mad with work like you did with Bobbie [*sic*] xxx And stay in there as long as you can. Yes, I have started, haven't I? But I want you to be very well when I do get home because you will have to do over-time, understand xxx xxx

Won't it be lovely, sweetheart... I wonder how many months old she will be by then? Well darling, as you know by now I expect, we have Caen at last. Perhaps we can get going now. I hope they look after you in there, duck. It's a pity we had to come out here just at this time. I might have been able to have had two or three days off to come and see you, but we shall just have to make the best of it, eh?

Does it seem to you a long time since we were married, duck. Eight years. And Bobbie [*sic*] six and a half now. And now Julia. Gee, it makes me feel old, yet 33 isn't old is it?[21]

Well dearest, we are still here at the same place. We have all, more or less, made ourselves comfortable here. But, of course, [I] would rather be in England. It would have been better if this had been Paris or some such big town with a bit of life now and again. Has Bobbie been alright [*sic*] with May...? I suppose he has. Has he been in to see you at all? And mum, Mabel and Ethel and everybody has been to see you, I expect, so you won't be lonely, will you duck.

I almost forgot, duck, thinking so much about Julia. I also received the cigs today. Thanks very much. It's grand to have Woodbines again. I hope everything at Crayford is still OK, duck,[22] and your mum and dad are still safe and sound, altho' I suppose they still have the planes over there the same as you there. They seem to get a lot of them down tho', duck, don't they, but they must do a great deal of damage as well as loss of life.

Well dear, I can't keep my mind off Julia at the moment so I'll finish now and try and write a long one tomorrow, so until then,

Cheerio My Darling God Bless
Ever Your Very Loving Eric xxx
For Bobbie [*sic*] and Julia xxx[23]

Julia's arrival was a timely distraction from the dull grind inside the commando perimeter. As July wore on, it was almost as though the war was being fought on another continent. While armoured formations clanked and clattered slowly southwards and American forces groped their way through the southern Cotentin, the commandos went nowhere. Doc almost certainly wasn't exaggerating when he wrote of days spent sunbathing with little to do but dream of happier days gone by and happier days, hopefully, to come. 'We have had two very hot days this week,' he wrote to Maud, 'and [it] reminds me of the good times we had at Minster. Bobbie [*sic*] would like that now, wouldn't he duck. I bet he would have a good time at Minster, don't you. I wonder just how long it will be before we can go again. It will take a long time to clear those towns tho' after the war, won't it. But, still, they will come again. All in good time, eh?[24]

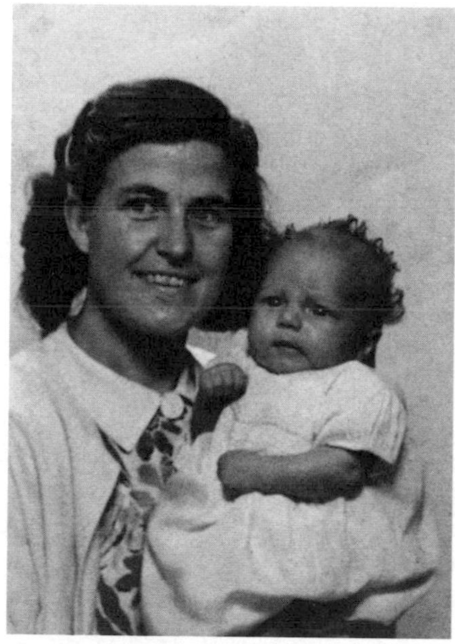

Maud and Julia, her 'commando baby' on 25 August 1944, aged seven weeks. The photo was sent to Eric in Normandy and signed 'To daddy with love'. (J. Wells)

Family matters were uppermost in his mind. Even the doodlebugs and his precious roses played second fiddle to thoughts of the daughter he had not seen. He imagined Maud fussing over her. He wondered who she looked like and was chuffed to learn the girl he called his 'commando baby' most resembled him. 'God forbid,' he joked. 'And she sleeps all the time, eh? That is something like me.' From all he heard, he thought 'she must be a grand little thing'. He tried to picture Bobby's excited face at seeing his sister for the first time, and he regretted not having been able to take him for a swim. 'I expect he would just about have managed to this year, don't you think so, dear?' he wrote. 'Still, perhaps this time next year will see us all together somewhere...'[25]

He couldn't wait for their future together to begin, but first there was a war to be won. Around Amfréville and along the high ground east of the Orne, they went on waiting. Waiting while downpours turned trenches into muddy pools to be baked hard by the sun. Waiting while mists of mosquitoes grew fat on the bloated carcasses of dead cattle. Waiting, above all, for the long-awaited breakout to begin.

As the end of July drew nearer each day seemed alike. 'Things are very much the same here, duck,' he wrote to Maud on 24 July. 'The time seems to fly by... Nearly seven weeks now. It doesn't seem that somehow and at others it seems years since we left England.'

Up Close and Personal

With an escort of a single armoured car, an American general with a short-fuse temper and a penchant for pearl-handled revolvers drove through mile after mile of newly liberated French countryside. George S. Patton was in his element. For the first time since D-Day, 'the German defences had not only been bent but broken by an Allied attack'.[1] Set free from the constricting Bocage country, troops and armour were pouring across Brittany in a torrent. In the south, the Germans had evacuated the regional capital of Rennes, leaving only a 'handful of drunks' to be rounded up. The speed of advance, after weeks of deadlock, was exhilarating. Roaring west towards Brest on 4 August, Patton 'whooped with joy every time they ran off a map and had to open a new one'.[2] Meanwhile, on the other side of the bridgehead, British airborne and commando units occupying the same positions they had held since D-Day had need only of a single, depressingly familiar, map. While the US Army's most controversial general exulted in his race across western France, Britain's elite special forces continued to sit tight in the Normandy sunshine, leaving a junior 'non-com' with time on his hands to indulge his homely fantasies.

Doc Harden was trying to picture his garden back in Northfleet. While he had been scrambling around the fields of Normandy, his wife had been harvesting a bumper crop of vegetables back in Colyer Road. Doc was pleased for her, but his passion was for the ornamental rather than the edible. 'Give me the roses, flowers and the lawn every time,' he had told her.[3] Now, with her attention focused on a baby daughter, he imagined his favourite roses rambling wild across a neglected garden. However, where once he might have urged her to devote more energy to caring for his prized flowers, now he was merely anxious to make sure she wasn't overdoing things so soon after giving birth. 'I hope you are not working too hard, duck,' he wrote. 'You will have to look after yourself for a time now before you start going mad.'[4] He was still finding it difficult to comprehend long-range fatherhood. 'It's a funny thing this, knowing you have a daughter and not being able to see her.' He hoped she wouldn't have grown too much before he could see her, just as he hoped the worst was over so far as the dreaded V1s were concerned. 'They must be rotten things to have around,' he said. 'Worse than it is here, I should think.' On that note, he signed off with his by now familiar refrain: 'Well sweetheart, no more news so will close...'

However, as was often the case, things were not quite what they seemed. From the relaxed tone of his 4 August letter Maud could have been forgiven for imagining her husband basking in the French sunshine while the war rumbled on elsewhere, much as it had been doing for the past six or seven weeks. In fact, he was no longer in the orchard that had been Four Five's home since abandoning Merville two days after landing in France. Together with No. 3 Commando, the Marines had finally moved out three days earlier, but their march was nothing on the scale of the American surge into Brittany. They had travelled less than 3 miles through the ruins of Amfréville and Bréville to an abandoned brickworks on the edge of the sprawling Bois de Bavent. There, they took over positions that had been occupied by units of 5 Parachute Brigade. But while the switch represented a welcome change of surroundings, 'it was by no means a rest cure'.[5] Indeed, the position, east of Le Mesnil crossroads, was, by common consent, far and away 'the most unpleasant defensive position held by Four Five'.[6]

Unbeknown to Maud when she read those disarmingly comforting lines from Normandy, Doc, Cabbie Harris, Cakes Cakebread and the rest of Four Five's long-suffering men were actually dug-in at the sharpest point of the eastern perimeter, within shouting distance of the enemy. 'We could often hear Jerry shouting and singing,' wrote Maj. Ian Beadle, E Troop commander, 'the latter always on Friday nights. Women's voices too!'[7] In places, the warring positions were only 50yds apart. So close were they that a road that ran through both the British and German lines had to be masked by a hessian curtain to make it safe to cross. With the ground between the two lines sown with mines and booby traps, no man's land lived up to its name. 'Patrolling was just a matter of moving up and down the hedgerows and the first people to throw grenades usually came off the best,' recalled Morris Steele.[8] He knew better than most, having come off worst in a bomb duel that resulted in him being evacuated with hand and head injuries. Only snipers ventured out with any regularity and even they had orders not to shoot for fear of provoking ghastly retribution from the enemy's close-range mortars. At Le Plein they had been bad enough, but at Le Mesnil they were positively murderous.

According to Ian Beadle's reckoning, Four Five were forced to endure as many as '10 or 15 stonks a day'. At first, they were caught unawares. Casualties, 'which had dwindled in previous weeks, began to mount again'.[9] To counter the threat, 'movement to and from the forward troops was restricted to the essential only'.[10] So near were they to the enemy's positions that they could actually hear the 'pop' of the bombs leaving the mortar barrels. Experience soon taught them that they had around 30 seconds to react before impact. It gave rise to a novel early-warning system. A duty NCO was detailed to blow a whistle as soon as he heard the tell-tale 'pop'. It worked well enough for the men in the front line, but was less successful in protecting men further back. Most vulnerable of all were the working parties carrying hot food and drink from the cookhouse 800yds back, through an orchard to the forward positions. A single bomb wiped out a four-man ration party, killing two. One of the wounded survivors recalled:

> Once you were about 600 yds back from our front line you could not hear the warning whistle and our four-man team was caught in this situation. I was very fortunate to be the most distance from the exploding mortar bomb but received a wound in the mouth which broke off a tooth and lacerated my tongue. My mouth was pouring with blood and I was in shock. I had no idea how serious my injury was but made my way to the casualty tent. I was seen by a doctor and given an injection in my arm and a cup of tea...[11]

For over a week, Four Five remained pinned down. B Troop, in reserve, lost five men injured in a single day and, overall, it was estimated that 400 bombs a day fell on the positions occupied by the two commando units.[12] Things became so bad that rations and ammunition had to be brought up at night by men wearing canvas shoes to deaden the noise. But no matter how much care was taken, nowhere felt safe at Le Mesnil, day or night. As if to prove the point, the Germans raided one of the commando listening posts in the early hours of 6 August. In a flurry of grenades, two men from A Troop were killed and another wounded.[13] It was, as Derrick Cakebread put it, a 'rough time' in what became known as 'Bomb Alley'.

Not that you'd have known it from Doc's letters home. 'We have had some very nice days here lately, duck,' he told Maud in a letter post-dated

8 August. 'I should think that in peace-time it was very much the same as Kent all around here, altho' there seem to be more apple orchards. I should like to have seen them in the spring... Well my dear, I'm afraid there's no more news that's different...'

He gave the impression of being more concerned with the V1 situation back home than his own discomfiture under mortar attack. From newspapers, he'd seen that the aerial assault on southern England was continuing. He sincerely hoped they all 'passed over' Colyer Road and wondered if Maud had taken to sleeping in their air-raid shelter again. Resolute as ever in his reticence, he maintained the lie, writing on 9 August:

> It's a job to know what to put in these letters, duck. There is no news worth writing about. We just go on here, one day very much the same as another.
>
> I am of course looking forward to the day when I shall see Julia. That will be a day for me sweetheart, and I suppose you are content now, eh?'

That same day the unit war diary reported 'enemy aircraft active', dropping flares and bombs to the west of the commando positions. Over the next five days the Germans kept up the pressure. Enemy mortars were 'active throughout the day' on 10 August, 'particularly busy' on 11 August and 'as active as ever' on 12 August. Enemy patrols were also reported, while aircraft carried out bombing sorties during the small hours. It was the same old story on 13 August. The war diary reported: 'Enemy aircraft again active during the night. His mortars opened up early in the morning and kept up a shoot at intervals throughout the day.' During the next 24 hours, sixty-five bombs fell on Four Five's position, five of them on the Commando Command Post. There was more aerial activity on 15 August, with bombs dropped north and south of Four Five's perimeter.

From somewhere inside the embattled lines, pocked by mortars and rank with the stench of dead livestock, Doc resumed his correspondence as though he were writing from a parallel universe. Leaving aside V1s for a moment, his first thoughts were for Julia:

> I shall like to see her. She sounds a lovely little thing. Hope it isn't too long... but all in good time, eh, duck. We shall have a lot to make up for won't we...

> We have nearly everything we want in the way of cigs and soap and so on. The food isn't too bad, duck, but too much stew. Yes, we are getting bread now. That makes a change.
>
> We could do with a spot of leave now. One chap in each Troop goes to a rest camp about every four days so, of course, it would take months almost for everyone of us to go. I should like to have gone while this hot weather is on. I miss the swimming as much as anything here, I think...
>
> All the war news is very good now, isn't it, duck?[14]

So it was. While Doc dreamed of walks along the beach at Minster and claimed to have 'no news worth writing about', the battle for Normandy was reaching its climax. Everywhere else, the Allied armies were advancing and the retreating German Army was desperately fighting to avoid encirclement. To the south, the narrow lanes around the tiny village of Falaise were choked with death and destruction. But even as the noose was tightening around the fugitive Wehrmacht, the scene confronting Four Five appeared dishearteningly familiar.

The dawn of 16 August showed every likelihood of following the same pattern as the previous fifteen days. 'Enemy AA and mortars again very active,' noted the war diary. At 12.10 a.m. signs of German patrol activity in front of C Troop was 'broken up' by bursts of Bren-gun fire. Then, for the first time in more than a fortnight, an eerie silence settled over the fields around Le Mesnil. At 3.40 a.m. a report reached Commando HQ that the enemy had 'faded away'. After a rare day of peace, Four Five peppered the enemy positions with mortars without retaliation. That night, patrols crept cautiously across no man's land. One approached to within 25yds of the German lines without hearing a sound. Another opened fire with Brens in an attempt to provoke a response. But there was none. By dawn, the reason was clear. The men who had made their lives a misery for the past two and a half weeks had gone. All of their activity in recent weeks had been nothing but a ruse to mask their planned withdrawal.

Less than 4 hours after the patrols returned, Operation Paddle, the prearranged plan for the pursuit, swung into action and Four Five were finally on the move.

Over the coming days there would be plenty for Doc to write about, if only there had been a pause in the action long enough to do so. After the stultifying weeks spent on the 'phoney front', the contrast could hardly

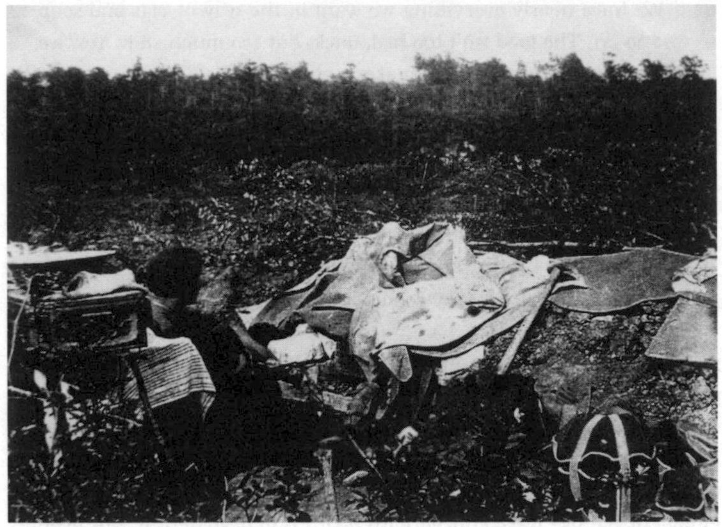

Trench warfare, Normandy style. Commando positions on the 'phoney front'. (via F. Harris)

have been more marked. It was a return to the first few frantic days after the landing, only this time the commandos had the whip hand, as they chased and harried the retreating Germans all the way back to the River Seine. 'It was our stock in trade,' recalled Fred Harris. 'Night infiltrations. River crossings. Bloody hairy stuff. The old Jerries were panicking a bit and one of our first jobs was to capture some high ground around a place called Angerville.'[15]

The 300ft-high Brucourt-Angerville ridge lay roughly 5 miles behind the enemy lines and dominated the German positions east of the River Dives. It overlooked all of the river crossings in the vicinity as well as a broad swathe of marshland, which the Germans had deliberately flooded with seawater to render it a barrier to tanks and infantry. To reach the high ground, this swamp would have to be negotiated. First, however, a route had to be found that avoided the enemy outposts. From Bavant, which had been occupied after the Germans pulled out of Le Mesnil, patrols from Four Five splashed across the inundated marsh to recce the enemy positions. Over two days, they pinpointed the German posts and found potential crossing points. These forays were the prelude to a full-scale brigade night infiltration: its objective was to capture the prominence as quickly as possible and then stay there. It would then be up to the Germans, as Brig. Mills-Roberts put it, 'to drive us off it if they could'.[16]

Organised, mounted and executed in a little over 12 hours, the plan was a simple one and did not appear to Peter Young to be 'a particularly promising expedition'.[17] But as long as the troops stayed close together, No. 3 Commando's pugnacious leader thought there was at least a chance of finding the objective. So it was that at 6.00 p.m. on 19 August, Four Five followed Nos 3 and 4 Commando over a duckboard bridge across the Dives en route to a forming-up position for the advance. It was hard going, but after struggling through a mist-shrouded marsh, they struck a railway line that they followed until they reached a canal, which they crossed via an improvised bridge. Advancing warily with Doc and the rest of A Troop was Lt Muir Beddall:

> The entire Brigade was advancing slowly in single file. The advance guard had laid white tape to ease direction finding – this was the first of many occasions on which this successful form of navigation was used. The night was pitch black and the Commandos, exhausted by weeks of action, stumbled and groped their way forward for what seemed an endless period of time.[18]

Peter Young was astonished at their progress and the lack of reaction to it. It seemed to him as though the brigade, plodding behind, was making enough noise to 'wake the dead', but, incredibly, they managed to pass through the German lines completely undetected. Under cover of darkness, the column wound its way slowly uphill. No. 4 Commando had already branched off towards its objective: another rise on the other side of a broad valley. The rest pushed on, moving across the shoulder of a steep hill behind the enemy's first line of defence. At the head of the column, the leading scouts approached a scattering of buildings on top of the objective. Their disbelief at finding none of the tracks or bridges guarded was matched by the shock felt by a hapless German soldier, who emerged from an outhouse carrying a tray of food and was confronted by a wild-looking group of commandos. He panicked, dropped his tray and bolted before a single shot dropped him dead in his tracks. Moments later, three horse-drawn guns blundered into No. 3 Commando's path. The result was carnage. In a frenzy of running and shooting, squads of men stormed the houses and the position was quickly won. The fighting was not entirely without loss to the commandos, however. Four Five suffered casualties capturing a house. According to Mills-Roberts, one of the

German machine gunners inside called out that they wanted to surrender, but as the commandos broke cover, the Germans opened fire, killing two and wounding several others. The consequences were dire. Enraged at seeing their mates slaughtered, the rest of the attacking party rushed forward and, as Mills-Roberts put it, 'cleared the place up thoroughly'.[19]

By 7.00 a.m., after what the Four Five war diary called a 'short fight', the high ground on either side of a valley was in commando hands. Around 1,600 men had stolen through the enemy's lines to occupy ground that was key to their defence. It was a spectacular coup, but now they were on their own: entirely cut off from supplies of any kind. As his men hurriedly dug in, Mills-Roberts knew it would only be a matter of time before the Germans reacted. He was right. Shells were soon straddling the weapon pits. A self-propelled gun clattered forward to shoot over open sights until counter battery fire rustled up by the commando's artillery liaison officer shooed it away. In the midst of it all, a fighting patrol ran into trouble.

The commandos were barely established on the ridge when orders were issued for A Troop to link up with No. 4 Commando. The aim was to clear a way through the valley and open up a supply route between the two hilltop positions along which ammunition, food and casualties could be ferried. It was a daunting proposition. Brian White had no idea of the strength or the location of the enemy, only that they were lying somewhere between him and his objective and were certain to be on the alert. Mills-Roberts watched them go 'briskly' down the hill to join a road that led across the waterlogged marsh straddling the valley. Accounts of what followed vary. According to Mills-Roberts, there was a sudden sound of 'distant crumping ... and a shell crater appeared just in the rear of the patrol, then a second shell landed in the middle of the patrol killing the patrol leader: two more shells fell in the same place and killed two men'.[20] But those on the patrol told a different story. Muir Beddall, who was in the leading section, recalled approaching some farm buildings on the other side of a bridge when he spotted a German looking over a low wall:

> Brian White came forward and ordered me to take my section to the left and come in at the rear as he charged down the road with the rest of the Troop. There was a stream or ditch on either side of this road. The Germans then opened up with a self-propelled anti-tank gun, and the first shell killed Brian White, as he bravely directed operations from the centre of the bridge, and two others.[21]

Among those making the attack was Bren gunner Fred Harris:

> As we followed the line of the brook we came under small-arms fire, so we did the usual thing. We took cover to find out what the situation was. And the next thing I saw was Brian White, he'd got to the bridge and was standing in the middle of it, waving us on. And at that moment a bloody shell hit him and blew him to pieces along with a marine called McFatter. It was an incredibly brave act. People talk about leading from the front, well Brian White definitely did that day.[22]

There was nothing Doc could do for either of them. Pinned down in front of the enemy strongpoint, the commandos could neither go forward nor backwards. As Doc dealt with the wounded as best he could, the patrol appeared to be caught in a trap from which there was no obvious escape without risking further loss. But, then, from the skies, came salvation. A rain of shells and smoke bombs poured down and, with Lt Tommy Thomas and Marine Derrick Cakebread lingering to give covering fire, the rest of the troop legged it back through the grey smother, taking their wounded with them.

Their retreat was the signal for a counter-attack on the positions occupied by No. 6 Commando. Around 250 Germans in camouflage jackets charged out of a wood, but were halted 100yds short of the commando posts. As they pulled back, another attack burst around the houses held by Four Five. Despite having endured heavy mortaring, E Troop beat off the enemy, at the cost of its commander wounded. But the Germans were not finished. In the afternoon they made a further assault, this time directed at the rear of the commando perimeter. The position, protecting Four Five HQ, was occupied by the remnants of A Troop under Tommy Thomas, who exacted revenge for their earlier losses. Thomas was said to have personally claimed an 'especially good bag with his rifle'.[23] It was the Germans' last throw of the dice. A little later a patrol pushing out from Four Five's perimeter found no sign of the enemy. That night, as rain beat down, engine noises were heard all along the enemy front. It was the sound of a mass withdrawal.

The following morning a commando force made up of A and B Troops under the leadership of Maj. Ian De'Ath, DSO, was sent west to clear a stretch of high ground known as the Brucourt feature. In temporary command of A Troop was Capt. E. Lee-Smith, a South Wales

Borderer attached to Commando Brigade HQ, who had brought up a jeep convoy laden with supplies the previous night. He was the troop's third commander in nine weeks of fighting. They met no opposition and shortly after midday they returned with a few German stragglers in tow and the news that the enemy had pulled out. By dusk, Four Five were concentrated south of the main Varaville-Branville road with its headquarters in a former German supply dump crammed with equipment and loot of all descriptions.

Over the next two days the brigade pressed on, sometimes on foot, occasionally in trucks, but the Germans were always one step ahead. During one night's halt in an abandoned arms dump, A Troop had the misfortune of suffering an infestation of fleas that, according to Fred Harris, 'used our string vests like scaling ladders!' Wrecked bridges hampered their progress, allowing retreat to outpace advance. Eventually, on 24 August, Four Five and No. 6 Commando were tasked with repeating their Angerville success by penetrating the enemy rearguard with orders to occupy the high ground west of Beuzeville.

Guided by a local *gendarme*, the commandos made a wide detour round German machine-gun posts beyond Pont l'Eveque. Fred Harris remembered it as a 'horrendous' night-long cross-country march. 'At every stop,' he wrote, 'some of us almost fell asleep standing up. It seemed like we were walking round in circles.'[24] With Four Five leading, the commandos eventually reached their objective unchallenged shortly before dawn and were already dug in when the first mortar bombs began falling. Just before midday, A Troop sent out a fighting patrol to tackle some troublesome snipers and reconnoitre as far as some railway bridges in front of Beuzeville. Harris, together with the rest of support section and troop headquarters, were left behind to provide covering fire:

> After a while, to our left, a horse-drawn wagon with two Germans on it came jogging down a lane. At the same time, across our front, no more than 200 yds away, a German patrol was making its way from left to right. They obviously hadn't a clue where we were. Amazingly, we saw one Jerry pick up a bit of timber and throw it at someone ahead of him, apparently skylarking... Our pulses were racing a bit now. I remember the TSM saying, 'Hold your fire until I give the order!' And it seemed an age before he called 'fire!' Both men on the wagon were despatched and we also fired at the patrol which then went to ground in tall grass or fern... Later, I was one of the group which went out to check on German casualties. I got,

> from the driver of the wagon, a Luger pistol with a wooden holster which converted it into a mini sub-machine pistol...[25]

Not long after, Tommy Thomas returned to report the bridges blown. On his way back, his patrol dealt with a number of snipers. The men of A Troop had succeeded in passing, 'with great aplomb, through that portion of the wood where enemy opposition was thickest'.[26] The rest of the day was spent strengthening their position to meet an anticipated counter-attack that never came. During the night more patrols were sent out to try and cut the Germans' line of retreat out of Beuzeville. It proved to be another wearying march to no avail. By the time they reached their goal, the Germans had already flitted.

And so the commandos' eleven-week-long Normandy campaign fizzled out in anti-climax. Not that many among Four Five were complaining. Withdrawn from the pursuit, they were able to relax out of range of the enemy's guns for the first time in eighty-three days. As a 48-hour rest was extended to a week, Doc and his pals revelled in the delights of newly liberated Beuzeville, Trouville and Honfleur:

> My Darling Sweetheart,
> We are now having a few days' rest and it is a real treat to be away from the sound of guns for a bit. From here we can go to two or three well known big towns and, altho' there are no pictures or shows of any sort, it does at least make a change to walk about and see shops and people. Yesterday we went to a town near here to hear the Plymouth Div band of the Royal Marines and it was a real treat to hear some good music again. From there we went on to what was a well-known seaside resort in peace time. It hasn't been knocked about much. The one thing we all missed most, I think, was the fact that we could not get a cup of tea anywhere, but, of course, these places have been free only a few days and it is far too early to have canteens there yet.
>
> About three from each troop have gone to Paris today for a march past or something, I expect. I received another letter from you yesterday, duck. Thanks very much. I'm glad you are doing well. This morning I received the cigs that Mabel had sent. That's about six weeks coming, I think, but just in time as we are a bit low on them. I had a letter from mum yesterday, too. Well, sweetheart, there's no room for more. Will write a letter later, so for now,

Cheerio Sweetheart God Bless
Ever Your Loving Eric xxx
For Bobbie [*sic*] and Julia xxx[27]

Two days later word reached him that he was heading home. On 7 September, Doc boarded a ship at Arromanches bound for Southampton and a reception camp at Petworth. There, he was given a new uniform, backdated pay and a rail warrant before being shipped off on leave. He was desperate to see his newborn daughter and desperately in need of rest and recuperation.

The Final Reunion

Eric's homecoming was a difficult one. To Maud, he seemed distant and withdrawn, while for his part he felt almost a stranger in his own home.

Though he didn't realise it, he was physically and emotionally exhausted. For almost three months he had been living on the edge, in more or less constant danger amid harrowing scenes of death and destruction. He had seen close comrades killed and maimed. He had endured day after day of unremitting strain, most notably during the tense standoff in Le Mesnil's 'Bomb Alley' and the hazardous night sorties deep behind enemy lines. All of this came after the fierce and bloody actions fought at Franceville and Merville in the wake of his fraught landing on D-Day.

Maud knew little of his ordeal. How could she? Eric's letters home had given little hint of the agonies he had suffered or witnessed. In his attempts to shield her from the worst, he had successfully masked war's grim realities behind a veneer of half-truths and humour. He made such a good job of it that Maud had no inkling of the psychological trauma he must have been experiencing on what was his first home leave from the combat zone.

In any case, she had concerns of her own to contend with. For almost two and a half years, she had been living the life of a single mother, balancing work with domestic duties, coping with shortages and enduring the terrors of air attack. It had been hard enough with one child. Now, with a baby daughter to bring up, almost on her own, she was feeling the strain. Bobby was becoming a handful. His schoolwork was suffering. It was a wearying and worrying time that had left her at a low ebb. She was feeling every bit of her thirty years: fretting about her looks and fearing that the old spark had gone from their relationship.

Given all they had been through, it was, perhaps, inevitable that tensions would bubble to the surface. Maud was worn out and in need of support and reassurance, and, though neither of them realised it,

Eric was almost certainly suffering the effects of battle fatigue. Their fortnight together was not what either of them would have wished, though Eric could not bring himself to admit it. Writing home from Petworth, he appeared oblivious to the strains that Maud had felt were glaringly obvious:

> Well sweetheart, for me it was a grand leave. Why you thought I was unhappy God knows because, sweetheart, I was happy. I may have been a little different, perhaps, but then it was strange to settle down after the past three months, believe me xxx.[1]

A few days later, reflecting on a leave that had left Maud feeling fraught and frayed, he returned to the subject:

> Did I seem all that different, duck. The only difference I felt was I was very tired at times and just didn't seem to have any strength for tumbles xxx Is that why you thought I was not happy, duck?
>
> We are a funny couple aren't we? Your trouble tho', duck, is you always put me up against Ray or Fred next door and one or two others. Well darling, I shall never be a steady old jogger. I should like to be, just for you, but it can't be done.
>
> But darling, I'm happy as I am. You shouldn't want telling that tho', really. Now I ask you, sweetheart, am I any different to what I was before I was in the army? For myself I don't think so.[2]

Not for the first time, he was missing the point. He appeared not to have recognised just how jaded and run-down Maud was. She was worn out and feeling unloved and she had misread the signs in Eric's unresponsiveness. The penny eventually dropped and his next letter yielded something of the reassurance she craved:

> Well darling and now how are you? Still fit and well? Still lots to do, eh? So you think you look an old hag, eh? Not a bit of it, darling. No mother could look after her family better than you do us three. I think we are lucky for all what you think sometimes! xxx I suppose you had your reasons for thinking that, but take my word for it, darling, we all three love you. See? xxx[3]

What to Eric seemed a simple misunderstanding easily mended took longer for Maud to shake off. His mentions in letters home of an occasional 'kiss waltz' and a variety of dance partners hardly helped. It wasn't long before he was having to explain himself again:

> You mentioned about girls in your last letter. Silly, girls don't worry about me, believe me, darling. I am too quiet for most of them and the easy sort don't worry me. So, you don't have to worry about me at all, darling. I have girl friends here and there but either they get fed-up with me or get fed-up with being friends. I don't know which it is...

Before long the mood had changed markedly, a sign perhaps that Maud had accepted that her concerns were unfounded. 'Well darling,' he wrote, 'you sound very happy indeed by your letter and that's how it always need be instead of worrying yourself whether I love you or not. You are silly that way, aren't you xxx.'[4]

The matter resolved, they focused again on the usual concerns: the children, the air raids, and the question of where Eric was headed next. 'There are a lot of buzzes going round, the main one is we are not going into billets this time,' he wrote from Petworth. A few days later, and in the absence of any training, the camp was still agog with rumours. 'We have been all go, getting things ship-shape,' he reported, 'but I expect we shall start as soon as we get to the new camp... As far as I know at the moment we go to this camp for a fortnight and then go into billets.' This time the 'buzz' was spot on. In early October, Four Five moved into Royal Marine barracks at Southsea, near Portsmouth, having been reinforced by eighty men from the Holding Commando and a number of officers and men who had recovered from wounds suffered in Normandy. These included Walter Bigland, Eric's former housemate from his Eastbourne days, who returned to find the unit busily engaged preparing for 'jungle warfare training, in readiness for shipping out to Burma'.[5]

Probably for fear of causing further upset, Eric did not mention the brigade's intended destination in his letters home, though Maud would find out soon enough. Nor did he make any reference to the issuing of tropical kit as a precursor to the move that would have seen them embarking on amphibious operations along the Arakanese coast. But he did speak of training being stepped up, first at Southsea and then at Bexhill-on-Sea where Four Five moved at the end of October.

What Eric called 'real training' got under way that same month. All too quickly, he found himself back in the old speed-marching routine.

After weeks of rest and light training, he was clearly out of practice. 'What a day yesterday, eh duck?' he wrote. 'We did a 16-mile forced march and did we get wet. We started at 10 a.m. and finished it at 2 p.m. Not bad, eh? We all had a full load too, but we felt it after all this time...'[6] Another march left him in agony. 'I had new boots on, so you can bet on what my feet were like when we had finished,' he told Maud. 'The first blisters I've had since the old 222 days.'[7]

The rigours of long-distance marching, however, were not the only thing that was irking him that autumn. Bexhill was only a few miles from Eastbourne, but the two towns were poles apart in Eric's eyes when it came to the way they treated the commandos foisted upon them. In a letter to his mother, he wrote disparagingly of the citizens of Bexhill and the town itself, which he described as a 'dump':

> I always thought it was a posh place. It may have been before the war but it isn't now. It is a very dirty little town and they had a very hard job to get us all billets here, as most of the people didn't want us here. Still, now that we have started to train again we won't see much of it.
>
> It wasn't too bad at Portsmouth. After all there were plenty of dances and pictures there and the biggest dance halls I have ever seen, too, I think, and all the people there were very good, always glad to [see] us, but they don't want us here at Bexhill.
>
> They could just as well [have] sent us to Eastbourne where most of our billets are still open. The people of Eastbourne even asked to have us back there but that's the army all over, isn't it?[8]

While he had no complaints about his own billet in Windsor Road – he reckoned it was 'one of the best', despite being 15 minutes' walk from headquarters – he immediately took against the town and its people. He criticised the lack of entertainment: there were only two dance halls, 'altho' that should not worry me at a time like this', and just three small cinemas. However, his biggest grouse was with the people who had shown their disdain for housing the commandos. He told Maud that the local police had been compelled to go round the town in search of the last billets, a task they completed with about half an hour to spare. Overall, he found the locals unfriendly and unwelcoming. Whenever he met any of them, he reckoned they were 'too proud to speak'. Try as he might, he couldn't ever imagine growing to like the town.[9]

Fortunately, there was 'all sorts of stuff and nonsense' to occupy him. There were full-scale exercises on the Sussex Downs, more speed marches along the coast and a variety of courses to attend. When he wasn't busy with these, there were medical duties to be done in hospitals and the unit's sick, which was situated in a block of seafront flats that he thought had probably been 'very grand' in peacetime. Duties and training aside, he spent as much time as he could away from Bexhill. He paid frequent visits to his old stomping ground at nearby Eastbourne; with friends, he went to dances at the Winter Gardens, though even these weren't what they once were,[10] and he called in to see his old landladies who were always happy to indulge and spoil him.

Weekend leaves were also reasonably plentiful and, for all its faults, Bexhill was at least near enough to Northfleet to allow regular trips home. They gave him a chance to dote on his 'commando baby' – he planted a second Kanzan cherry tree in her honour – and to check on Bobby's progress. As a violinist of no mean ability, he was desperate to pass on his love of music to his children. He became obsessed with acquiring a piano for Bobby to learn on and he imagined a time when he, Bobby and Julia would play together as a family trio:

> Wouldn't it be grand to have him on the piano and Julia on the violin, eh? They should like it alright [*sic*] because I do, if that has anything to do with it. I hope she does better than I did tho', if she does start... Still I could always give her a hand with it, couldn't I? xxx Show her how it is done sort of thing xxx...[11]

Eric's leaves home, hurried as they were, undoubtedly helped to sweeten the pill of separation, though the joy of reunion was not without its anxious moments. One weekend leave in particular had unfortunate consequences. The first Eric knew about it all was in a letter from Maud telling him that she thought she might have fallen pregnant again. He hoped that she was wrong. Neither of them were ready for a third child so soon after Julia's birth. 'Poor old duck,' he wrote on 27 October. 'God, you must be at your wits end to know what to do... You must be worried out of your life...' In another letter he added: 'Gee duck... It would be rotten to have to go through all that again.' As usual, he tried to put a brave face on things. 'It can't be helped now,' he said. He wasn't averse to a larger family, but now wasn't the best of times to be bringing another child into the world. 'We have a couple of good kids... haven't we, duck? xxx Let's hope it stays at two, for now anyway.'

Maud, for one, had plenty on her plate as it was without another baby to worry about. Thankfully, however, it proved to be a false alarm, though the uncertainty lingered for weeks afterwards, adding to the stress of everyday life on the home front. Most worrying of all that autumn was the renewed menace from the air. Scarcely had the danger from the V1 onslaught receded than a second and far more terrifying terror weapon was unleashed against civilian targets in England.

The V2 rocket offensive opened with attacks on London the day Eric returned from France. Since then, they had wrought widespread destruction in the capital and the regions around it. Once again, the communities along the Thames found themselves under attack, only this time from lethal rockets that struck without warning. Like many others, Eric had believed the capture of V1 launch sites in France would signal the end of Hitler's terror campaign, but the arrival of a doodlebug in Swanscombe on 8 November had disabused him of that notion. Five days later, a V2 struck Gravesend, leaving four dead and more than seventy people injured. 'Gee, that was a close one, wasn't it,' he wrote after hearing the news.

Although details are scant, it appears that Maud and the children were caught up in the drama, possibly briefly having to evacuate their home. 'I'm glad you are safe and sound,' he wrote. 'Poor old duck, it must have been rotten for you to have to get the two kids out like that...'[12] That same week fifteen V2s fell on London. Another twelve came down outside. November was a grim month capped by more tragedy when another rocket rocked Gravesend again. Eight people died in the blast on 29 November and more than fifty were injured.

The prospect of ten days' Christmas leave offered welcome relief from such wretched news. For weeks beforehand, Eric could scarcely contain his excitement at the thought of a grand family gathering. He urged Maud to ask Ethel to seek out 'anything extra' for the festivities. 'There seems to be a chance of her being able to get hold of some turkeys this year,' he wrote. 'It should be just like old times.'[13] So it turned out. His great expectations were fully met in a homecoming to remember. He was still bubbling about it when he wrote home from Bexhill days later. 'Did you enjoy the party, duck?' he wrote. 'I think the adults liked it as much as the kids, don't you?'[14]

Party over, Eric departed a frozen Northfleet, locked in the icy embrace of one of the worst winters of the war. Pipes were iced up and roads had been turned into skating rinks. It was just as he'd predicted back in November when he'd been caught in a snow flurry on his way to the firing range. 'It seems as if we shall have a stiff winter,' he had written then. But the outlook was bleaker than either he or Maud could have imagined as the joy of Christmas together dissolved into a tearful parting. 'Poor old duck,' he wrote from Bexhill, 'you can't get used to me going each time can you?'[15]

It was the last time they would ever see each other.

The Road to Brachterbeek

The war wasn't going to plan. All hopes of delivering a knockout blow before Christmas had been shattered by the defeat of Operation Market Garden, the over-ambitious airborne attempt to seize a bridgehead across the River Rhine. Then, in mid-December, as the men of Four Five were preparing for their festive leave, the Germans launched a massive counter-offensive in the west, which had thrown the Allies into disarray. A gap 30 miles wide was torn in the US First Army front and, as Doc headed home, panzers were pouring through the breach in a desperate attempt to drive across the Meuse and capture the Allies' vital supply port of Antwerp. By Christmas Eve, the German advance bulged 50 miles into Allied territory with its tip 4 miles from the banks of the Meuse. Shocked by the setback and the enormity of American losses, Churchill called for a quarter of a million more men to be found to reinforce the Western Front. Among those hurriedly despatched were the men of 6th Airborne Division who had fought side by side with the Commando Brigade in Normandy. By the time Doc arrived back in Bexhill at the end of December, it seemed only a matter of time before they would be joining them. 'The news isn't so good these days,' he wrote to his mother. 'It looks, after all, as tho' we shall have to go back.' He could not hide his frustration and bafflement at the enemy's ability, even with its backs to the wall, to inflict further embarrassment on the Allies. 'It beats me how he beats us back each time. Still, we shall put a stop to that when we get out there again, eh?'[1]

He was less explicit to Maud. There seemed no point in worrying her until he had definite news. Resorting to his time-honoured approach, he insisted 'there is very little news'[2] and kept his letter brief. He asked after everyone. He discussed the weather – 'they haven't had it half so cold here, duck, as it has been at home' – and he talked about getting another set of dentures. However, it was what he didn't say that was now uppermost in his mind: that the Ardennes offensive had altered everything and that the long-anticipated move to the Far East had been postponed indefinitely.

The signs were already there. While the brigade was enjoying its Christmas leave, its commander had been summoned to Lt Gen. Sir Miles Dempsey's Second Army Headquarters in Holland. Back in Bexhill, all the talk was of a rapid deployment. Confirmation did not come immediately, but it hardly took a genius to work out where they were headed. To his mother, Doc wrote:

> A few lines before we get going, wherever we are going. I suppose by the time you get this I shall be well on the way. Of course, they haven't told us anything. We can only put two and two together. I hope it is not so cold when we get there tho'. It has been very cold here with plenty of snow, but today the thaw has come with lots of rain...
>
> I should think we shall be away untill [*sic*] it's all finished this time. Still, it's better than Burma, isn't it? As long as that doesn't come after tho'...[3]

Events were moving fast. A few days after returning from leave Four Five was paraded together. Derrick Cakebread recalled:

> We had just done a field firing exercise when they called us together and announced we were wanted back in Europe. Whoever it was spoke to us said the Jerries had pushed the Yankees back on the Ardennes and we'd got to go back to help 'em out. They gave us five days to change everything. We had to take all the tropical kit back and get our normal gear. And that was all there was to it.[4]

In fact, even as the commandos were returning their 'jungle greens' to the quartermasters' stores, the Germans were in full retreat. But by then the die was cast and orders were issued for No. 1 Commando Brigade's journey overseas. For the second time in a little more than seven months, the brigade was preparing to embark for the European theatre of war, though in very different circumstances and with personnel much changed from the first occasion. Since returning from Normandy, 46 Royal Marine Commando had replaced No. 4

commando and there had been many comings and goings among the other units. As Four Five was restored to full strength, A Troop, in common with most of the other troops, was given an infusion of new blood. Out went Capt. Lee-Smith, back to a brigade staff job, and in came 29-year-old Capt. Dudley Coventry. The troop's fourth commander was, like Lee-Smith before him, an army man. A pre-war regular, he was a gentleman ranker who had soldiered with the Royal Norfolk Regiment before being commissioned into the East Lancashires. He was a flamboyant character, his square-jawed, hard-eyed good looks embellished by a preposterously big ginger handlebar moustache. Thus far, his war had been an unconventional one. Spells with No. 5 Commando and the Parachute Regiment had been followed by cross-Channel forays with small-scale raiding forces, during which he gained a reputation as a fearless leader. He was joined in A Troop by Lt Robert Cory, whose own war had been no less eventful.

The new section commander had joined the Royal Marines as a regular officer at the beginning of the war. He spent more than a year and a half training before being posted to the cruiser HMS *Dorsetshire* shortly after her participation in the sinking of the *Bismarck*. South Atlantic patrols were followed by a brief and disastrous attachment to the Eastern Fleet based in Ceylon (Sri Lanka). Steaming for a secret anchorage at the southern tip of the Maldives, *Dorsetshire*, in company with the cruiser *Cornwall*, fell prey to Japanese dive-bombers. The devastating attack on the afternoon of 5 April 1942 lasted just 11 minutes and left more than 1,000 men from the two ships' companies floundering in the hot oily water. Cory, in command of a gun turret, had slid down the side of the ship as she sank, stern-first, 8 minutes after being struck by the first of at least five direct hits. Picked up by navy destroyers after spending 28 hours in the water clinging to wreckage, he was one of around 570 survivors from a crew of 800. Returning to the UK, he was posted to HMS *Belfast*, and served with her on the Arctic run to North Russia and on D-Day, when she acted as flagship to Task Force J in support of the Canadian landings on Juno Beach. But after three years spent at sea, he thought it was time to do some soldiering and volunteered for the commandos. A few months later, after completing his commando training, he was ordered to join Four Five at Bexhill.

The reorganisation extended beyond troop level to include the medical section. Hugh Smith, who had distinguished himself during the desperate fighting at Franceville Plage and Merville, departed and in his place as medical officer came 23-year-old John Tulloch. A fine athlete and talented footballer, he had graduated from Edinburgh University in 1943 before volunteering for special service. A spell with 10 (IA) Commando was curtailed by a parachute-training accident and he went to France as brigade medical officer; he was therefore well known to Four Five. He took charge of an experienced medical team, consisting of a sergeant and two privates attached to headquarters and six troop medical orderlies, of which Doc Harden was one. In preparation for the unit's planned move to Burma, Tulloch had spent two weeks on a course at the School of Tropical Medicine, but thereafter he had busied himself at Bexhill, doing sick parades, route marches and generally getting to know the men in his section. Included among these, as a supernumerary, was the unit's new chaplain. Known as the 'Bishop', Reg Haw was another veteran of the Normandy fighting. He had landed on D-Day with 47 Royal Marine Commando and was among a few to go ashore without getting his feet wet, a fact he attributed to his status as padre. After all, he liked to tell people, 'one baptism a day was enough for any chaplain'.[5] With his down-to-earth banter, he was a popular addition to the medical section, and a man that Tulloch would come to see as his 'constant companion and support' during the difficult days that lay ahead.

The altered plans meant that final preparations were carried out in a rush and there was no time for the usual embarkation leave. Shortly before leaving Bexhill on 13 January, Doc wrote home disappointedly:

> My Darling Sweetheart,
> ... I haven't written up to now because we didn't know for sure when we would be going, but as far as we know now we shall be going today or tomorrow. Well, sweetheart, I did think we would have had another weekend before we went, but there it is, the army all over, isn't it.
>
> I suppose it will be a very long time before I see you three again. This time I expect we shall be there until it is all over...

With that he changed the subject to the weather, recent incidents involving V2 rockets and the children:

> How is Julia now, duck? [She had caught a chill over Christmas] And Bobbie's [*sic*] tooth? Has it troubled him since. It would be

better to let it come out on its own, but if it hurts him too much have it out. There's nothing worse than tooth ache. How is he going with the piano? I do hope he will take to it and, as you say, he can then teach you. Has Hilda heard from Harry yet? I heard that they are not going back to Italy for three months. Let's hope that is true. It will give him a chance to get home once or twice before they do go again, won't it.

Well, darling, xxx for this time that's all. I'll write as soon as possible when we get going. The letters should not take too long each way this time, that's if it is where we think it is.

Well darling, don't worry too much. I'll look after myself as much as possible,

Cheerio Darling God Bless
Ever Your Loving Eric xxx
For Bobbie [*sic*] and Julia xxx[6]

From a transit camp at Purfleet, Doc travelled with the rest of Four Five through a frozen landscape to the north bank of the Thames. Their destination was the docks at Tilbury. As he boarded the ship that would carry him away for the last time, he could recognise across the river all the familiar landmarks he'd known as a boy. It was hard to imagine that somewhere on the shore opposite, Maud and the children would be going about their daily routine little realising how near he was to them. Once aboard, he passed the time by scribbling a few lines home. There wasn't a lot to say. He wondered if Maud had received some money he'd sent home along with his kitbag and he hoped that there hadn't been any more rockets around Northfleet. But mostly, it was more of the same: questions about Julia's cold, Bobby's piano lessons – 'Tell him I shall expect him to be able to play me something when I come home' – and his mother's plans since repairs to her house in Factory Road had been completed. For the rest, he simply wanted to offer some comforting words:

Well darling, for the third time I am going across. I should be used to it by now, shouldn't I? And so should you, but I suppose it will always be the same with you, won't it xxx

Try not to worry, duck. I'll take as good care of myself as possible. We hope to be there some time on Mon. I hope it isn't too rough. Last night at the camp we went to see an ENSA [show]. It was very good indeed. There was a sextet well known on the wireless, I believe. I forget their name (you know how good my memory is). There were also two singers. They were very good. They sang among others 'Ome Alone'. Also, there were three chaps just fooling about and were they good!

Of course, duck, we don't know for sure where we are going. If we did we couldn't say, but, of course, each chap has his own idea where and what...

Well darling, there is very little more to write about. I suppose we shall have to wait till we land before we can get this off to post, so for now,

Goodnight Darling God Bless
Ever Your Loving Eric
For Bobbie and Julie [*sic*] xxx[7]

Four Five landed in Ostend on 15 January, a week after Hitler had sanctioned a limited withdrawal from the tip of the bulge and the same day that divisions from the First and Third US Armies had linked up at the sharp end of a pincer movement designed to nip out the Ardennes salient. For two days, while Four Five languished in a Belgian Army barracks formerly occupied by German troops, the retreat continued. Hitler's Ardennes gamble had failed and the action was petering out as the units of the Commando Brigade briefly went their separate ways to bolster depleted British formations: 3 Commando to 11th Armoured Division, 46 RM Commando to Antwerp on anti-sabotage duties and Four Five together with 6 Commando to 15th (Scottish) Division on the snow-fringed banks of the River Maas.

A train carried them through the wintry Dutch flatlands as far as the town of Helmond, a few miles east of Eindhoven. 'We were all freezing cold,' wrote Derrick Cakebread. 'The snow was deep and there was no heating on the train. Nor anywhere else in Holland, or so it seemed'.[8] Doc snatched a few moments to dash off a quick letter:

My Darling Sweetheart xxx
Just a few lines. Haven't much time. I should think we shall have some mail perhaps by tomorrow or the next day. We have had quite a good time since being here. Very cold tho'. But it doesn't seem to be quite so cold today. This is quite a nice town and should think in peace-time it was a grand place.

It hasn't been damaged a lot. Seems funny to write about a place and you don't even know where or what it is, doesn't it? Well duck, I hope you three are well and fit as I am at the moment. Well darling, can't stop for more as they have to go in now, so will write again tomorrow. Look after yourself for me,

Cheerio Darling God Bless
Ever Your Loving Eric xxx
For Bobbie [*sic*] and Julia xxx[9]

The rumble of gunfire was a reminder that they were back within earshot of the front line. In Helmond, a convoy of trucks was standing by to ferry them a few miles south to the village of Asten, where they spent the night billeted with families. For Derrick Cakebread that meant sleeping in a straw-covered attic with around twenty others above rooms shared by a Dutch family and their livestock. Doc was luckier. He was one of five commandos lodging in a loft with a large family consisting of a mother and father together with their nine children. Despite the cramped conditions, he was struck by the warmth of the Dutch people:

Dear Mum and All,
A few lines while we have time and a little comfort. Well, I hope everybody is OK... We are in [censored] and from what little we have seen of them, they beat the French hands down.

All the towns look neat and clean and the people are grand. What a difference to the French. You feel that they really want you and put themselves out no end for you. At the moment we are all in different houses... We go out to our meals to the Comdo [Commando] cookhouse.

We shall only be here a few days I expect and then perhaps the front line. They have had lots of snow here but at the moment it is mostly slush with a very cold wind. It will be a long time before we return this time, I think...

Your Loving Son and Brother Eric.[10]

It was still bitterly cold on the morning of 19 January. They shook themselves out of their straw bedding and headed off on the last stage of their journey to the frozen foxholes around Baarlo on the outskirts of Venlo on the Dutch-German border. The 10th Highland Light Infantry seemed only too glad to be taking their leave of the icy riverside scrapings. As the commandos tumbled down into listening posts and formed standing patrols, they could have been forgiven for having a sense of *deja vu.* The weather apart, it was Le Mesnil all over again, even down to the daily dose of mortaring, which added to their discomfort. With only parachute smocks over their battle dress, the men of Four Five were singularly ill equipped for their wintry watch in sub-zero temperatures. Frostbite was a serious risk. At night, it became necessary to relieve sentries so frequently as to defeat the purpose of posting them. Fortunately, however, the Germans, manning a similar straggle of posts on the other side of the partially frozen Maas, were disinclined towards any action beyond trying to keep warm themselves.

For three nights the commandos shivered and froze until on 22 January they were unexpectedly freed from their role in another wartime standoff that had been remarkable only for the appalling coldness. There was no time to rest, however. No sooner had they swapped places with the 8th Royal Scots Fusiliers than they were clambering aboard trucks for the 20-mile journey south along pitted roads to the small town of Echt in a narrow corridor of Dutch territory sandwiched between Belgium and Germany. Signs of recent heavy fighting were everywhere. The snow-shrouded fields were stained black with a litter of incinerated tanks and shattered houses from which curls of smoke were still plainly visible.

Echt itself presented a grim spectacle in the fading light of a winter's afternoon. Rubble-strewn streets were lined with ruins. The disfigured walls promised grim retribution to the town's liberators with grisly graffiti urging the defenders to 'Remember Aachen' and 'Exterminate the slayers of our women and children'.[11] Disgorging from the trucks, the commandos settled down amid the contorted remains of houses for what promised to be another uncomfortable night made worse by the warning to prepare for action the next day. In the freezing darkness, plans were laid and briefings made for an advance towards Linne via two straggling villages situated in a loop in the Maas. Four Five's objective was to capture the second of these. Its name was Brachterbeek.

Hundreds of miles away, back home in Northfleet, Maud went about her business oblivious of the events unfolding in a tiny corner of Holland. The previous evening she had received two letters from Doc.

Neither gave any inkling of trouble. The first had been written three days before, shortly before Four Five reached the line of the Maas:

> My Darling Sweetheart xxx
> Here we are again, my dear. How is everything and everybody? Julia better yet? And Bobbie [*sic*], is he alright?
>
> Well dearest, it is very cold here and tonight the wind is very high. The snow has gone from here quite a lot, a lot of slush about now. Hope Bobbie [*sic*] likes the piano, darling. We have had a long train journey here, about 17 hours on the train, the rest by lorry. The train had wood seats... Very cold.
>
> There are very good transit camps all over the place now, tho'. If we have to go a long way, we stop and have a hot meal. That helps a lot too. I hope you have finished with the cold weather now, duck, and no burst pipes.
>
> Did you get my kit-bag alright, duck? All my shirts and shoes and things were in it. I sent it the day we left Bexhill...
>
> Well darling, I don't know for how long it will be this time. Three months at least, I should think. Perhaps six. Who knows?
>
> Well, my darling, little more to write about this time, so until tomorrow...[12]

The second letter, written on 19 January, contained £2. It was just a brief note by way of an explanation for some photographs he had ordered. They were pictures of his first troop commander, Buzz Grewcock:

> Darling xxx
> I forgot to tell you in the other letter. There are four photos on their way to you. They will be about three weeks, I should think. They are where the officer is shaking hands with Laycock. He was our troop commander who was killed that night in Bréville. He was the best officer in the whole Commando. The best always go like that don't they...
>
> Cheerio Darling
> Eric xxx[13]

Maud tucked the letter carefully back into its envelope. Later, she would return to it and, in pencil, add the date and time of its arrival: 'Monday evening, 21.1.45'. It was the last word she would receive from him.

Advance to Contact

Stiff with cold and eyes red-rimmed with tiredness, the men of A Troop were slow to rouse in the pre-dawn darkness of 23 January. Few had managed more than forty winks of shivering sleep in their ruined refuges. Eve-of-battle nerves and sub-zero temperatures had seen to that. Amid the usual moans and groans there were half-hearted attempts at humour, but as frosty morning followed freezing night there was little to laugh about. The mood was edgy as Robert Cory shook himself into action. Outside, engines growled and tanks jarred and jolted into clattering life. The last time he'd seen action it was from inside one of HMS *Belfast*'s hulking turrets, blazing away at the Normandy shoreline. He had come close to death in the bomb-churned waters of the Indian Ocean. This was an altogether different test, however. More than five years after joining the Marines, he was about to lead his section into combat for the first time. Going out into the mush of churned snow, he called his section together. As they lined up a flickering red glow caught his eye. It was Doc, sucking on a Woodbine. In a sudden release of tension, Cory barked: 'Put that bloody cigarette out.'[1] With that they took their places in the long column shuffling out of Echt.

What Robert Cory described as an 'advance to contact' marked the next stage in a limited offensive designed to overrun the last remaining area still occupied by the Germans west of the River Roer. Launched seven days earlier as the Ardennes battle dragged on to its inevitable conclusion, Operation Blackcock had developed into a vicious slogging match waged in the main by the 'poor bloody infantry' in conditions described as 'unspeakably bad'.[2] Always bitterly cold, 'it thawed, froze, fogged, snowed and rained, sometimes all five in a mushy mixture within 24 hours'.[3] And yet there had been no letup as the men of 12th Corps edged their way slowly but determinedly forward day after dismal day, 'from river to river and brook to brook, from copse to copse, hamlet to hamlet and house to house'.[4] In that narrow triangle of frozen polder fields, with Roermond at the apex, with the sides bordered on the west by the Maas and the Juliana Canal and on the east by the meandering intricacies of the rivers Wurm and Roer, the Germans had constructed three defensive trench systems protected by trip wires and minefields in advance of the Siegfried Line.

Variously known as the Heinsberg salient or the Roermond triangle, it had become a fortress held by two German divisions, the 176th and 183rd, stiffened by the addition of a regiment of parachutists who more than justified their fearsome reputation. Fallschirmjäger Regiment Hubner was a first-class fighting unit. Ordered to fight to the bitter end, many in its ranks did precisely that, selling their lives dearly with a display of fanatical bravery worthy of a better cause. Theirs was a tragic resistance whereby the wastage of life and courage availed nothing but 'a vain, empty, suicidal, self-inflicted total defeat' that grew worse with every hour. Starved of reserves, they fought one delaying action after another as 52nd (Lowland) Division battled to clear the ground towards Heinsberg while 7th Armoured Division and 43rd (Wessex) Division struggled to mop up the flanks. On 21 January, Regiment Hubner's stubborn defence of the small village of St Joost had cost two battalions of the Durham Light Infantry and the Rifle Brigade almost seventy casualties. It was only after the most bitter of house-to-house fighting involving flame-throwing tanks that they were defeated, leaving 100 dead to be counted amid the torched ruins. Three days earlier, two Scottish battalions had suffered more than 100 casualties clearing a couple of neighbouring villages just inside the German frontier.

By the time No. 1 Commando Brigade entered the fray, no one in 12th Corps was under any illusions about the will of the enemy to resist or about the grit and determination that would be required to turn them out of their skilfully sited defensive positions. Nor was there any misapprehension that this was anything other than an infantry-style operation involving commandos. Codenamed 'Dolphin', the Commando Brigade thrust on 23 January was merely part of 7th Armoured Division's two-pronged advance intended to clear the enemy from its left flank between the Maas and the railway linking Sittard to Roermond. The aim was to capture the villages of Maasbracht and Brachterbeek as a preliminary to the seizure of Linne, a fortified village on the far side of a stream called the Montforterbeek. This in itself was a prelude to the division's assault on Montfort, a move designed to ease 52nd (Lowland) Division's advance. If past experience was anything to go by, it promised to be a difficult day, fraught with all the usual hazards of a journey into the unknown. To that extent, it was not dissimilar to any of the more notable infiltrations carried out by the brigade in the latter stages of the Normandy campaign. The big difference was that they had been carried out under cover of darkness; the approach to Linne was timed to take place in broad daylight. Furthermore, it would mean marching through flat, open country clad in airborne smocks and green berets that rendered the wearers doubly conspicuous against the gleaming white backdrop of snow-shrouded fields. To compensate for such disadvantages, the brigade had, at least in theory, the support of a handful of Cromwell tanks belonging to C Squadron, 1st Royal Tank Regiment (RTR), some armoured cars manned by the 11th Hussars and the guns of 3rd Regiment, Royal Horse Artillery.

The only route towards Maasbracht and Brachterbeek that appeared to offer any cover was along the course of a dried-up stream, but, in the absence of a reconnaissance, it was discounted. Instead, it was decided to assault Maasbracht from the west, having wound their way across the iced-over Juliana Canal near Berkelaar before re-crossing via a footbridge. All of this was to be done before daylight, with artillery concentrations on the eastern end of the twin objectives covering the final advance. By 8.30 a.m. all was ready and No. 6 Commando moved out of their forming-up position on Stevensweerd.

A last-minute recce carried out by the 11th Hussars seemed to indicate Maasbracht to be only lightly held, but the commandos were taking no chances. Around 9.00 a.m., No. 6 Commando re-crossed the canal and, with Four Five and brigade HQ trailing back as far as Berkelaar, pushed on, supported by 1st RTR's white-painted Cromwells. At any moment, they might have expected to come under fire, if not from Maasbracht, then from mortars or artillery ranged further back, but there was nothing, only an eerie silence. In the crisp, bright morning light, they strode warily through a virtually deserted main street that only the day before had been occupied by German troops. It was all rather perplexing. They had now been on the go for 1½ hours without the slightest sign of any opposition. A few minutes later, their job done, No. 6 Commando settled down in easy occupation, while Four Five carried on towards the next-door village of Brachterbeek.

As they marched through Maasbracht, a 'wildly excited' Dutch policeman suddenly appeared at the side of the road and began handing out apples to the passing commandos. Robert Cory's section of A Troop took the lead, and as they headed out on either side of the snow-packed road, they were cheered by No. 6 Commando. It wasn't long before they were beyond the row of houses and out into open country again; files of silent men, their 'steps making little noise in the crisp, flaky snow, which dazzled the eye wherever one looked'.[5] The air was fresh and clean and to Four Five's intelligence officer, Bryan Samain, 'it was difficult to believe that somewhere before us an alert, hard-fighting enemy lay in wait, determined to give battle'.[6] At the head of the column, Cory was just as puzzled. 'There was no information about enemy dispositions ... and we approached Brachterbeek without knowledge that the Germans had withdrawn from there too,' he later wrote.[7] Along the way, he passed by a camouflaged Cromwell tank, incongruously parked by the side of the road:

> The tank commander said he was having a bit of trouble with the conditions, but would I like him to take us in. What he was meant to be doing there, I have no idea, but I declined his offer, saying 'not until we had been fired on', as I reckoned that, in the circumstances, he might be rather a liability. However, I told him that the CO was not far back and might want to use him.[8]

Brachterbeek was reached by 10.30 a.m. Once again, there was no opposition, although unlike Maasbracht the village had not been abandoned. As Cory's men searched through the houses, they saw the first ominous signs of trouble. It was written in the frightened faces of the villagers. 'They were,' he later wrote, 'considerably excited and agitated'. With good reason. They were certain that 'the Germans could not be far away'. But where? And in what strength? With no clear idea of what they were heading for, A Troop received orders to push on. Their route now took them south-eastwards, following the road as it led out of Brachterbeek through open country towards a junction some 300yds distant. Beyond it stood Maasbracht railway station. Before moving off, Dudley Coventry reorganised the troop. Having led into Brachterbeek, Cory's section stood aside to let Tommy Thomas, the Military Cross hero of Operation Vixen, take over at the front. After a brief pause, Cory then fell in some 150yds behind and slightly to the left. Ignoring the road, he led his men across a field that lay between the village and the Montforterbeek. Just beyond it, clearly visible, was the tower of a windmill, standing alongside the road that led into Linne. Bringing up the rear was troop headquarters, led by Coventry and including among its number TSM Harry 'Wiggy' Bennett, marines Johnny Haville and Dickie Mason, the troops' mortar team, and Doc.

Support section, A Troop. Johnny Haville is third from left, with TSM 'Wiggy' Bennett, capless, fifth from left. Neil Patrick is standing second from left and Derrick 'Cakes' Cakebread is sitting far left next to Haville. (via D. Cakebread)

There was a discernible tension in the air. The behaviour of the inhabitants had put everyone on their guard, yet it remained eerily quiet, with the silence broken only by the jostle of equipment and the scrunch of boots on hard-packed snow. At the rear of Thomas' party, on the right of the road as it sloped towards the fields, Bren gunner Fred Harris was struck by the almost unnatural serenity. Ahead, beyond the silent column of marines, he could see the station buildings just the other side of a road junction where a row of cottages dribbled round the corner. Still nothing stirred. There appeared to be no sign of life anywhere. Walt Bigland was beginning to feel the effects of their long trek. Part of a sub-section commanded by Sgt 'Dolly' Gray, he had been lugging his Bren gun for the best part of 4 hours and was only too happy to exchange it for fellow marine Neil Patrick's Sten gun.

Patrick hadn't been included among the leading party. He'd been back with troop headquarters when they set off towards the station. Not long after they had gone, however, Dudley Coventry had given him a message to deliver verbally to Lt Thomas. The gist of it was to look out for a patrol from 7th Armoured Division's Reconnaissance Regiment, which was thought to be 'possibly' somewhere ahead of them. Heading down the road, he had overtaken Cory's section, who were plodding somewhere across the field to the left, without even noticing them.[9] He eventually caught up with Thomas' section when they were within 50yds of the small row of cottages leading to the station crossroads. All was perfectly peaceful, but he had hardly had time to deliver his message and swap weapons when everything changed:

> Thomas' reaction to my message was to whip his rifle to his shoulder and shoot a person emerging from the station buildings. I reminded him of my message, to which he replied: 'The man is wearing black equipment.' He was right ... the man was a German soldier wearing black equipment on top of a white snow suit![10]

According to Patrick, the South African's deadly accurate shot acted as the 'starting gun' for hostilities to commence, and this they did with a vengeance. As the enemy soldier crumpled to the ground, fire erupted around them as a hail of bullets sprayed the road. For a few seconds it was chaos as the commandos scattered in all directions in a mad scramble for cover. Fred Harris and his number two, Don Vinten, dived for a shallow roadside ditch as bullets tore lumps out of the snow. Walt Bigland flung himself after them, but the ditch gave little protection. Even after scrunching his body into the tightest of balls Walter reckoned that at least half of it was exposed above road level. Their plight appeared hopeless: they had walked into a trap from which there seemed no escape. As bullets skipped across the road, mortar bombs began peppering the fields, showering them with clumps of snow and ice as they lay pinned to the ground, scarcely daring to move. Just when all seemed lost, Bigland caught sight of a figure darting across the open road. He was carrying a Bren gun, his Bren gun. 'It was Neil Patrick. I couldn't believe what I was seeing. There was heavy fire coming in at us, but there he was, running forward. I saw him put the Bren on a gate post and open fire.'[11]

When the commandos dived for cover, Patrick had found himself lying alongside Sgt Gray, close to some bungalow-like buildings. Having decided a walk back to troop HQ was no longer an attractive proposition he had thrown his lot in with Gray's sub-section:

> My active participation in the battle did not last very long. I... took up a position on the pavement close to the bungalows, loosed off a

> couple of magazines in order to keep the German heads down and allow the rest of the lads to seek a safe haven in their respective buildings...[12]

The second part of his plan worked perfectly. While he blazed away, the rest of the section scurried across the road into the cluster of empty houses. Walt Bigland made it safely into one that appeared to be on fire. On the count of three, Fred Harris and Don Vinten leapt up and sprinted 30yds diagonally across the bullet-swept road to the last cottage in line:

> I went feet first at the door, the intention being to boot it in. Unfortunately, it didn't turn out like that. I simply bounced off what was a very stout door. My Bren clattered to the ground and the Germans in the station spotted me. A machine-gunner sent several bursts at the building and along the road. But luckily there was a shallow recess in the doorway. As I squeezed myself into it a burst of fire hit the brickwork spattering my face with chippings and shredding my leather jerkin and parachute jacket. One of my pockets was ripped away and two 'Mills bombs' dropped to the ground. It was pretty hairy and definitely not a place to dwell in. My Bren gun lay about six feet away and self-preservation was the order of the day. Don had managed to smash a window through which he'd climbed into the house. So I turned and made a break for it and got in the same way. I then returned to the door, opened it from the inside and retrieved my Bren with the help of a 'twig' broom...[13]

By then, most of the section had reached the relative safety of the houses, but the marine who'd made it possible for them to escape was now himself in deadly danger. 'At least one German machine-gunner had not read the script,' Patrick later wrote, 'and I was hit almost immediately.'[14] Regaining consciousness seconds later, he heard one of the marines calling out: 'Jock has had it. He has been hit in the head':

> My reaction to this news was fuelled by sheer rage and a wish for retribution, to the extent that I took my gun out in the middle of the road, where I had a better view of the station buildings, lay down in the snow, fired off all the ammunition I had left in the general direction of the station windows where their fire was obviously coming from. During this time I was also exhorting the

> fatherless Germans to come out and fight. At this stage, I really feel I was certifiable!
>
> Fortunately, this state of mind did not last long and, reason prevailing, I returned with my gun to Sgt Gray's bungalow...[15]

Inside the cottages, Fred Harris and Don Vinten moved through to the back and, from a rear window, spotted signs of life at a windmill some way behind on the other side of a bridge over the Montforterbeek. 'We exchanged fire several times,' wrote Harris, 'but it shortly went quiet... To all intents and purposes we were pinned down, not knowing what was going on.'[16] Holed up in a neighbouring cottage, Walt Bigland felt similarly isolated. 'We were cut off from everything,' he said.[17] Told to keep watch from the back, he suddenly saw distant movement across the field. He could just make out the figures of three men darting through the snow to some dark shapes on the ground. Though he didn't know it then, it was the first inkling that anyone in the forward section had about the drama going on behind them.

At the moment the Germans opened fire, Robert Cory's section had been spread across the field, trudging through snow sometimes halfway up to their knees. As machine guns raked the ground and mortar bombs blew geysers of snow, Cory saw Tommy Thomas' men scuttling towards the buildings near the station crossroads before losing sight of them. 'We were completely exposed but, astonishingly, no one was hit,' he wrote.[18] After that things happened fast. To his right, he could see two large clamps of potatoes covered with mud and straw. Over to the left was an electricity pylon, its severed cables hanging forlornly to the ground, and beyond it, the dark, dominating presence of the windmill that Fred Harris would shortly spray with his Bren gun. It didn't take a genius to work out that the potato clamps, some 4ft high by 20–30ft wide, represented the only source of protection on that bullet-swept field. Instinct took over as the section suddenly took off in a wild surge before throwing themselves behind the nearest clamp. All bar one of them made it safely under cover. Looking around, Cory noticed a solitary marine coolly taking aim from a prone position under the slight, snow-covered camber of the road. He was evidently shooting at some 'shadowy figures moving over to our far left from where the fire seemed to be coming'.[19] 'I thought this to be highly dangerous (which it certainly was) and called him in behind the clamp.'[20]

From the cover of the potato stack, Cory's section, which included his batman (marine officer's assistant) Marine Whitney, together with

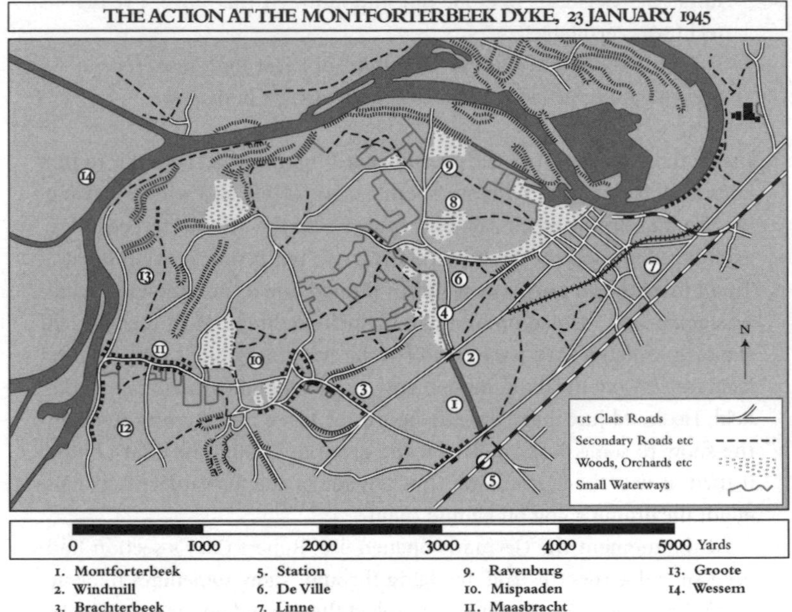

45 RM Commando's advance towards Brachterbeek on 23 January 1945.

marines Wales, Weston and Wheeler, replied fitfully to the barrage of incoming fire. Given that the Germans were wearing white camouflage suits, Cory suspected their efforts were probably ineffectual. Amid the hiatus, he conferred with Tim Cook, his section sergeant. A risky plan was already forming in his mind:

> I thought that 'Tommy' might be heavily involved in some close quarter engagement in the buildings ahead and, clearly, we were not much use where we were. I thought of [putting down a] smoke [screen] but with only phosphorous grenades that was not much of an idea and obviously we had to get forward to 'Tommy'. I told Sgt Cook to get bayonets fixed and sent Whitney back to Troop HQ in the farmhouse at the crossroads [some way behind] to say that I was going to make a dash for the buildings where Tommy had disappeared.[21]

Decision reached, Cory told Weston to stay where he was and give what covering fire he could with his Bren. Then, on his order, they leapt out and went for it, hell for leather, straight into a storm of fire:

> Almost immediately Wales and Wheeler went down and I was hit in the arm which knocked me over. I picked myself up but was then hit three times in my leg, presumably by a machine gun burst, and went down, face first in the snow...[22]

The charge had turned into a bloodbath. Realising the futility of trying to advance further in the face of the enemy's overwhelming firepower, Tim Cook led the survivors to shelter behind the second potato clamp, some 20yds from where his badly wounded section leader lay struggling for breath, his lifeblood draining into the snow. Weighed down by his pack and equipment, not to mention a 'useless' arm and leg, Cory could not move, let alone turn himself over. For a moment, he thought he was going to suffocate in the snow. But, just as he started to fear the worst, he felt something tearing at his straps:

> Sgt Cook [had] crawled back to me, under continuing heavy fire, and cut away my equipment so that he could turn me on my back. He then bound on field dressings which the others threw to him from behind the clamp. During this time he was constantly under fire and I kept telling him to get back under cover, which he quietly refused to do until he had done all he could for me...[23]

Having finished patching up his officer, Cook, who was miraculously still unscathed, dashed back behind the potato clamp. Cory lay on his back in the open, his head swimming with shock and pain, as the bitter cold that would leave him with severely frostbitten feet took its grip. Time lost all meaning, but a little while after, he saw Marine Whitney running past on his return trip from troop HQ, 'presumably with orders from Dudley Coventry for the section to stay put'.[24] Later still, he heard one of the unit's jeeps revving spectacularly as it hurtled down the road, its crew cheering madly, en route for Tommy Thomas' beleaguered section. That was all he remembered until, quite suddenly, he realised he was no longer alone. Someone was kneeling beside him, calmly checking his wounds while a rain of bullets from unseen machine gunners and riflemen kicked up puffs of snow around them. He recognised him instantly. It was Doc Harden, the same Doc Harden he had admonished a few hours earlier for sneaking a quick drag on a cigarette as they prepared to move out of Echt. Cory's befuddled brain was working overtime, but Doc appeared unhurried:

> I think he gave me a shot of morphine and said he would 'be back'. I told him on no account to do so and, I guess, that's the last thing I ever said to him.[25]

16

No Greater Love

Like everybody else in A Troop, Johnny Haville had been surprised by the fury of the fire unleashed against them. One moment he had been marching down the road with the rest of headquarters section and the next he was running for dear life back to a brick farmhouse near the edge of the village they had only just left. Taking cover inside, he listened to the crash of mortars and what sounded uncomfortably like shellfire mingling with the ceaseless rattle of machine guns and rifles. It sounded as though all hell had been let loose. In the confusion of shouting and shooting it took a while for the awful truth to register: A Troop was in dire peril, with one section out of sight and apparently cut-off near the station, another section seemingly cut to ribbons and pinned down in a veritable no man's land, and headquarters section powerless to intervene because of the sheer weight of enemy fire.

While Dudley Coventry worked through his decidedly limited options, Haville and his fellow mortar man, Dickie Mason, were ordered out to take up a defensive position in enemy slit trenches by a small hedge at the rear of the Vossen farmhouse. From there, they could see a machine-gun post sited in the windmill, 400yds to the left on the other side of the Montforterbeek, directing steady bursts towards where Cory's section was desperately seeking shelter. It was this gun, with its clear view across the fields straddling the station road, that was causing most concern, though there were, in fact, more hidden machine guns and riflemen firing from positions as close as 200yds away. Further forward they could hear, if not see, the fierce struggle going on around the station crossroads. Then, in the midst of it all, they noticed something else in front of them that seemed to defy belief. It took a moment to work out what was going on, but then they realised that the solitary figure going from one wounded man to another was Doc. How he came to be there and how he wasn't struck by any of the countless rounds spattering the snow, they had no idea. All they knew was that he was the only one moving in a landscape where every other single living person appeared frozen to the spot.

Haville looked on in awe and later recorded:

> He had gone out on his own initiative with his medical bag and was kneeling beside them, tending to their needs, applying field dressings and, no doubt, morphine where necessary; going from one to the other in turn with no regard for his own safety until he had completed his task in his own time. Watching him one couldn't but admire his coolness and dedication. How long he was out there I wouldn't hazard a guess but it was a considerable period. Then, to cap it all, he came staggering back, carrying Marine Wheeler over his shoulder...[1]

Wheeler was wounded in the leg and, according to TSM 'Wiggy' Bennett, Doc did his level best to throw the Germans off their aim by zigzagging back to the farmhouse. At this point, it was unclear just how many times A Troop's medic had been out in the open. Official accounts vary, but Bobby Cory was certain that he made at least four separate journeys, each time in the face of a hail of fire; the first time to treat the wounded where they lay and the next three times to bring them in. If correct, then Wheeler was rescued following Doc's second venture into no man's land. But, according to Wiggy Bennett, there was a period after bringing in Wheeler when Doc was unaccounted for, giving rise to the suspicion voiced by the troop sergeant major that he had made further unseen and unrecorded visits to the wounded. Bennett wrote:

> We made Wheeler comfortable and we then lost touch with Harden for about half an hour, during which time we believe, acting under his own initiative, he went out to the wounded again, or probably twice.[2]

What is certain is that Doc was undeterred by the fire that had penned one section in buildings near the station junction and pinned another to the frozen ground behind. His only thoughts were for the wounded, lying where they had fallen. Marine Wales was his main concern. His wound appeared to be haemorrhaging. Something needed to be done and done fast. Having caught his breath, he prepared for another dash into no man's land, but Dudley Coventry was having none of it.

There were few men in Four Five more fearless than Coventry, yet he was adamant that Doc should not risk his life again. Doc made a vain attempt to plead his case. Uppermost in his mind were the effects of the freezing temperatures on the two injured men lying out in the snow. If their wounds didn't kill them, the cold certainly would. Such was the intensity of fire, however, that Coventry quite reasonably judged that his chances of reaching them alive, let alone returning with them across 120yds of open ground in the face of small-arms and mortar fire were so infinitesimal as to render such a mission suicidal. Doc was ordered to stay put while tanks were ordered up and a smoke screen laid down to cover any further attempts at rescue.[3]

It wasn't the first time that vehicles had tried to break the deadlock. As soon as it was realised that A Troop had run into trouble and was in danger of being destroyed piecemeal, Lt Col Gray had ordered F Troop's four jeeps, bristling with machine guns, to drive forward in support. It was these jeeps that Cory had heard 'hurtling down the road' as he lay out in the open, wounded and unable to move. However, what sounded like a spectacular charge in the manner of the cavalry riding to the rescue of a beleaguered patrol quickly turned to bloody farce as the jeep crews mistook their firing position for the area occupied by Tommy Thomas' section. The cheering that made such an impression on Cory had been the result of a misunderstanding of the shouts and waves coming from the men at A Troop headquarters. Rather than urging them on to the relief of Thomas' men, they were actually trying to stop them driving headlong into the same trap. By the time they realised their mistake it was too late. Barely 100yds beyond A Troop headquarters the leading jeep was pelted with heavy machine-gun fire. Fred Harris saw it suddenly veer off the road, heard a loud crash and assumed it had hit a wall. In fact, with its driver and another man wounded, it had ploughed into a ditch. On board was the jeeps' commander, Cpl Frank Middis:

> I took over from the driver and managed to get our jeep out of the ditch and caught up with the rest of the section at a farmhouse which was occupied by Lieut Thomas and a few men from A Troop. We pulled up at a barn wall which we thought would shelter us from the enemy fire but soon came under machine gun fire again which caused more casualties...[4]

Far from riding to the rescue, the jeep crews were now pinned down themselves. They remained so for some time, with bullets peppering their vehicles, until the very men they had set out to relieve came to their rescue! Not for the first time, Thomas was the saviour. Working his way as close as possible to the trapped men, he tossed them some smoke grenades, which Middis set off before they all dashed round the corner and into the building, bringing their wounded with them.

Even as they were scrambling to safety, the fate of Lt Cory and Marine Wales was hanging in the balance. Dudley Coventry was convinced that their best hope of recovery lay with the Cromwell tanks of 1st RTR's C Squadron. Doc, on the other hand, was just as strongly of the opinion that they would be too late to save them. As far as he was concerned, their only means of survival depended on the speediest possible rescue. All of his training had taught him that he had to act fast. He had done all that he could in the circumstances, but he knew it wouldn't be enough to keep them alive indefinitely. Aside from the dangers of haemorrhaging, his greatest worry was that shock brought on by exposure to the bitter cold would kill them before they could be brought in. That day there was 17 degrees of frost, more than enough to freeze the life out of those men if nothing was done quickly.

Frustrated by the delay that he feared would prove fatal, he made up his mind to circumvent his troop commander. What he decided flew in the face of all principles of military discipline and made a mockery of all the promises he'd made to Maud to take good care of himself. In those moments, however, he appears to have been motivated by a sense of duty higher than those to either his wife or senior officer: it was a commando medic's duty to his comrades. It wasn't a case of being rash or reckless; it was simply a matter of balancing risk against the certainty of death for Cory and Wales if nothing was done soon. While the fighting continued unabated outside, Doc laid bare his plan to TSM Bennett. According to Bennett, he was 'cool and calm' and 'gave no thought to his own safety provided the wounded could be got in'.[5] The two of them then took the idea to Johnny Haville and Dickie Mason. 'TSM Bennett and Doc approached ... to ask if we would volunteer as a stretcher party and try to recover the wounded,' recalled Haville. '"Doc" said they would certainly die if left out in the snow and in such a low temperature.'[6] Without argument or, indeed, any discussion whatsoever, they agreed to do so.

It is not clear how long after the initial rescue that this took place. Nor is it known for certain whether Doc hatched his plan before or after any intervention by the tanks. Indeed, it is not clear whether an attempt was actually made. Neither the 1st RTR war diary nor its unit history make explicit mention of trying to come to A Troop's aid, and Bobby Cory certainly had no recollection of either hearing or seeing any tanks while he was lying in the open. What is indisputable is that the tanks had problems at Brachterbeek.[7] Chief among them was the open ground that made it difficult to reach firing positions without making themselves easy targets for panzerfausts, the German equivalent of the bazooka or PIAT (Projector, Infantry, Anti-Tank) gun. Nor were they helped by the artillery's smoke screen. A lack of wind was blamed for two failures. All the smoke did, according to John Day, was provoke yet fiercer retaliation as the Germans intensified their mortar and small-arms fire in anticipation of a masked advance. Tanks or no tanks, and Johnny Haville always maintained that the rescue effort was renewed only after the failure of the armour to make headway, there was no question about what happened next.

In broad daylight, with Doc leading, the three men left the farmhouse, first making for the cover of the hedge. They were all unarmed. Haville and Mason had discarded all their equipment and sacrificed weapons for speed. They paused momentarily. Then, with nothing but their courage to sustain them, they set off through a gap in the hedge:

> We ... started to run to the casualties who were lying about 120 yds to our front. Doc carried the stretcher and was wearing his red cross [armband] but that did not deter the Germans who immediately fired upon us with machine guns that came from the direction of the windmill to our left. As I ran through the snow I could see bursts of fire kicking up the ground in front of my feet and I wondered what I'd let myself in for, but we continued running, keeping as low as possible till we reached the wounded. Here, we lay down while strapping Marine Wales on the stretcher first. Doc said he would take the front shafts while Richard and I took one each at the rear and we ran, crouching on the return journey, amid small arms fire and the frightening explosion of mortar shells, thankful to reach our HQ in one piece.[8]

Even as they reached cover, artillery fire was registering on the ground around. Doc's attention, however, was focused on his patient. Of the two wounded men lying out in the open, he had recognised that Wales was the most urgent case. But, tragically, during their dash back, the young marine had been hit again. Inside the farmhouse, Doc did all he could for him. Working fast, he tried to halt the bleeding while giving TSM Bennett

A Troop men. Fred Harris is standing on the left. The marine next to him is believed to be Marine Fred Wale, who was known as Wales in Four Five. (F. Harris)

and others in the building a crash course in dealing with a haemorrhage case. Sadly, it was all in vain. The wound that Wales received while being carried out would prove fatal, but Doc knew none of this. He was already busy planning his next move, seemingly undaunted, if not entirely unscathed by his heart-pounding endeavours. It was at this point that Doc told Johnny Haville that his smock had been ripped, either by bullets or shell fragments. What he omitted to mention was that he had also been wounded in the side. When Haville later discovered this, he was astonished 'as nothing seemed to hamper his movements'.[9]

Doc was like a man possessed. Nothing, it seemed, could prevent him carrying out his mission. Not the Germans and certainly not Dudley Coventry. Having started without orders, he had deliberately ignored his troop leader's unambiguous order telling him to stop. What Coventry made of it is not clear. Perhaps he had come round to the idea that faint though the hope was, it was the only chance available to save Cory. Either that or he preferred to turn a blind eye to such an impossibly brave act of insubordination. Whatever his feelings, he made no further attempt to hold Doc back. In any case, it would probably have been pointless. Wound or no wound, A Troop's medic wasn't going to quit now. One more trip would do it, just over a 100yd sprint and back again. What thoughts ran through his mind as he caught his breath before making that final effort can only be imagined. If it occurred to him that he might be chancing his arm one too many times, then he kept it to himself. Truth was, there wasn't long to think about anything much, still less to speak. According to Johnny Haville, Doc was too wrapped up in what he was doing to waste time talking:

> We said very little to each other on these trips, knowing what we were facing and being at the mercy of such fiends. The few words that Eric said were of how we could get these unfortunate chaps to safety and comfort them. That was just his way...[10]

After what he described as 'a short rest', the three of them steeled themselves for the last time and, silent prayers said, rushed out again. Fire was still coming in from the flank, but they covered the ground quickly and safely, dropping down alongside Cory, who was frozen and barely conscious. They worked fast as bullets zipped past them, Haville and Mason lifting Cory while Doc slid the stretcher beneath him. Then, straps secured, they were up and running again, heads bowed forward in the same formation as before: Doc at the front and the other two with one shaft apiece. Incredibly, their luck was holding. They were just about halfway, possibly even nearer, to the hedge and safety when Haville heard a click, 'as if something had passed my left ear'. That same instant, Doc collapsed mid-stride. He was dead before he hit the ground, without uttering a sound.

Behind his prostrate body, there was momentary confusion. It had all happened in the blink of an eye. One moment they were moving, the next they were on the ground, with the stretcher, with Cory on it, lying almost on top of Doc. It took a few seconds for Haville and Mason to take it all in, but even then they could scarcely believe that the man who had risked so much for so long as to seem almost indestructible had been struck down within sight of their journey's end. Bullets were buzzing around them as Haville crawled forward to make sure. A single shot had caught Doc in the back of the head and exited through 'a small round hole in the centre of his forehead without shedding a drop of blood'.[11] The click he had heard was the sound of the bullet passing between him and Mason on its deadly path.

With Doc lying dead beside them, they were now faced with a terrible dilemma. Cory was in agony. The fall had jarred his already grievous wounds. It was clear that he needed to be treated swiftly to stand any

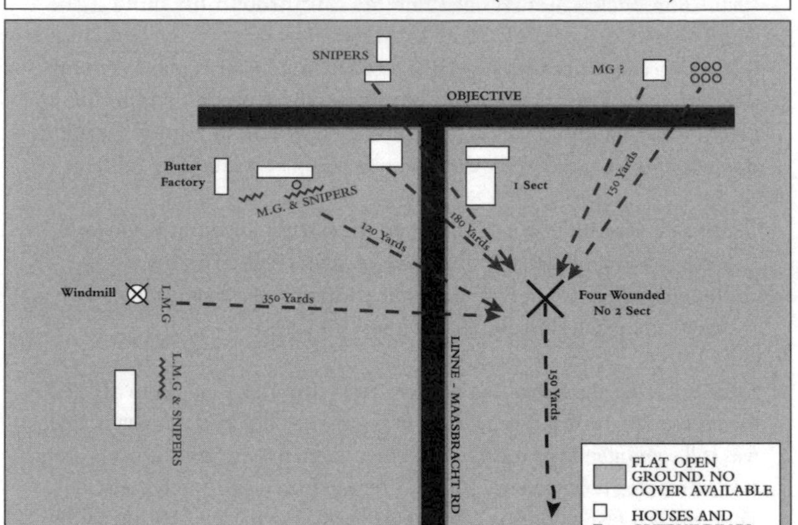

Rough sketch plan showing the scene of the VC action.

chance of surviving and equally clear that the Germans had them in their sights. To try and lift the stretcher was out of the question. Cory was in no doubt about what had to be done. As soon as he realised what had happened to Doc, he made his decision. 'As fire was still coming in, indeed it never stopped, I told them to leave me on the stretcher and get back under cover.'[12]

History repeated itself, however, as, for the second time that morning, his order was ignored. Even then, trapped as they were, face down in a frozen flatland with bullets singing inches above their heads, Haville couldn't help but admire the gesture. 'Here,' he thought, 'was a very gallant officer':

> I told him we would get him back somehow in spite of our serious situation. Obviously, a sniper to our rear had his sights on us and it would have been fatal to stand up and carry the stretcher. I suggested to Richard that if he eased up the front of the stretcher, I would push

> from behind and, by crawling along, use it as a sled. This we found to be successful on the hard snow but very strenuous.[13]

Leaving Doc where he'd fallen, they edged ever nearer to safety. Progress was painfully slow. Then, just a few yards short of the hedge, they saw a figure crawling out to help them. It was Wiggy Bennett. 'How I got out I don't know,' he later recounted. 'We sledged Mr Cory on our stomachs. It was only a hundred yards… I don't know how long it took us. It seemed like hours. We could only push the stretcher a few inches at a time…' Brave though his action was, this was an exaggeration. Both Haville and Cory agreed that by the time Bennett reached them they were no more than 20yds from A Troop headquarters; however, there is no denying that the troop sergeant major's intervention helped ensure a swifter end to their prolonged ordeal. Finally, with one last shove, the three of them managed to push the wounded officer out of harm's way. Safely inside the building, Cory was laid out on the floor. Despite the waves of pain, he passed what information he could to Coventry, 'especially about the windmill which seemed important at the time'. After that he thanked his saviours profusely and was then 'promptly very sick'.[14]

Back in Brachterbeek, John Tulloch had no idea of the rescue mission that had been taking place just a few hundred yards from his regimental aid post. The first he knew of A Troop's troubles was when Four Five's second-in-command, Maj. Ben de Courcy-Ireland came to see him in the early afternoon. Their conversation was brief. 'We've made contact with A Troop,' said Courcy-Ireland. 'They have a lot of wounded. I think that you should go up and see what needs to be done.'[15] Tulloch agreed. A map was produced. He was shown the rough location of Tommy Thomas' marooned section and the route to take, and that was it. There was no word about the enemy machine guns that still had the remnants of Cory's section bottled up in no man's land. Nor was there any mention of the fate of F Troop's jeeps or of the wounded in need of treatment at troop headquarters.

Cursory briefing complete, Tulloch called for his driver, Marine Elliot, and set off in one of the medical section's three jeeps. They hadn't gone far when they were waved down by a marine on the edge of the village. 'You can't go any further,' he warned. 'If you go beyond the houses you come under fire. I've been sent with a message for A Troop and whenever I leave the houses I have been fired on.' Tulloch explained his mission and there followed what he described as a brief discussion that ended with the marine hopping aboard. Seconds later, the last house flashed by and they were out in the open, a fluttering Red Cross flag as their only protection. But it counted for nothing. Almost immediately, they drew heavy fire from over on the left, in the direction of the windmill:

> That first burst missed us but we could feel the second burst hit the body of the jeep below our seats. Elliot kept going ... slightly varying his speed on the snow-covered road. The third burst also missed but was closer and the fourth burst a tyre. I said to Elliot, 'Don't slow down.' He managed to keep reasonable control as we slithered along the road. The fifth burst also missed us and then we were at the farmyard entrance at the left of the road and just short of the T-junction [in fact, it was the station crossroads]...[16]

A sergeant who was sheltering close by waved them into the yard, where they slid to a halt. Leaving Elliot to change the bullet-punctured tyre, Tulloch went straight to the wounded, who were lying in what he took to be a stable. As he went inside, the sergeant called after him, 'The doc is here' and a cheer went up. Tulloch examined each one in turn, covering wounds with field dressings or, in the worst cases, shell dressings. Fortunately, he had brought plenty with him, even stuffing some inside his smock. Scraps of wood lying around were used as makeshift splints. The immediate treatment completed, he wandered out into the yard to be greeted by the astonishing sight of his two remaining jeeps, crammed with medical equipment, drawing up. 'What on earth are you doing here?' he called out angrily. 'Major Courcy-Ireland felt that you would need more transport and sent us up,' came the sheepish reply. Like him, they had displayed Red Cross flags to little effect, but, unlike him, they had miraculously escaped the fire directed at them unscathed.

Overcoming his annoyance at having all his medical stores placed in jeopardy, Tulloch decided to make the most of the situation. He was just about to load all the wounded aboard when Tommy Thomas appeared and told him that there were more casualties in a house on the other side of the road, nearer to the station junction. Tulloch was in a quandary. He knew that he wouldn't be able to leave without them, but he couldn't see any way of reaching them. The road was completely exposed to enemy fire and there was still a shoot-out going on between the holed-up commandos and the Germans in the station. The only solution he could think of was to call a truce and to recover them under the banner of the Red Cross. It was undoubtedly a risky plan, particularly so in view of the rough reception given to the jeeps, but in the absence of any better ideas he thought it worth a try:[17]

> I asked that our side stop firing and see what happened. They did and I stuck the red cross flag from my jeep out of the farm yard gate so that the Germans could see it. Firing stopped. So I walked out across the road carrying the flag, up the garden path to the house opposite. There was a sergeant waving me round to the back, so I went. There were four walking wounded whom I looked at and dressed. Then the sergeant said, 'There is one more marine wounded in a trench in the front garden. We haven't been able to go out and get him.' So I asked for a volunteer to help me and several came forward...[18]

Picking one, Tulloch disappeared round the side of the house, still carrying his flag. Again, the Germans held their fire and they were able to move out into the garden. They found the marine, who Tulloch recognised as the inside-left of the unit football's team, lying, 'cold and miserable', at the bottom of the trench with a bad shoulder wound. 'Getting him [out] was difficult, but we managed and carried him into the house. The sergeant had taken a door off its hinges to use as a stretcher. I went out and stood in the T-junction with the flag while the "stretcher" was carried across to the farmyard.' Some walking wounded took advantage of the ceasefire to cross over as well.

Once in the yard, Tulloch immediately began preparing their evacuation. His own jeep having been repaired, the wounded, totalling thirteen men from A and F Troops, were 'sardined' into the three vehicles, with two stretcher cases slung on a frame on top of the jeep. Then they were off, bumping and revving their way back to Brachterbeek. The truce that had amazingly held for so long was now over and the battle resumed. 'There was a lot of firing,' said Tulloch, though whether any of it was deliberately directed at the convoy is not clear. But by varying their pace to make 'an irregular target', they all made it back safely, though with their vehicles sporting a variety of damage.[19]

Leaving the jeeps to find the nearest casualty clearing station, Tulloch set off for Four Five's headquarters. On the way, he was met by Brig. Mills-Roberts. He wanted to know what the situation was with A Troop. Tulloch told him what little he knew and then continued on his way to headquarters where he handed Nicol Gray a note that Tommy Thomas had asked him to deliver. With that, he headed back to the regimental aid post for a well-deserved, but all too brief, rest.[20]

Armed with Thomas' hand-delivered 'sit-rep', Gray, meanwhile, left his headquarters with a small party that included a runner and his personal wireless operator, Frank Burton.[21] The advance to the station had stalled. A Troop was partially cut off and, having concurred with Dudley Coventry, Gray realised it was impractical to attempt a withdrawal in daylight. It was time to change tack. By then, it was clear that the Germans were holding the Montforterbeek in considerable strength and were unwilling to budge without the stiffest resistance. So, ordering the isolated sections to hold on until dark, he radioed fresh orders to B and E Troops to move eastwards out of Brachterbeek and seize a bridgehead over the stream with the support of four Cromwell tanks.

The advance didn't begin well. Just after passing a small copse halfway to the stream, E Troop, who were leading, were blasted by machine-gun fire from an embankment above them. Two marines died instantly and three more were wounded, one of them fatally.[22] With the line of advance temporarily blocked, Capt. John Day, B Troop's commander, decided to move further left, hoping to outflank the enemy position. At this point, the supporting tanks turned up, but, not for the first time, their value was limited. A marsh directly in front of them meant that they were unable to move forward. After a 'conflab' with E Troop's commander Maj. Ian Beadle, Day returned to his troop with a plan to try and find a way across the marsh on foot. He told Lt Peter Riley to carry out the 'recce' with his section, taking care to avoid trouble. Then he headed back to discuss tactics with Beadle and the tanks commander. No sooner had they begun, however, than sounds of action carried across the Montforterbeek. Fearing the worst, and imagining that the tanks would have to shoot them through after all, Day dashed off after Riley, 'mentally cursing him for falling into the same trap as A and E Troops':

> We had no problem crossing the marsh and I soon found myself jumping the narrow stream... A few yards [on] I could see Peter Riley and some of his men searching a group of Germans. A quick word with Peter confirmed that he had the situation under control and I left him to it, concentrating on getting the Troop into a defensive position.[23]

As luck would have it, Riley's advance could hardly have been better timed. At the moment he crossed the Montforterbeek, a party of about a dozen Germans were pulling back from the direction E Troop were approaching. Despite Day's instruction, his first instinct was to attack. With his section sergeant close behind, Riley doubled forward, firing his

Thompson sub-machine gun. The Germans were taken completely by surprise. Three died in that initial charge. Five more were taken prisoner, one of them wounded. The remainder fled.[24] When Day arrived, he found them occupying a wooded gully, one end merging with the trees lining the Montforterbeek and the other pointing across open fields towards Linne. Known thereafter as Riley's Gully, it offered good fields of fire on either side but was overlooked by the same troublesome windmill that had been a thorn in A Troop's side throughout the day. Nevertheless, it gave Four Five a vital foothold on the far bank of the main German defences. Sending a sub-section to cover the rear, Day dug in along the rim of the gully facing the windmill, which was partially demolished shortly afterwards by 1st RTR in what the B Troop commander considered their 'most useful' contribution to an otherwise disappointing effort. As darkness fell, D Troop moved up to reinforce their gains, and, for the remainder of the day and night, they clung on, being fitfully mortared by the enemy, shelled by their own side and counter-attacked by a force of about forty men who were comfortably beaten back. In capturing and holding a bridgehead over the Montforterbeek, Day had accomplished his primary objective and opened the way to Linne, but in later years he would chide himself for not doing more. By occupying the gully, he had effectively turned the Germans' flank. Had he realised it, or so he reasoned, he could have pushed south, mopping up the enemy lining the stream, thus relieving the pressure on A Troop.

The isolated groups of marines pinned behind potato clamps and cut off in cottages and barns had no option but to hang on and wait for darkness. Theirs was the most miserable and the longest drawn-out ordeal of that frantically hard-fought day. For more than 8 wearying hours, they were trapped, unable to advance or withdraw and chilled to the bone in temperatures that plunged to -15°C. 'I don't remember ever having been so cold,' said Derrick Cakebread.[25]

It had been a frustrating day for A Troop's sniper. Having survived the initial 'murderous fire', he had found a perfect position in an attic. Then, with his sights fixed to the maximum 1,000yd range, he began firing, only to be ordered to stop by TSM Wiggy Bennett because they were about to use the farmhouse as a first-aid station. He spent the rest of the day as an observer while the battle raged on around him and various relief attempts came to nought. For much of the time, the small parties of men holed up in the cottages near the station were clueless as to what was going on. 'We were virtually out of the fight,' reckoned Fred Harris. 'There was the occasional exchange of small arms fire, but all we could basically do was stay alert and wait.'[26] One of the few men to run the gauntlet of fire around the dismembered sections of A Troop was the padre. Without a thought for his own safety, Reg Haw had dashed from the village to take over Doc's duties at troop headquarters, where he remained an inspirational figure throughout the rest of the action.[27]

Eventually, as the short afternoon light faded, Tommy Thomas decided to risk sending a man back to troop headquarters for further instructions. Section Cpl Don Thomas was selected to go. Earlier that day he had seen someone struggling in the snow, apparently trying to assist men lying wounded in the field behind, but he had been too far away and the smoke from shells had been too thick for him clearly to see who it was. In any case, he'd been too busy with his own troubles, trying to 'subdue' the opposition around the station, to pay too much attention to what was going on elsewhere. Now, however, as he flitted back across the darkened field, he found himself passing the potato clamps and the body of Doc Harden, still lying in the snow. Where earlier it would have been almost suicidal to move amid the blizzard of bullets it was now still and peaceful. He didn't tarry. Continuing on to troop headquarters, he was told by Dudley Coventry to return immediately with orders for the survivors of the stranded sections to pull back.[28]

Shortly before the withdrawal began, two 'stretcher jeeps' reached troop headquarters. John Tulloch had come to fetch the wounded. It was the first that he knew of Doc's death or his selfless heroism. Not long afterwards, at around 8 p.m., the remnants of A Troop began emerging out of the darkness, some of them guided by Dutch civilians, all of them exhausted by their prolonged resistance. As Lt Cory was being loaded onto a jeep, he heard someone mutter that he was 'lucky to have a Blighty'[29] and then noticed Sgt Cook and members of his own section returning. They were carrying with them his green beret and Doc's lifeless body.[30]

Of all the painful losses suffered by Four Five that day none was more keenly felt than that of Doc Harden. Quiet, dedicated and selfless, he had been a father figure to many of the younger marines. In action and out of it, he'd always put the needs of others before his own. He was always there, always ready to help, always passing round his battered packets of Woodbines. Now he was gone. As night blotted out the battlefield, Johnny Haville was moved beyond words by the respect and reverence displayed by the men of A Troop as they brought Doc in.

The pity and poignancy of that deathly scene would stay with him for a long time afterwards. It seemed to him as if they could not bear to be parted from him, as though 'they wanted to keep him with them'.[31]

17

For Valour

The telegram boy paused before approaching the door. Bobby was playing on a pair of roller skates outside and the two of them chatted briefly. Maud was inside, doing the washing, when she heard the knock. The moment she opened the door she knew instantly it was the news she had dreaded. It was 29 January 1945, the day her world fell apart.

The standard message was brief, the few words saying little and yet saying everything:

> 4.35 HAMMERSMITH OHMS 31
> PRIORITY CC MRS HARDEN 195 COLYER RD NORTHFLEET KENT
> 977 DEEPLY REGRET TO INFORM YOU 11006144 L/CPL H E
> HARDEN RAMC WAS KILLED IN ACTION 23 JANUARY LETTER
> FOLLOWS = RAMC RECORDS +

For six days she had unknowingly been living a lie, a lie in which all of the dreams and hopes she had shared with Eric for so long were still alive and still seemed possible. But in that shattering moment it must have dawned on her that it had all been a terrible illusion. There would be no family holidays to Minster after the war was over, no long walks along the beach, no swimming lessons for Bobby and no musical gatherings round the piano. She felt crushed. The man she had loved for thirteen years, her soulmate and the father of her two children had been snatched from her by a war he could have sat out. It scarcely seemed possible. Barely a month had gone by since their tearful parting, less than a fortnight since he'd returned to the front line. Those first uncertain days had been hard enough, not knowing where he was or what he was headed into:

> I haven't yet got used to the idea of you been [*sic*] gone again. I wonder where you are, dear, if you are where you thought you

> were going. When you write, Eric, say, Yes you were right, if you are the ones who started the new break through in Holland. They only mention Infantry on the wireless, but there [*sic*] Comdo's don't get any credit, do they?
>
> What sort of a landing did you have, dear? I hope it was better and safer than before, and hope you won't have to creep through cornfields after not having any sleep for a week...[1]

As the icy weather returned, leaving the streets of Northfleet ankle-deep in snow, her thoughts drifted back to happier times spent together:

> There was a lovely moon here last night, darling and it did look pretty on the snow. Like when we were courting and used to sit down in it and declare we were not cold although we froze to the ground almost.[2]

Doc Harden's original grave in Maasbracht. (Army Medical Services Museum)

It was colder than she could ever recall. 'I freeze at night with two eiderdowns and Bobby to try to warm me, so I bet you are cold there, sweetheart.'[3] She had imagined him shivering in a hole in the ground as he read, with a mixture of relief and pride, that Julia was 'better' after her Christmas sickness and that Bobby had risen to third in his class at school. Of Julia, Maud added: 'You'd see a difference in her even now. She's still as good, Eric, and cries even less now.' There was all the family gossip to pass on too. Brother-in-law Harry was back in Italy, having recovered from his wounds, and Ena had given her a bonnet and coat for Julia. Then there were the updates on Bobby's piano lessons and news from the St John Ambulance. The ambulance he'd taken charge of amid much pomp and circumstance was back in 'dock' again and in need of repairs, if only the spare parts were available. The branch was searching for a full-time driver and Maud hoped he wouldn't be tempted to rejoin the moment he got back. 'Wait a few weeks,' she said, 'then you can, love.' She closed by urging him to 'keep touching that bit of wood' for luck and to 'take care, love, great care',[4] little realising that his luck was about to run out and that this letter, like all the others she had written since he departed for Ostend, would never be read by him.

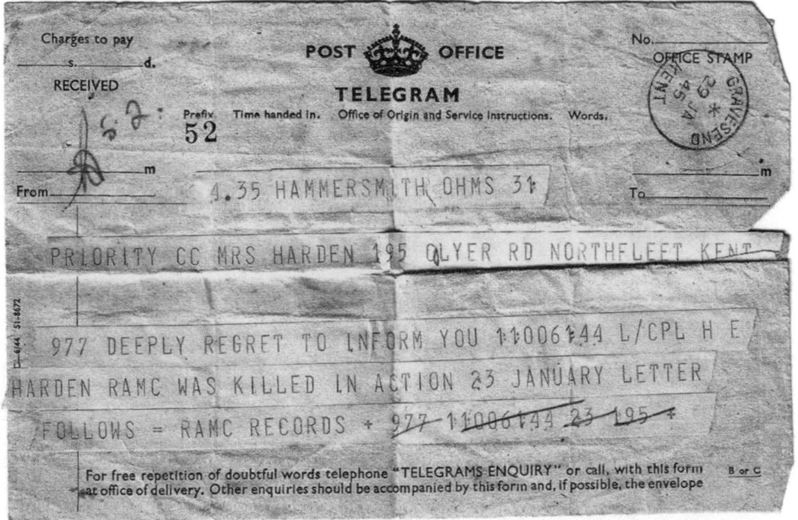

Charges to pay s. d.
RECEIVED

POST OFFICE
TELEGRAM

No.
OFFICE STAMP
GRAVESEND KENT 29 JA 45

Prefix. 52 Time handed in. Office of Origin and Service Instructions. Words.

From To

4.35 HAMMERSMITH OHMS 31

PRIORITY CC MRS HARDEN 195 COLYER RD NORTHFLEET KENT

977 DEEPLY REGRET TO INFORM YOU 11006144 L/CPL H E
HARDEN RAMC WAS KILLED IN ACTION 23 JANUARY LETTER
FOLLOWS = RAMC RECORDS + 977 11006144 23 195 +

For free repetition of doubtful words telephone "TELEGRAMS ENQUIRY" or call, with this form at office of delivery. Other enquiries should be accompanied by this form and, if possible, the envelope

B or C

The telegram announcing Eric's death reached Maud on 29 January 1945. (via J. Wells)

Eric had been dead three days when she posted her final letter. It was just two pages long, written on the last sheets of notepaper she had:

> How are you, dear? Just about frozen through, I bet. Don't forget to say if you want your winter underwear sent. I've got some more soap, too, when you need it, Eric. Would you like any gloves or helmet knitted, darling? Whatever you want it's up to you to ask for. Won't they give you the sack dear, no, I didn't think they would somehow.
>
> I bet Ethel[5] is cold in the shop too, this weather. I wouldn't like her job. I bet, too, it's pretty over there, that's if you get time to see it and are not too frozen to admire it. You can tell it's cold by the different birds in the garden, even seagulls today and I've only ever once before see them in the garden and that was the first winter we had here.
>
> Julia is getting on fine now, Eric, and says Dad as plain as you like. Of course, she does not know it, but it pleases Bobby. If she doesn't want her hood up, she gets that stick down and throws it out and then looks round for applause. She keeps us busy now picking up the things she throws out. Bobby (and me) is doing five finger exercises but his fingers are hardly long enough yet. Still he keeps at it. I don't know if I'll ever learn it as I can't read the music quick enough yet, still, I'll have a go as I would like to be able to play it.
>
> May and Jill[6] are coming for the weekend, dear, if it's not too bad. I hope they come as it gets lonely sometimes.
>
> How is your ear now Eric[7] I hope the noise won't make it worse. We had another form to fill in about our damage and before they do anything we will get even another one. Still, I'd be glad to get it mended.
>
> Now I'll close till Saturday, Sweetheart.
> All our love and Take care – God bless then.
> Yrs Ever Lovingly Maud.[8]

Across the bottom of the letter she'd squeezed in no fewer than twelve kisses, adding nine more from Bobby and Julia along the side, before apologetically squeezing it into the small envelope that was all she had left in the house. A few days later, the same envelope, post-dated 'Gravesend 7pm 26 Jan 1945', would be returned to her unopened, the single word 'DECEASED' written in the top left corner and a purple stamp almost but not quite obscuring Eric's name. It simply stated: 'It is regretted that this item could not be delivered because the addressee is reported deceased.'

Maud was desolate. 'He was my life itself,' she wrote. 'Only when I visit his resting place will I realise it is true.'[9] Just as she was struggling to come to terms with the emptiness left by her heartbreaking loss, so his pals in Four Five were finding it hard to believe that the ever-smiling, generous-spirited medic they knew as Doc was no longer with them. 'I cannot tell you how much the boys of A Troop miss Eric,' wrote Dickie Mason, 'as he was not only one of the boys, but a father to us, as we could talk to him, and tell all our troubles to him, and he would not say a wrong word about anyone...'[10] Of them all, none took his death harder than his closest mate, Sid Gliddon. He was serving as a medical orderly attached to No. 3 Commando the day he was killed. The shock was considerable. The two of them had been inseparable, spending every spare minute they could together:

> I can't describe how I felt ... could not believe it... You can just imagine how very much I miss him... Believe me ... we all thought the world of Eric... We use[d] to talk so much of what we were going to do after the war, and he was coming to Penzance to have a holiday and I was coming up to see you all. How much we had planned...[11]

Both Gliddon and Mason were among those members of A Troop who gathered at his graveside for the burial service conducted by Four Five's padre, Reg Haw. It was held in a small field near to a monastery in Maasbracht where the commando returned on 24 January. Four Five had lost five men killed (another would die of wounds a day later) and thirty men wounded, a large proportion of them from A Troop. Doc was buried alongside his comrades. 'We laid him to rest reverently, with our prayers and affection,' wrote Haw. 'A cross inscribed with his name, rank, number and unit and the date of his death marks his grave.'[12] As the frozen earth closed in on his friend, Sid Gliddon couldn't help but think of Maud and the two children. 'Eric used to talk so much about them and you,' he wrote to Maud.[13]

In their grief, the men of A Troop drew comfort from two things: firstly, that his death had come quickly and without suffering[14] and, secondly, that he had lost his life in the midst of a display of gallantry that was unsurpassed in all of the commando's service from D-Day onwards. In the days following the action, his magnificent courage was the talk of Four Five. There had been many acts of bravery that day around Brachterbeek: Neil Patrick's single-handed stand that gave his mates a chance to reach cover; Peter Riley charging headlong into a bunch of Germans on the far side of the Montforterbeek; John Tulloch's fire-swept rescue mission; Johnny Haville and Dickie Mason's double crossing of no man's land to bring in A Troop's wounded. But of all the myriad acts of individual heroism the self-sacrifice of Doc Harden stood out as something exceptional, even superhuman. His was not a hotheaded explosion of mad courage, but a coolly calculated and prolonged display of selfless devotion that went far beyond the call of duty. He had crossed and re-crossed 120yds of open ground raked by fire from enemy positions as close as 400yds at least six, and possibly eight, times, all on his own initiative. Having been ordered to cease his self-ordained mission, he could reasonably have refrained from further risks without a stain on his character, but he chose to carry on to the bitter end, and as a result of his dedication and determination, two lives had been saved at the cost of his own. The effort to honour his memory began straight away.

John Tulloch had spent most of 24 January reorganising his depleted medical section. One of his headquarters party was switched to A Troop in place of Doc and Reg Haw made the numbers up. Back in Maasbracht, they had jointly selected a deserted house to use as a sick bay, complete with a 'liberated' double mattress. Before either of them could test it out, however, Tulloch was called that evening to see the adjutant who promptly told him: 'We are thinking of putting two people up for the VC and Harden is one of them':

> My reaction was, 'How marvellous. A fighting man and an RAMC man. What could be better for the unit.' Discussion followed – the Brigadier had to endorse the recommendation and might only approve one and Harden might be the unlucky one. I wanted him put forward as number one choice, because the other was still alive. He had another chance for the VC but Harden had not; again, the Brigadier could change that. We parted with the adjutant saying that he would discuss it with the colonel and let me know. Eventually, the adjutant told me that only Harden's name was being put forward, so I was satisfied...[15]

The first inkling that Maud had of Eric's heroism came in a letter from Nicol Gray. It was written on 6 February during a lull in the fighting.

The Montforterbeek had been cleared, Linne had been captured unopposed and Four Five were back near the scene of the Brachterbeek action, having recently suffered grievous losses in a night raid across the Maas.[16] There was a thaw and the once-frozen ground around the station and ruined windmill had turned to mush. On a single sheet of looted notepaper bearing the name of the local government in the area – Gemeente Maasbracht – Four Five's commanding officer tried to find the right tone between compassion and soldierly pride. It was seven months to the day since he had taken command of the commando in the middle of its first action. In that time, it had been his sad duty to write all too many such letters to grieving parents and wives, but none quite like this one, none where he considered the dead man worthy of the highest honour:

> Dear Mrs Harden,
> I write to tell you how very sorry I am that your husband has been killed in action. His death has hit us all very hard for he was trusted, loved and respected by all ranks of the Commando. He lost or rather gave his life to save lives of our wounded. Three times he went out to bring in casualties who would have died but for him. On the third time he was bringing in his badly wounded officer, Mr Cory, when he was killed instantly. I shall always be proud of having had Harden in my unit. He was a very brave and gallant man and his devotion to duty and his comrades was a fine example to us all. I have recommended him for the Victoria Cross and I hope that he will be granted it.
> We have buried him peacefully beside some of his comrades.
> Let me know if I can help in any way.
> Again, you have my sympathy,
> Yours sincerely,
> W N Gray.

It was unusual but not without precedent for a commanding officer to inform a relative that their loved one had been put in for a posthumous award. Normally such matters are dealt with in the strictest confidence, partly for fear of raising false expectations. Of all those recommended for the VC, relatively few are granted and many are downgraded to lesser awards. Compelling though Doc Harden's case was, Gray would have known better than most that receiving official approval was by no means a foregone conclusion. Up to February 1945 only 1,300 awards had been made since the institution of the Victoria Cross 'For Valour' at the end of the Crimean War, almost ninety years earlier. In that time, the standard required to earn the VC had risen immeasurably, so that during the entire course of a Second World War involving millions of British and Commonwealth servicemen and women just 182 were awarded. Of those, the overwhelming majority were given for what might be termed aggressive or offensive-spirited actions. Only five recognised exclusively life-saving acts of supreme bravery on the battlefield and, up to January 1945, none had been a granted to a member of the Royal Army Medical Corps in more than five years of global conflict.

Maud dutifully passed Colonel Gray's letter to Eric's mother for relatives to read, little knowing that she would be setting off an unfortunate chain reaction with unforeseen consequences. Somehow, news of the letter either leaked out or was passed to the local newspaper, which ran with the story of the butcher's shop manager who had been 'mentioned for VC'. By 16 February, Eric's heroism was headline news and, in the days that followed, as more letters and reports arrived, the

Brigadier D. Mills-Roberts, D.S.O., M.C., Irish Guards.

HEADQUARTERS
FIRST COMMANDO BRIGADE

B.L.A.

My dear Mrs Harden,

All of us in the First Commando Brigade are terribly proud of the V.C. which your husband won.

He was a man in a million & his courage was of the highest type. It is easier to be brave with a weapon in ones hand than carrying a stretcher, & all of us realise that.

Lance Corporal Harden will be missed by all who knew him in this Brigade, but his name will never be forgotten.

Brigadier Mills-Roberts letter of congratulation on the award of the VC: 'He was a man in a million'. (via J. Wells)

stories multiplied. A number of them quoted extracts from a letter to Maud written by Four Five's chaplain Reg Haw the day after Nicol Gray's letter. In it, he wrote of Eric's 'exceptional gallantry and bravery ... regardless of his own safety' before alluding to his VC recommendation. 'Others will tell you of your husband's bravery,' he said, 'and it may be that his name may soon become famous.'[17] Among those joining in the tributes was Wiggy Bennett, whose 'eyewitness' account put flesh on the bare bones of the story. Related to a 'military observer', his dramatic, if not entirely accurate, rendering was widely published.[18] After bringing in two men, one of them with the help of Haville and Mason, Bennett recounted that 'Harden's smock was ripped to pieces by bullets, but he took no notice and carried on'. He described Eric as a 'first-class fellow' who was 'loved' by all the commandos 'for his efforts on their behalf'.[19]

The publicity flew in the face of all military protocol. Maud, who was an entirely innocent party in the leak, was deeply embarrassed by the episode, but nevertheless shouldered the responsibility for it.[20] Most concerning of all to her was the thought that someone's indiscretion might adversely affect the chances of Eric's courage being posthumously recognised. 'Don't let his memory suffer through my love,' she pleaded in one newspaper story. She was backed by Lord Harris, the acting commissioner of the St John Ambulance Brigade in Kent. Remembering Eric as a man who, prior to the war, 'won golden opinions by his service to the Brigade and to his fellows', Lord Harris pledged his full support:

> Undoubtedly his action deserves some very high award, and I can only hope that this unfortunate premature publicity will not in any way prejudice his case which I am taking up with the proper authorities.[21]

While all of this was going on, more letters continued to arrive from home and abroad, each one supplying new fragments of information to add to a mosaic of courageous self-sacrifice. From Eric's troop commander, Dudley Coventry, Maud learned for the first time that Eric had disobeyed orders in carrying out his 'magnificent work'. Writing on 18 February, shortly before being relieved by American forces, Coventry said that it was 'entirely due to his heroism and calmness that the lives of one marine and one officer were saved...' He added:

> I should also like to mention that he went out the first time on his own initiative, although I had told him previously not to do so.

He did this magnificent work fully aware of the dangers it involved, and I'm afraid it's impossible to speak highly enough of his great work and unselfishness in giving his life to save others.

I had known your husband in England, and had been treated by him on various occasions, so I wish you to realise that I did appreciate his worth before I came out here. He was a friend of every man in my troop, and I might say the whole Commando.

In expressing his 'greatest sympathy', he concluded with his own salute:

If there were only more men in the world like your husband the war would either be over by now, or never started.

Even as Dudley Coventry was delivering his own insightful observations, another correspondent with particular reason to be grateful was composing her own heartfelt tribute. Far away from the war-torn borderland of Holland and Germany, in the peaceful Dorset village of Purse Caundle, near Sherborne, Annette Cory searched for the words to express her thanks and her sorrow:

Dear Mrs Harden,
I am writing to send my deepest sympathy to you. I feel it especially, as your husband was killed bringing my husband in. I would like you to know how very much we feel for you. My husband said that L/Cpl Harden was quite marvellous, and extraordinarily brave, and if it had not been for him, my husband would have died.

If there is anything that we could do for you, will you please let us know...[22]

Finally, there came the telegram that lifted the guilt-laden cloud of uncertainty that had been hanging over her. It was the confirmation from the War Office that the King had been 'graciously pleased to approve the posthumous award of the Victoria Cross' to L/Cpl Henry Eric Harden of the Royal Army Medical Corps. Officially announced on 8 March, the corps' first and only VC of the war recognised his 'superb devotion to duty and personal courage of the very highest order'.[23] The first of two VCs given for acts of bravery during Operation Blackcock's wearisome fighting, it capped a long list of awards to the men of Four Five for their part in the fighting around Brachterbeek on 23 January. There were Military Crosses for Doc's senior officer, John Tulloch, and for Peter Riley, and Military Medals for A Troop's Neil Patrick and Nicol Gray's wireless operator Frank Burton. To these, in the fullness of time, would be added periodic awards that were, at least in part, made in recognition of gallant deeds performed that day: a Distinguished Service Cross to the Revd Reg Haw, RNVR, and Military Medals to Wiggy Bennett and Peter Riley's section sergeant Bill Noakes.[24]

Amid all the rejoicing at so many honours, there was, however, disappointment at two glaring omissions from the list: Johnny Haville and Dickie Mason. Many in Four Five considered their bravery ranked only marginally below the exceptional courage shown by Doc Harden. As volunteer stretcher-bearers, they had risked their lives in the face of a galling fire on two occasions and were instrumental in ensuring that the rescue mission he initiated was completed in the most difficult circumstances imaginable. Most assumed they would be in line for the Distinguished Conduct Medal, an award second only to the VC, or, at the very least, the Military Medal. As it was, Haville received an oak leaf mention in despatches, the lowest-ranked honour, and Mason got nothing. 'It was shameful, pathetic and terribly sad,' said Fred Harris.[25] Many in A Troop were simply dumbfounded at so obvious an injustice and the fact that one of them should have been totally ignored in what was a shared effort merely made it worse. 'We couldn't believe it,' said Derrick Cakebread. 'Something had gone badly wrong, but how or what we never knew.'[26] Fifty years on, the failure to adequately recognise their courageous contribution still rankled with Bobby Cory. 'It was absolutely disgraceful,' he said. 'Nobody in the Commando could ever understand why it should have been.'[27] Haville and Mason, he wrote, 'deserved better'.[28] It was, on the face of it, a baffling oversight made all the more incomprehensible by the belated honour to Wiggy Bennett, even though his Military Medal was not solely for the brief assistance rendered at Brachterbeek.[29]

Eric's VC, the 132nd award of the war and the fifth to a Kentish man, unleashed another wave of publicity and another surge of correspondence. Headlines hailed the unselfish heroism of the medic who 'Disobeyed Orders to Seek Shelter and Went Out to Help Wounded'. In one story he was the 'VC [who] Went Where Tanks Couldn't' and in another the 'First Aid VC'. Maj. Gen. Lewis Lyne, GOC 7th Armoured Division, to which the Commando Brigade was attached at the time of the Blackcock operations, called it a 'superbly gallant action'. He added: 'I have known many brave and unselfish actions in this war but I can think of none comparable with this one.'[30] The secretary of state for war agreed. Speaking on the floor of the House of Commons on 13 March, the Rt Hon. Sir James Grigg singled out the commando medic for especial praise. He told assembled members of Parliament: 'I do not remember ever reading anything more heroic.'[31] Many were moved beyond measure by the story of uncommon battlefield valour that they interpreted as a saga of supreme sacrifice. 'In his gallant act,' wrote Justina, Lady Dunbar-Nasmith, the deputy superintendent-in-chief of the St John Ambulance Brigade, and whose husband was also a VC holder, 'we of St John see the fine tradition of the Knights Hospitallers being carried into modern warfare.'[32] Derek Mills-Roberts, who had endorsed Nicol Gray's original recommendation, was of much the same opinion. Pausing in the midst of preparations for Operation Widgeon, the Rhine river crossing, the commando brigadier whose qualities as a fighting man were evidenced in his DSO and MC, described Eric as 'a man in a million' whose 'courage was of the highest type' and added: 'It is easier to be brave with a weapon in one's hand than carrying a stretcher, and all of us realise that.'[33]

The renewed publicity brought with it additional emotional strain that Maud bore steadfastly, without fuss or complaint. Thrust ill-prepared into the glare of an undesired spotlight, she appeared to draw strength from Eric's courageous example. 'I am very proud to have been the wife of such a brave man and to know that he was happy as my husband,' she wrote.[34] She took solace from the fact that he had been 'killed outright' and 'did not lose his life in vain'. To Reg Haw, she wrote:

> I can quite well picture him acting as he did, bravely, without a thought for himself, giving his life for others... He had everything to live for yet it counted for nothing when his comrades needed his help. He was all I lived for and I thank God for eight years of our life we spent together. He loved his two children so much, yet, that others might live, he was taken from us.

She concluded her brave letter with her own loving tribute:

> As a son, husband and father, as well as a soldier, he was everything good, straight and true, and, in life, as in death, everyone was proud of him.[35]

Maud hid her grief behind a veil of duty to her children and to her husband's memory. She urged friends and strangers who wrote offering their sympathy not to feel 'too badly'. Eric, she said, 'must have known at the time what it meant and he did it willingly'.[36] According to her daughter, she 'carried the whole family through it all with complete dignity, self-control and modesty, and with the courage that so many had seen in her…' It did not go unnoticed. Reg Haw remarked on her 'magnificent spirit'[37] while Derek Mills-Roberts thought she had conducted herself bravely, 'like the wife of a hero'.[38] Publicly at least, she remained resolute and strong, while suffering in silence the aching pain of loss. 'I miss him most when our little boy says "Good night" to him every night,' she once confided. Johnny Haville saw in her self-effacement striking parallels with her husband's quiet determination. 'I just can't help but admire you in your courage and words, to me they seem so typical of Eric's life,' he wrote.[39]

Her modesty was no affectation. When she attended the Buckingham Palace investiture to receive Eric's VC, she asked the king if he would present it not to her, but to Bobby. To her way of thinking, he had more right to it than she did. It was, as she explained to a journalist, a medal that would forever remind him 'how brave his daddy was'. To understand the meaning of that bravery he need look no further than a letter that reached Colyer Road in April 1945. It came from the Royal Naval Hospital at Sherborne in Dorset and was the hardest letter Bobby Cory had ever had to write:

> My dear Mrs Harden,
> I've been wanting to write to you for so long now – since January 23rd to be exact – but just haven't been able. But how I am to convey the gratitude and admiration I feel for your husband and the very deep sympathy I feel for you in your loss I don't know. To owe someone your life is to owe the greatest thing on earth, but not only did he save my life, but gave his own in doing it and I can't even thank him. He was a great man, a man we were all proud to have with us and whose memory will always be alive and an inspiration to all of us and the nation as a whole. While England continues to produce men like him, she will always be the greatest of nations. His VC is unquestionably the most well deserved of the war and I would like to congratulate him and thank him through you, though I would give anything to be able to do it personally. May we all follow his splendid example. How thankful I am that death came to him suddenly and not after long suffering, and that must be a relief to you too.

I myself am progressing well now. My arm is out of plaster now and I am able to move about on crutches which makes things more pleasant. I don't know how long I shall be in hospital though. I expect it will be some months yet. But it is going well and the doctors are, I know, well pleased with the progress.

Once again, Mrs Harden may I humbly and sincerely thank you and sympathise with you, and if there is anything, I mean anything, that I or my wife can do for you, please don't hesitate to let us know.

God bless you,
Yours sincerely,
Robert Cory.[40]

In the days and weeks that followed, as the war in Europe drew ever nearer to its inevitable conclusion, more details continued to emerge about Eric's time in Four Five. Wiggy Bennett had been waiting for weeks to write to Maud on behalf of 'all the other lads' of A Troop, but such had been the frenetic speed of their advance across Germany that there simply hadn't been time. Finally, after a month that had seen them cross the rivers Rhine, Weser and Aller, there was a chance to draw breath. On 21 April, from a billet in Luneberg, south of Hamburg, where Four Five awaited its final assignment, Bennett remembered 'one of the greatest men it has ever been my pleasure to meet':

Both in and out of action, he was my right hand man. Nothing was too much trouble for him if it would help the chaps. He was always to be seen helping out of action with the cooking and rations apart from his own job. We have missed him terrific [*sic*] and he is always in our thoughts. We are always talking of him. There will never be another 'Doc' in our Troop... Always cheerfull [*sic*] and full of life, he was honestly loved by us all.[41]

Comforting though such words were, they still represented only a fragmentary picture. There were still gaps to be filled, questions to be answered, particularly about Eric's final moments. In particular, Maud wanted to know what, if anything, he had talked about during the moments leading up to his death. Johnny Haville did his best to help, but there was little to tell. 'If any words do occur to us that he said, and may be of comfort to you, we'll let you know,' he wrote. There is no evidence, however, to suggest either he or Dickie Mason ever did recall any more.

Instead, Haville joined the, by now, long list of people in saluting a man he was 'honoured' to count as a friend and whose 'cheerfulness and kindness never changed'. 'He was one of the very best... It seems a shame that the best have to go first, which is always the case.' Setting aside any feelings of injustice at his own niggardly treatment, Haville paid wholesome tribute to the medic whose 'fine qualities' he had already seen displayed during the fighting in Normandy:

> When his award was announced on the wireless I felt very proud knowing I'd shared those trips with such a great man. He so richly deserved his VC to let the world know of such courage and sacrifice...[42]

Bobby Cory understood those sentiments better than anyone. Barely a month earlier, he'd left hospital for the first time since being wounded. With his wife at the wheel of a small two-seater car, he'd driven through Devon and into Cornwall. The sun was shining and villages along the way were decked with bunting and flags. It was 8 May 1945: VE-Day, a day he never thought he'd live to see. The celebrations spilled out onto the streets as he motored westwards, one of the luckiest men alive with a debt he could never repay.

Sixteen days later another letter dropped on the mat at 195 Colyer Road. It came from Dickie Mason. 'I am most sorry Eric is not here to see Victory,' he told Maud, 'as it is men like him who make a better world.'[43]

Acts of Remembrance

Bob Harden had no idea what came over him. One minute he was at the back of the coach lost in thought and the next he was leaning over the driver, urging him to stop. Rain was drumming down from a leaden sky. The surrounding fields, sodden and desolate, lay half-swallowed in a grey murk. It was the afternoon of Sunday 22 January 1995 on the road out of Brachterbeek and Bob wasn't about to let pass a heaven-sent opportunity to finally lay so many ghosts to rest. It was time, at last, to confront the past and discover the truth about his father's sacrifice.

As a child of 7, Bob, or Bobby as he was still known then, had marked the first Armistice Day since the war's end in Westminster Abbey. In a moving ceremony, captured on film by a Pathé news team, he had placed a cross on the Tomb of the Unknown Warrior. Walking slowly between tall lighted candles, a tiny figure dwarfed by the abbey's epic grandeur, he symbolised all of the nation's children who had lost parents in the six-year-long conflict that had destroyed so many dreams. In the years that followed, Bob would accompany his mother, his sister and Aunt Mabel on a family pilgrimage to visit Nederweert War Cemetery where his father's body had been re-interred. He found a lovingly tended garden of peace that his father would have appreciated better than most and a four-line inscription that would come to sum up a life snatched away, a life that already seemed less real and more a part of legend. Carved beneath the outline of the Victoria Cross, it read:

Greater Love
Hath No Man Than This.
That A Man Lay Down
His Life For His Friends.

Bob's sister Julia returned twice more to Nederweert, in 1954 and 1955, on tours organised by the British Legion for children whose fathers had been killed or had died of wounds during the fighting in Holland. For Julia, like Bob, the short trips to the countryside midway between Helmond and Echt were part of a far longer emotional journey in search of a closer understanding of the father that Bob barely knew and Julia did not know at all. Each time she returned, Julia was struck by the great kindness of her Dutch hosts and the extraordinary esteem in which they held their British liberators.

Back home in Kent, people were no less supportive. Their father's unselfish heroism struck a chord with his fellow townspeople and their pride in his posthumous honour was reflected in an outpouring of generosity. The citizens of Northfleet contributed magnificently to a local memorial fund, championed by a local newspaper. 'This must not be a small effort,' it declared. 'Our support ... must be in keeping with the self-sacrifice of this gallant soldier. Anything less would be a reflection on the dignity of Gravesend and Northfleet and the honour of its people.' The response was headed by contributions from the Local War Relief and Services' Comfort Fund and Gravesend Civil Defence Services. Among hundreds of individual donations was one from a man in Essex who simply signed himself 'A Last War VC'. The monies raised helped to pay off the mortgage on the family's home in Colyer Road. Meanwhile, another fund launched by Sir Alexander Hood, director general of the Army Medical Services, drew donations from far and wide. They included sums of money raised by the Commando Association, the Royal Army Medical Corps, the St John Ambulance Brigade, the Master Butchers' Association and from a host of fundraising events that included a special concert staged at the Royal Herbert Hospital where Eric had carried out ward duties in 1942. In all, more than £10,000 was raised, most of which was spent on Bob and Julia's education, with the remainder providing a small income for Maud to supplement her war widow's pension. Julia described it as 'overwhelming, astounding and humbling'.[1] But wonderful though it was, no amount of financial assistance could ever compensate for the loss of a husband and father. Nor was the gesture entirely pain-free.

Bob, in particular, suffered further unintentional upset when a decision, taken in his best interests by the trust's administrators, backfired. Deeply unhappy and unsettled, he lasted barely two terms at a boarding school in London before switching to Eltham College and, eventually, King Edward VII Sea School in preparation for a career in the

Julia lays a wreath on her father's grave during a visit to Holland organised by the Royal British Legion in 1955.

Merchant Navy. Having learned from the experience, Maud insisted that Julia go as a day pupil to Our Lady's High School in Dartford and, later, St Joseph's Convent High School in Gravesend.

Through all of the distress and upheaval, Maud remained the family's rock, just as she had been in the immediate aftermath of Eric's death. When her mother died in 1949, she shared with her sister, May, who was also a war widow, the task of caring for their increasingly infirm father until his death. Yet despite all her struggles, she made every effort to ensure that Bob and Julia had as happy and as normal a childhood as possible. She took them on visits to a London still scarred by war and she fulfilled Eric's dreams of family holidays with summer trips to Allhallows, Cornwall and Lulworth Cove. During this time, she continued to shield her children from her own grieving and what her daughter has called 'her core of loneliness'.[2] For Maud, though she did eventually remarry in 1956,[3] the pain of Eric's loss would never fully go away, and was only ever in part eased by the proliferation of honours and memorials that followed in the wake of his Victoria Cross.

Writing in March 1945, immediately after the *London Gazette* announcement of the VC, Brig. Derek Mills-Roberts had assured Maud that Eric's 'name will never be forgotten'. He was right. In Britain and in Holland, his courage has been, and continues to be, commemorated on plaques and in portraits, in road names and in churches, in barrack blocks and medical centres and in battlefield pilgrimages and services of remembrance.[4] Not surprisingly, his home town of Northfleet led the way. A portrait in oils by W.O. Millar, the principal of the Gravesend School of Art, was unveiled amid much pomp in Northfleet Council Chamber and is now displayed alongside a painting of Gravesend VC winner Robert Palmer in Gravesham Council Chamber. In 1952, the town's new St John Ambulance Brigade headquarters was named Eric Harden VC Memorial Hall in his honour. Plaques were placed on the houses in Colyer Road and Factory Road where he had lived, and in Lawn Road School where he was taught and where he served as an ambulance driver during the Blitz. His sister Mabel arranged for another to be put up at a block of flats where she lived with a rose garden aptly sited at the back, and his sister Ethel, for whom he managed the butcher's shop, provided, in his memory, the angel setting for the new altar beside a commemorative plaque in All Saints' church. Elsewhere, Harden Road and nearby Henry Gardens, a new development of special-needs housing, serve as enduring reminders of his great courage.

Northfleet has, indeed, done its bravest son proud, but so too have generations of Dutch people. Henry Hardenstraat, a road opposite the Commonwealth War Graves Commission cemetery in Nederweert, is a notable tribute to a foreign soldier, but nowhere is the commando medic more revered than in the scattering of rural communities around Brachterbeek. The bridge that spans the Montforterbeek bears two memorial plaques, one in Dutch, the other in English, and, not far from Harden Bridge, in the garden of the windmill that was such a malevolent feature of the winter's day battle all those years ago, a small chapel has been built in memory of Eric and the men of Four Five. More recently, villagers, including parties of local schoolchildren, joined with veterans to dedicate a memorial cross and plaque on the field where the man the people of Brachterbeek call 'Our Hero' met his death. In a modern twist, a geocaching canister[5] was placed on the battlefield site, which, together with others placed on the bridge and at Nederweert War Cemetery, helps to form a Harden triangle of remembrance.

Over the years, the men of Four Five forged close links with the towns and villages around Maasbracht and Brachterbeek. Annual pilgrimages, coordinated by local schoolteacher Peter Roufs and the Liberators Reception Committee, helped keep alive the memories that an ever-dwindling band of survivors have carried with them for more than half a century. At Smeets' family pension and in Fred Peets' Café, the stories and the drink have flowed liberally as ex-commandos like Derrick Cakebread, John Day and Fred Harris relived their lost youth. In good humour and high spirits, they have been drawn back, in appreciation of the myriad kindnesses shown to them by the Dutch people and to revisit in happier circumstances the scenes of battle seared forever into their consciousness. They remembered the days in January 1945 when life appeared to hang by a thread and they remembered the mates less fortunate than themselves who did not make it home. In particular, of course, they remembered Eric Harden, the man they knew as 'Doc'.

They recalled a cheery, friendly man, always willing to help a mate, always prepared to put his own needs second to those of his comrades in A Troop. Fred Harris remembered his pride at being 'in the marines'. 'He was a quiet, gentle man in keeping with his military profession,' he added. 'But even though he was 10 years older than most of us, he was still one of the boys.'[6] To Neil Patrick, Doc was 'quiet, unassuming, generally cheerful and dedicated, a good friend, top class comrade, and a great loss to all of us in A Troop'.[7] 'He was a bloody good medical man,' added Derrick Cakebread. He had served alongside Doc from D-Day through to Brachterbeek and he had always found him 'dependable and resourceful':

> He was like the rest of the Commandos; we had been trained to do a job and Doc did it always to the best of his ability. You could always rely on him. He was always there when you wanted or needed him.[8]

Never was that more true than on that bleakest of January days in 1945 when the men of A Troop lay trapped in a snow-covered potato field on the edge of Brachterbeek. Neil Patrick, whose own courage was a distinguishing feature of the desperate fighting, felt Doc's reaction to the crisis and his unselfish feats of rescue were 'typical of the man'.[9] Others, who were more closely involved in the drama, remained deeply affected by his sacrifice half a century on, none more so than Bobby Cory, who owed his life to him, and Johnny Haville, who had been an active participant in two of the rescues.

For Cory, the events of 23 January 1945 retained a haunting clarity. He had never forgotten that wretched day, nor was he ever likely to. The scars from the wounds he received near Brachterbeek were a daily reminder, but the psychological scars were even more evident the day I met him at his home in north Suffolk in late 1994. Recalling the 'advance to contact' that had gone horribly wrong, he struggled to keep in check raw emotions that were shot through with gratitude and guilt. For almost half a century he had lived with the knowledge that his life had been spared at the cost of another's. There were times during our conversation when the burden seemed too much to bear. In a short, scribbled note to me, he had described Doc's actions as 'one of, if not the most, outstanding acts of gallantry throughout all the hostilities and one for which I certainly owe my life'.[10] Only by honouring Doc's memory was he able to repay a part of what he saw as a lifelong debt. It was something he was committed to doing for the rest of his life.

As one of the last survivors of the gallant band of rescuers, Haville, too, found himself inextricably linked to Four Five's greatest hero. In later years, he was frequently called upon to recount Doc's final moments. Never once did he seek to steal the limelight from his 'very gallant comrade'. In a letter written to me almost five decades after the fighting at Brachterbeek, he insisted that Doc would 'always be remembered by those who took part in the action and witnessed his wonderful example of courage and devotion to his fellow men'.[11] By then a frail, yet dignified man, he also reflected on the qualities of a man whose death would forever be associated with his own miraculous survival:

> For the few months I knew Eric Harden it was apparent that he was a steady, dedicated man with a sense of humour... always happy doing his job whether it was dressing a minor wound, attending blisters or helping to make a meal behind the lines.
>
> He liked what he called a 'civvy' Woodbine, not the ones bought at the NAAFI, the small packets of five sent from home. They were invariably flattened in the post, but he still enjoyed them and often handed them around.
>
> During the hot weather in France, when the enemy were [*sic*] in full retreat and we were marching in full kit in an effort to overtake, Eric would pass around his water bottle, not filled with water but Calvados! He had always something to offer...[12]

As well as ensuring that Doc's heroism has not been forgotten, veterans such as Fred Harris, Johnny Haville and Bobby Cory were able to perform one more valuable duty. Their stories helped to fill a void that served to draw Bob Harden and his sister, Julia, closer to a father they had spent their lives grieving for without ever really feeling his presence. Almost all of their 'memories' of him were second- or third-hand. The last time Julia saw her father she was six months old. Bob's only recollections were hazy ones of short wartime leaves spent together and of feeling shy in his father's company. Their lives have, in a very real sense, been journeys of self-discovery, as Julia has observed:

> The wonderful friends I have gained over the years would sometimes ask why I cried at such times as The Last Post, war films, war poetry? How could I grieve for a relationship I never had? I believe a large part was because I was always aware of my mother's and brother's loss... As I grew up I became increasingly aware of what I also had lost, the relationship that is always labelled father/daughter...[13]

At the same time, she has had to contend with all that it means to be the daughter of a war hero who continues to be venerated almost seventy years after his death. She finds it 'oddly peculiar' to think that, as well as being her father, Eric Harden VC has also become public property: an iconic figure with a near-mythological status all of his own. Yet hard as it has been to come to terms with this, she believes it was much harder for her brother, Bob:

> My brother was a hero's son and especially, therefore, had to live with the expectations of some who did not understand the dark side of that inheritance. As Harden VC's daughter my burden has not been so great in that way. I have been allowed to come to terms slowly with being 'special' in a way that had absolutely nothing to do with me – I did not choose to be born, I have done nothing.[14]

Something of the confusion of emotions may be gleaned from Bob's correspondence with Four Five veterans as his own quest for information about his father gathered momentum in the 1990s. Following a reunion at Arbroath, he wrote: 'So many names, so many faces – and so little time in which to meet and talk to them.'[15] There had been few among the commando gathering from A Troop, but those who were present had nothing but praise for Doc. Hearing their stories and how highly they thought of him filled Bob with a feeling of immense pride tinged with great sadness. 'My own memories of him are so few,' he added.[16]

Bobby Cory and Johnny Haville in Nederweert war cemetery at the grave of Doc Harden, 22 January 1995. (via J. Wells)

Not only that, but the picture he carried in his head of his father's brave final action had become increasingly muddled the more versions he had heard and read.

His mind was still in turmoil when he received a telephone call from an officer in the Royal Army Medical Corps stationed in Germany, inviting him to attend a memorial service in Holland to commemorate the 50th anniversary of his father's VC action. Marines from 45 Royal Marine Commando would be joined by wartime veterans and serving soldiers from RAMC units based in Germany. Among the guests of honour were Bobby Cory, who Bob remembered meeting once as a child almost fifty years earlier, and Johnny Haville, who he had never met before. The service at Nederweert War Cemetery, in pouring rain that reminded Bob of the monsoon season in India, was emotionally charged, but it was the visit to the battlefield that followed that would live longest in the memory. The night before, Bob had chatted with Johnny Haville and told him of his confusion about what happened on 23 January 1945. He even drew a diagram to better explain what he understood to be the story.

Haville told him that it was incorrect and assured him he would put him right, and that was how they left it until the afternoon of the battlefield tour when the coach wound its way through Echt and Maasbracht towards Brachterbeek, along the route the commandos had followed half a century before. As they approached the road that led to Harden Bridge, the coach paused while the Dutch tour guide related a story that Bob had heard before but which he now knew to be wrong. Moments later they were on their way again, splashing muddy water across the rain-washed road, until Bob's sudden intervention brought them to a grinding halt.

Joined by Bobby Cory and Johnny Haville, Bob stepped off the coach into the deluge. He could wait no longer. He wanted to hear, in their own words, what had actually taken place and where. 'There, in the pouring rain,' he later wrote, 'they began to tell me their story.'[17] Within seconds, they were joined by the detachment of Royal Marines. Then, the lads from the RAMC joined in, quickly followed by senior officers and the Dutch tour guide. They all listened as Bobby Cory recalled what happened to his section, 'his walking stick pointing in every direction', and then it was Johnny Haville's turn to recount the story of the heroic rescue mission initiated and led by Doc. Later, after laying wreaths on the bridge, the entire party returned to Brachterbeek and Cory, Haville and Bob walked the ground that was the scene of his father's last mortal act. 'At last,' he wrote, I now have a clear mind and an inner peace.'[18]

Seven years later, just nine months after his mother's death, Bob Harden succumbed to leukaemia, aged 64. At his request, their ashes were scattered in Holland not far from where Eric Harden, 'Doc' to his mates, had repeatedly scaled peaks of valour with a display of unselfishness that Maud thought so typical of the 'brave, straight, true man' she had loved and lost and that inspired Johnny Haville to write his own moving epitaph for the last medic to win the nation's highest military honour:

> An ordinary man, yet so extra-ordinary.

Appendix

The Heroes of Brachterbeek

Citations for action fought by Four Five on 23 January 1945.

Victoria Cross

Lance-Corporal Henry Eric Harden (No 11006144), Royal Army Medical Corps, attached 45 Royal Marine Commando:

> In North-west Europe on 23rd January, 1945, the leading section of a Royal Marine Commando Troop was pinned to the ground by intense enemy machine-gun fire from well-concealed positions. As it was impossible to engage the enemy from the open owing to lack of cover, the section was ordered to make for some nearby houses. This was accomplished, but one officer and three other ranks casualties were left lying in the open.
>
> The whole Troop position was under continuous heavy and accurate shell and mortar fire. L/Cpl Harden, the RAMC orderly attached to the Troop, at once went forward a distance of 120 yards, into the open under a hail of enemy machine gun and rifle fire directed from four positions, all within 300 yards, and with the greatest coolness and bravery remained in the open while he attended to the four casualties. After dressing the wounds of three of them, he carried one of them back to cover. L/Cpl Harden was then ordered not to go forward again and an attempt was made to bring in the other casualties with the aid of tanks, but this proved unsuccessful owing to the heavy and accurate fire of enemy anti-tank guns. A further attempt was then made to recover the casualties under a smoke screen, but this only increased the enemy fire in the vicinity of the casualties.

L/Cpl Harden then insisted on going forward again with a volunteer stretcher party, and succeeded in bringing back another badly wounded man.

L/Cpl Harden went out a third time, again with a stretcher party, and after starting on the return journey with a wounded officer, under very heavy enemy small arms and mortar fire, he was killed.

Throughout this long period L/Cpl Harden displayed superb devotion to duty and personal courage of the very highest order, and there is no doubt that it had a most steadying effect upon the other troops in the area at a most critical time. His action was directly responsible for saving the lives of the wounded brought in. His complete contempt of all personal danger, and the magnificent example he set of cool courage and determination to continue with his work, whatever the odds, was an inspiration to his comrades, and will never be forgotten by those who saw it.

Military Cross

Immediate award

Captain John Alexander Tulloch (291123), Royal Army Medical Corps, attached 45 Royal Marine Commando:

On the morning of 23rd January 1945 during the advance to contact from Brachterbeek towards Linne, the leading Troop of 45 Royal Marine Commando was pinned by heavy enemy small arms fire in some buildings. The Troop was isolated all day, all attempts to relieve them under cover of smoke or artillery produced no results. The Squadron of tanks co-operating could not be used to evacuate wounded owing to the proximity of enemy SP guns and bazookas.

In spite of knowing this Captain Tulloch twice ran the gauntlet of 400 yards open ground in his jeep to evacuate wounded. On the first occasion his jeep had two tyres burst by bullets and other damage but this did not deter his second venture which was equally hazardous.

His devotion to duty was remarkable and directly responsible for saving lives of casualties who otherwise would have had no real attention and must have died of exposure. His conduct had a direct bearing on the morale of the Troop which continued to fight on until withdrawal after dark was possible.

Temporary Lieutenant Harold George Riley, 45 Royal Marine Commando:

23rd January 1945 – Linne
On 23rd January, B Troop 45 (RM) Commando was held up by heavy enemy machine-gun and rifle fire during the advance on Linne. Lieut Riley was ordered to take his section and probe forward on the left. As soon as the section moved off, they drew heavy machine-gun and mortar fire on themselves from two well-sited and dug enemy posts. Lieut Riley immediately assaulted these positions, leading his section with great dash and resolution. In the face of fierce resistance two machine-gun posts were cleared by him with grenade and Thompson Sub Machine Gun fire, all the enemy being killed.

Before the remainder of his Troop could come to his assistance the enemy counter-attacked vigorously. There was no time to arrange a defensive position. Lieut Riley, followed by his men, met the enemy in the open and broke up the attack, killing 12 and wounding several more.

Throughout the whole day's fighting, Lieut Riley's coolness and high spirits were an outstanding example and inspiration to all ranks. The success in obtaining the footing across the Vloot Beek (Montforterbeek), from which the final attack on Linne was launched, was largely due to Lieut Riley's aggressive action.

Distinguished Service Cross

Immediate award

Naval Chaplain Reginald Haw, 45 Royal Marine Commando:

23rd January 1945 – Brachterbeek
This officer has been the Chaplain with 45 (RM) Commando throughout its operations in North West Europe since its arrival in that theatre on 17th January 1945. On 23rd January 1945 the Commando were advancing to contact in the Brachterbeek area. The leading Troop made contact with German Paratroops, and a fierce encounter developed. The two leading Troops were pinned in very open country under constant Spandau, mortar and SP fire. Within a short time the medical orderly of the leading Troop was killed and an immediate replacement was called for

to attend the casualties. The Rev Haw on his own initiative ran the gauntlet of a hail of fire and took over the duties of the dead medical orderly. Throughout the ensuing action the Rev Haw tended wounded and evacuated them to the Regimental Aid Post. During the more difficult periods he moved about positions under fire giving cheerful encouragement to the men. During this action his complete disregard of personal danger, and his cheerful banter to the troops inspired all who saw it.

Since this operation the unit has been very actively employed, in particular in the attack on Wesel across the River Rhine on the night 23rd/24th March, the attack on Leese across the River Wiser on 7th April and in forming the bridgehead across the River Aller from 10th April to 14th April. On all these occasions, and also during the intermediate stages, the Chaplain's example of courage, cheerfulness and complete disregard for his own safety has done more than anything else to maintain the morale and determination of the troops. He has won the devotion and confidence of all ranks by his untiring efforts at all times for the spiritual, social and medical welfare of the troops which have seldom been surpassed in or out of action.

Military Medal

Immediate awards

Marine Neil John Patrick (PO X 117198), 45 Royal Marine Commando:

23rd January 1945 – Brachterbeek
Marine Patrick was the Bren gunner of a section advancing to contact over very open ground. Suddenly the section came under very heavy small arms fire from two well-concealed enemy machine-gun positions who had withheld their fire until Marine Patrick's section had approached to within 100 yards. The section was immediately pinned near a small bank close to the road.

Marine Patrick realised the danger and disregarding the accurate enemy fire which was pinning down his section, he dashed 20 yards across the open to a position from which he could engage the enemy posts. This he did with great effect although the position afforded no cover.

His prompt action and initiative and complete disregard for personal safety enabled his section to regain the initiative and liquidate the enemy posts.

Marine Patrick's conduct was a shining example of the finest aggressive spirit.

Marine Francis Burton (PLY X 105925), 45 Royal Marine Commando:

23rd January 1945 – Vloot Beek (Montforterbeek)
On 23rd January 1945 during the initial battle for the bridgehead at Vloot Beek from which the final attack on Linne was launched, Marine Burton was carrying the Commando Rover set [CO's wireless]. Marine followed his Commanding Officer from Commando HQ to visit the forward Troops, who were hotly engaged. On the way, Marine Burton encountered heavy mortar fire and also came under accurate rifle fire. After some 300 yards had been covered Marine Burton was badly hit in his right arm. Although obviously in great pain and with a useless right arm, Marine Burton continued to follow his Commanding Officer, maintaining vital communications and passing orders for supporting fire to aid the forward troops. This he continued to do, refusing to return to the Regimental Aid Post until another signaller was obtained to take over the set.

Marine Burton's conduct was a shining example of a signaller's devotion to duty and loyalty to his Unit.

Periodic awards

Acting Troop Sergeant Major Henry Bennett (Ch X 512), 40 and 45 Royal Marine Commando:

North West European Campaign – 6th June [1944] to 7th May 1945.
TSM Bennett rejoined his unit in Normandy after being badly wounded. He insisted on rejoining in spite of having a permanently damaged elbow. Since rejoining, TSM Bennett's Troop has been in hard fighting and has suffered many casualties. On two separate occasions, all the officers of the Troop were killed or wounded and TSM Bennett had to command under difficult circumstances. He fully justified his unit's faith in him on each occasion.

He has in addition personally distinguished himself in action on several occasions, the outstanding example being the time when he went out to bring in the body of L/Cpl Harden, VC, at Maasbracht, during the action for which Harden's decoration was awarded. TSM Bennett had proved himself in many severe tests to be not only a very brave man but also a determined, aggressive and skilful leader. When out of action he has done sterling work in re-forming his Troop and keeping morale high and aggressive spirit to the fore. Successes which the Troop has had are to a very considerable degree due to TSM Bennett's leadership and magnificent performance right through the campaign.

Temporary Sergeant William James Noakes (Ex.977), 45 Royal Marine Commando:

North West European Campaign – 6th June [1944] to 7th May, 1945
Sgt Noakes landed with his unit on D Day near Ouistreham. During this landing he distinguished himself by getting out gangways on the LCI(s) after the seamen had become casualties. On D+1 he again showed himself to be a cool and aggressive leader, on this occasion during street fighting at Sallenelles. His subaltern was killed and Sgt Noakes rose to the occasion and commanded his section with skill and courage. After those early days he went out on many difficult patrols at night. For his patrol work he gained the respect of his officers and the complete confidence of his men. Since then Sgt Noakes has been in hard fighting, a lot of which was at very close quarters, at Angerville (20th August 1944), Linne (January 1945), in addition to being in an assault Troop in the forcing of the rivers Maas, Rhine, Weser, Aller and Elbe. In all these actions his unit was involved in stiff fighting. Sgt Noakes was on each occasion absolutely reliable, cool and aggressive. He has never missed a chance of inflicting casualties on the enemy. His loyalty to his unit and his devotion to duty are quite outstanding and his personal courage and disregard of danger beyond question.

Notes

Prologue

1. Letter to Eric, post-dated 22 January 1945.
2. Letter to Eric, 22 January 1945.
3. Letter to Eric, post-dated 22 January 1945.
4. Letter to Eric, 29 January 1945.

Chapter 1: Your Very Own Eric

1. Letter to Maud, December1934.
2. Letter to Maud, undated.
3. Interview with the author, 2012.
4. Pavitt, A., *Memories of Northfleet by the Riverside* (self-published, 2010).
5. Maude died tragically young, aged 18, in 1928, following an operation for appendicitis. At the time she was employed by Henley's Telegraph Works where her youngest sister Hilda later worked.
6. Interview with the author.
7. *Ibid.*
8. Haynes (*née* Harden), J.E., *Memories of Uncle Eric.*
9. Interview with the author. Eric's mother is described as a small, strong-minded woman of Victorian sensibilities.
10. Maud was born on 27 April 1914 in Peckham, South London. Her parents moved to 102 Crayford Way, Crayford, in 1920. One of her brothers, Bob, died in 1911.
11. Harden, J., *Eric Harden VC, RAMC (45 RM Commando): My Family's Story* (Menin House, 2011)
12. *Ibid.*
13. Letter to Maud, December 1934.
14. Letter to Maud, 5 April 1935.

15. Cecil and May were Maud's brother and sister.
16. Letter to Maud, 28 July 1934.
17. Letter to Maud, 5 April 1935.
18. Letter to Maud, undated.
19. Haynes, *Memories of Uncle Eric.*
20. Letter to Maud, April 1936.
21. *Ibid.*

Chapter 2: Lost Peace

1. Priestley, J.B., *English Journey* (William Heinemann, 1934).
2. Orwell, G., *Coming Up For Air* (Victor Gollancz, 1939).
3. Letter to Maud, 14 April 1936.
4. Interview with the author, 2012.
5. Holt, D., '16 August 1940 air raid', in *Northfleet WWII Memories* (Gravesham Library).
6. *The Reporter*, 24 August 1940.
7. Recollections of Joyce Brown (*née* Hull).
8. *Ibid.*
9. Harden, J., *Eric Harden VC, RAMC (45 RM Commando): My Family's Story* (Menin House, 2011)
10. Interview with the author, 2012.
11. Harden, J., *Op cit.*

Chapter 3: Gunner Harden

1. Letter to Maud, April 1942.
2. *Ibid.*
3. *Ibid.*
4. Letter to Maud, April 1942.
5. Letter to Maud, April 1942.
6. Letter to Maud, April 1942.
7. Letter to Maud, 26 April 1942.
8. Letter to Maud, 29 April 1942.
9. Letter to Maud, 26 April 1942.
10. Letter to Maud, 14 May 1942.
11. Letter to Maud, 5 May 1942.
12. Letter to Maud, 11 May 1942.
13. Letter to Maud, 14 May 1942.
14. This was almost certainly a comment in deference to his brother-in-law, Ray Gurney, who was a sergeant instructor in the Royal Artillery. Eric

greatly admired him and couldn't help but wonder what Ray would have made of his gun team. He imagined the two of them could 'talk for hours on end' about gunnery (Letters, 14 and 18 May).

15. Letter to Maud, 18 May 1942.
16. Letter to Maud, 23 May 1942.
17. Letter to Maud, June 1942.
18. *Ibid.*
19. Letter to Maud, June 1942. The veleta cheese mentioned by Eric was a soft processed cheese spread.
20. Letter to Maud, 29 May 1942.
21. Letter to Maud, 3 June 1942.
22. The factory was operated by Molins, peacetime manufacturers of cigarette machines. Having signed the Official Secrets Act, Maud would never speak about her work. The only thing she ever told her son or daughter about her time there was about the promiscuity of the factory girls.
23. Letter to Maud, June 1942.
24. Letter to Maud, 31 May 1942.
25. Letter to Maud, June 1942.
26. Letter to Maud, 3 June 1942.

Chapter 4: Medical Matters

1. Letter to Maud, 18 June 1942.
2. *Ibid.*
3. Letter to Maud, 21 June 1942.
4. Letter to Maud, 26 June 1942.
5. Bill Harden, his elder brother was serving in the Royal Navy.
6. Letter to Maud, 11 July 1942.
7. Letter to Maud, July 1942.
8. *Ibid.*
9. Interview with the author, 2012.
10. Letter to Maud, October 1942.
11. Letter to Maud, 6 October 1942.
12. Letter to Maud, October 1942.
13. Letter to Maud, 21 October 21, 1942.
14. *Ibid.*
15. Letter to Maud, October 1942.
16. Letter to Maud, October 1942.
17. Letter to Maud, 30 October 1942.
18. Letter to Maud, November 1942.
19. Letter to Maud, November 1942.

20. Letter to Maud, November 1942. The comment about carrying on 'like they do at work' was a reference to the behaviour of some of Maud's fellow workers at the Molins factory.
21. Letter to Maud, 30 October 1942.
22. *Ibid.*
23. Letter to Maud, 31 October 1942.
24. *Ibid.*
25. Letter to Maud, November 1942.
26. Letter to Maud, November 1942.
27. Letter to Maud, November 1942.
28. Letter to Maud, November 1942.
29. Letter to Maud, November 1942.
30. Letter to Maud, November 1942.

Chapter 5: With the Marines

1. Letter to Maud, 8 December 1942.
2. Letter to Maud, January 1943.
3. Letter to Maud, 7 January 1943.
4. Letter to Maud, 5 March 1943.
5. Letter to Maud, 17 April 1943.
6. Letter to Maud, 4 May 1943.
7. Letter to Maud, 13 January 1943. She was right to do so. By May, his friendship with Connie appeared to have fizzled out. In a letter dated 1 May, Eric wrote Maud: 'Oh by the way, sweetheart, I haven't heard from Leeds since I've been back, so I think we can call finis don't you. Did I hear you take a long sigh then xxx.'
8. Letter to Maud, January 1943.
9. *Ibid.*
10. Letter to Maud, 18 January 1943.
11. *Ibid.*
12. *Ibid.*
13. Letter to Maud, 20 January 1943.
14. Letter to Maud, 9 February 1943.
15. Letter to Maud, February 1943.
16. Letter to Maud, 4 March 1943.
17. Letter to Maud, March 1943.
18. Letter to Maud, April 1943.
19. *Ibid.*
20. Letter to Maud, 1 May 1943.
21. Letter to Maud, 10 May 1943.
22. *Ibid.*

23. Letter to Maud, May 1943. In fact, only one aircraft came down in the town, though another was thought to have crashed into the sea. The low-level attack carried out by twenty-two Focke Wulf 190 fighter bombers on Sunday, May 23, 1943 was Bournemouth's worst raid of the war. The Metropole Hotel and Beales' department store were virtually destroyed and the death toll topped 200, with 131 servicemen among the dead, and many more injured.
24. Letter to Maud, 3 June 1943.
25. *Ibid.*
26. Letter to Maud, 4 June 1943.
27. Letter to Maud, 21 June 1943.
28. *Ibid.*
29. Letter to Maud, 24 June 1943.
30. Letter to Maud, 24 June 1943. As a further thank you, two marines bought Eric a pint of beer, little realising he was a tee-totaller. 'I don't know how I got it down,' he told Maud.
31. Letter to Maud, 28 June 1943.
32. *Ibid.*
33. Letter to Maud, 6 July 1943.
34. Letter to Maud, 21 July 1943.
35. Letter to Maud, 4 August 1943.
36. Letter to Maud, 11 August 1943.
37. Letter to Maud, 12 August 1943.
38. Letter to Maud, 20 August 1943.
39. Letter to Maud, 23 August 1943.
40. *Ibid.*
41. Letter to Maud, 23 August 1943.
42. Letter to Maud, 28 August 1943.
43. Letter to Maud, September 1943. Almost six months earlier, Eric had been worrying that the war might drag on too long! Writing to Maud on 25 March, he commented on the latest war news: 'I wonder if Mr Churchill will be right when he says that the war won't be over until well into 1945. Gee, that's a long time to wait, isn't it duck! And I thought that it would finish this year too.'
44. Letter to Maud, 10 September 1943.
45. Letter to Maud, 15 September 1943.
46. *Ibid.*

Chapter 6: The Green Beret

1. The training programme for Four Five on 11 November called for all troops to muster at Ayr's Low Green for a 20-mile march in denims, steel

helmets and full fighting order, carrying weapons save for 2-inch mortars, personal ammunition, six magazines per Bren gun. The same week's activities included commando drill, firing practice, completing the assault course and cliff climbing.

2. Letter to Maud, October 1943.
3. *Ibid.*
4. *Ibid.*
5. Letter to Maud, October 1943. Weeks later, back in Ayr, he would add to the sense of secrecy by insisting that Maud not address any post to 45 Commando during his stay in Scotland.
6. Fred Harris, a 5th Battalion marine who became a Bren gunner in Four Five's A Troop, felt this to be an unfair slur. He disputed the notion that the marines were 'pressed men'. 'We were formed on parade at Burley and told what was going to happen to us, that we were going to become Royal Marine Commandos, and that anybody wishing to become a commando should take one pace forward and practically the whole battalion took one pace forward. So, in my mind, that was volunteering for the commandos.' (IWM Sound Archive)
7. Letter to Maud, 15 November 1943.
8. Letter to Maud, 10 November 1943.
9. Letter to Maud, 4 November 1943.
10. Letter to Maud, 29 October 1943.
11. Letter to Maud, 21 November 1943.
12. Letter to Maud, 10 November 1943.
13. Letter to Maud, post-dated 15 November 1943.
14. *Ibid.*
15. *Ibid.*
16. *Ibid.*
17. Letter to Maud, 25 November 1943.
18. Letter to Maud, December 1943.
19. In spite of the conditions and the relentless hardship of the training routine, turnout among the would-be commandos was expected to be immaculate with weapons and equipment well-polished and spotless.
20. Letter to Maud, December 1943. Daughter Julia recalls her mother saying that Eric had 'rescued' a marine from the water after he fell from a rope bridge. 'Seems he got into an argument about it with the officer, as they were supposed to leave "casualties". Dad thought that was a bit much during training exercises.'
21. This was almost certainly Marine Derrick Cakebread, a young Londoner who recovered to become a sniper who served with Eric in A Troop. He broke a bone in his foot during the first 5 miles of the march, but somehow managed to complete it and was deemed to have passed the course.

22. Fred Harris recalled having to complete the last mile in respirators. 'That was pretty killing. You couldn't see where you were [going]. They were misted up, sweaty...' During one of the exercises in the mountains, he said they took with them a potato and a piece of raw meat. 'We were supposed to go up there and cook it, but when you got up fairly high there wasn't a dry twig to be seen anywhere. Everything was damp. We just ate the stuff raw, almost.' (IWM Sound Archive)
23. Letter to Maud, 15 December 1943.

Chapter 7: On the Eastbourne Front

1. Letter to Maud, post-dated 5 January 1944.
2. Letter to Maud, 16 January 1944.
3. Eric had a taste for Worcester apples, which were a local orchard specialty around Northfleet and Southfleet. Bobby would polish them before sending them to his father!
4. A spell of leave followed shortly after reaching Eastbourne, probably negating the need to write about the incident.
5. '45 Vintage Newsletter' no. 9, March 1998, 'From those who were in peril on the sea'.
6. *Ibid.*
7. *Ibid.*
8. Interview with the author, 2012. The Streeters made such a good impression that Walter Bigland recalls his parents staying there after the war as paying guests! They also maintained a friendship with Maud Harden after the war, becoming 'Eastbourne aunties' to daughter Julia.
9. Letter to Maud, 2 March 1944.
10. Oranges were a rarity in ration-fed Britain during and immediately after the Second World War. Incidentally, the double orange ration was for a journey along the coast to see Field Marshal Montgomery. Eric dismissed it in couple of sentences: 'This morning we all went to Brighton to see Monty, or at least he came to see us. It was a good turn out too, of course there was a lot of spit and polish.'
11. Letter to Maud, 8 February 1944.
12. Letter to Maud, 20 March 1944.
13. Verity Rowbottom (*née* Day), who was 6 at the time, recalled her grandmother had just come in from the back of the house when the bomb exploded in Factory Road.

> She said, 'I think we're going to get it tonight' and then, bang. It was really frightening. Apparently, that night I wouldn't go to bed, which was lucky because all the ceilings came down upstairs. As

> soon as the siren went we all got under the stairs except for gran who was on her way when the bomb landed, flattening the houses opposite. It was terrible. The whole fireplace in the sitting room was blown out, the front door was blown off, other doors were all skew whiff, and loads of stuff was blown off the walls. I was taken out through the back and we walked to auntie Ethel's place in the High Street where we stayed for a couple of days.
>
> (Interview with the author)

Hettie Victoria Cotterill died in the bombing along with her 10-year-old son Derek. Such was the ferocity of the blast, no trace of the boy's body was ever found.

14. Letter to Maud, 23 March 1944.
15. Letter to Maud, February 1944.
16. Letter to Maud, 27 April 1944. Eric and Maud didn't own a car. They used to borrow one owned by his sister, Ethel.
17. *Ibid.*
18. Letter to Maud, 24 March 1944.
19. Letter to Maud, 8 February 1944.
20. Letter to Maud, marked Eastbourne 1944. Typical of these invasion schemes was Exercise Beetroot II, carried out on 19 February. Four Five's role was to land at Chapman's Pool and seize and hold a vital road junction before pressing on to secure a pass at Corfe Castle. A Troop's objective (codeword 'Portsmouth') was to clear a pillbox, secure the beach and then dig in astride the Swanage-Langton Matravers road. Among a multitude of instructions issued there were orders not to damage roads!
21. Letter to Maud, marked Eastbourne 1944.
22. Letter to Maud, marked Eastbourne 1944.
23. IWM Sound Records.
24. Letter to Maud, 11 March 1944.
25. Letter to Maud, 11 May 1944.
26. Histories of Four Five give the departure date as 26 May but Eric's letters clearly state it to have been a day earlier.
27. Harris, F.L., 'My Life' (unpublished manuscript).
28. Letter to Maud, 25 May 1944.
29. *Ibid.*
30. Letter to Maud, 31 May 1944.

Chapter 8: Preparing to Make History

1. IWM Sound Archives.
2. *Ibid.*

3. Cakebread, D., 'My Personal Story of D-Day and the Normandy Campaign' (unpublished manuscript).
4. Day, J., *A Plain Russet-Coated Captain* (Arthur H. Stockwell, 1993).
5. *March Past, A Memoir by Lord Lovat* (Weidenfeld & Nicolson, 1979).
6. Day, J., *Op. cit.*
7. *March Past, Op. cit.*
8 Harris, F.L., 'My Life' (unpublished manuscript).
9. *Ibid.*
10. 'Chronicles of D-Day, collected by Cdr Rupert Curtis DSC' (unpublished manuscript, IWM).
11. Interview with author, 2012.
12. Interview with author, 2012.
13. 'Chronicles of D-Day', Op. cit.
14. *Ibid.*

Chapter 9: The Longest Day

1. Curtis DSC, Cdr R., 'D-Day: We Landed the Commandos', in 'Chronicles of D-Day' (unpublished manuscript, IWM)
2. IWM Sound Archives.
3. *Ibid.*
4. Cdr Rupert Curtis.
5. Rupert Curtis maintained that the loss of life would have been much heavier had the German gun batteries been using incendiary or high-explosive ammunition instead of solid shot. Curtis estimated that half of the brigade might not have got ashore but for the fact that the enemy used the wrong type of ammunition.
6. Harris, F.L., 'My Life' (unpublished manuscript).
7. *Ibid.*
8. Letter to Maud, 2 July 1944. It was the only written reference he made to the D-Day landings that has survived.
9. John Tulloch, brigade HQ medical officer and later MO of Four Five, taken from an unpublished memoir passed to the author by his widow, 2012.
10. Cakebread, D., 'My Personal Story of D-Day and the Normandy Campaign' (unpublished manuscript).
11. Interview with the author, 2012.
12. John Tulloch, Op. cit.
13. Young DSO MC (2 bars), Lt Col P., *Storm From the Sea* (Wm Kimber, 1958).
14. Interview with author, 2012.
15. Interview with author, 2012.
16. Day, J., *A Plain Russet-Coated Captain* (Arthur H. Stockwell, 1993).
17. Cakebread, D., Op. cit.

18. Interview with the author, 2012.
19. Ambrose, S., *Pegasus Bridge* (George Allen & Unwin, 1984).
20. Cakebread, D., *Op. cit.*
21. Interview with the author, 2012.
22. Nicol Gray was awarded the Distinguished Service Order for his leadership on D-Day and the days that followed. He later earned a second award bar and was described by a marine on his staff as 'the bravest man he ever knew'.
23. Cakebread, D., *Op. cit.*
24. Emlyn Jones, from 'Chronicles of D-Day' (unpublished manuscript, IWM Archives).
25. IWM Sound Archives.
26. Interview with the author, 2012.
27. *Ibid.*
28. Samain, B., *Commando Men: The Story of a Royal Marine Commando in North-West Europe* (Stevens and Sons, 1948).

Chapter 10: Fighting for Survival

1. Letter to Maud, 24 June 1944.
2. RSM John Henry Grimsey and Cpl John Arthur Watson, KIA 7 June 1944.
3. Day, Capt. J.E., *The Story of 45 Royal Marine Commando* (privately published).
4. The commando was Cpl Richard Arlen, a German member of No. 3 Troop, 10 (Inter-Allied) Commando attached to Four Five. According to Ian Dear's history of Ten Commando (Leo Cooper, 1987), Arlen, a prize fighter in civilian life who had vowed to win the VC, had responded angrily to being fired at while under a white flag. 'He went back to his position, collected his tommy gun, and rushed forward to assault the machine-gun position that had fired at him and was immediately killed.'
5. Harris, F.L., 'My Life' (unpublished manuscript).
6. All three were killed, though not in Franceville. L/Cpl Frederick Thomas Stallwood and Marine Thomas Albert Lovett are both listed as killed in action on 8 June 1944 while Marine Leslie James Lee is listed as having died on 9 June.
7. Day, Capt. J.E., *Op. cit.* Captain Smith was awarded a Military Cross for his gallantry at Franceville. During the retreat from Merville, he assisted Jock Rushforth, the wounded commander of C Troop, to reach Le Plein.
8. *Ibid.*
9. Letter to Maud, 27 June 1944.
10. Letter to Maud, 24 June 1944.
11. '45 Vintage Newsletter' no. 2, John Shepherd (E Troop).

12. 45 RM Commando War Diary, National Archives. The unit record appears to be wrong here. L/Cpl Alexander Crystal Dryburgh was killed on 10 June and two more men from E Troop were wounded.
13. Samain, B., *Commando Men: The Story of a Royal Marine Commando in North-West Europe* (Stevens and Sons, 1948).
14. Day, Capt. J.E., *Op. cit.*
15. '45 Vintage Newsletter' no. 6, Neil Patrick (A Troop).
16. Letter to Maud, 24 June 1944.

Chapter 11:Vixen,V1s and a 'Commando Baby'

1. Letter to Mabel dated 19 June. In it, he thanked his sister for paying a visit to Maud. 'I expect she will be worried for a time now,' he wrote. 'I suppose things are very much the same at home aren't they, except, of course, you are all very worried about us chaps over here. The RAF are doing well here, Mabel, and, by god, we are thankfull [*sic*].'
2. Letter to Maud, 17 June 1944.
3. Letter to Maud, 19 June 1944.
4. Marine J.K. Crooks, quoted in Young, D., *Four Five* (Leo Cooper, 1972).
5. Mills-Roberts CBE, DSO, MC, Brig. D., *Clash by Night: A Commando Chronicle* (William Kimber, 1956).
6. *Ibid.*
7. *Ibid.*
8. 45 RM Commando War Diary, National Archives.
9. Day, Capt. J.E., *The Story of 45 Royal Marine Commando* (privately published).
10. Samain, B., *Commando Men: The Story of a Royal Marine Commando in North-West Europe* (Stevens and Sons, 1948).
11. Letter to his mother 'and all', 29 June 1944.
12. Letter to Maud, 29 June 1944.
13. Interview with author.
14. '45 Vintage Newsletter' no. 10, Jim Bailey (E Troop).
15. Letter to Maud, 24 July 1944.
16. '45 Vintage Newsletter' no. 10, Jim Bailey (E Troop).
17. Letter to Maud, 7 July 1944.
18. Letter to Maud, 24 July 1944. In a reference to the V1 menace, he told his 'Mum and All': 'I expect they will soon find something to beat it, don't you?' (Letter, 29 June).
19. His brother-in-law, Cecil Pullen, who was serving in the Air Transport Auxiliary, had made the family's Anderson shelter habitable again.
20. Bates, H.E., 'The Battle of the Flying Bomb' (unpublished manuscript). Quoted in Longmate, N., *The Doodlebugs: The Story of the Flying Bombs* (Hutchinson, 1981). Sussex also suffered badly from the V1s. Doc received

regular correspondence from his former landladies in one of which they said it 'isn't very healthy in Eastbourne these days'.

21. He had inadvertently added a year to his age. He was only 32.
22. A reference to Maud's parents who lived in Crayford, near the Vickers factory. In a letter written on 24 July, there is the suggestion that their house had suffered damage during the V1 onslaught: 'I hope your mother is still OK, Maud. I don't suppose Pa would like to move down with you, would he. He likes his own home better even if it is nearly blown down. But it must be rotten for them all the same. They must have a few of them [V1s] over there. They seem to get very near to the works don't they?'
23. Letter to Maud, 10 July 1944.
24. Letter to Maud, post-dated 20 July 1944.
25. Letter to Maud, 28 July 1944.

Chapter 12: Up Close and Personal

1. D'Este, C., *Decision in Normandy* (Robson Books, 2000)
2. Beevor, A., *D-Day: The Battle for Normandy* (Viking, 2009)
3. Letter to Maud, 12 July 1944.
4. Letter to Maud, 4 August 1944.
5. Young, D., *Four Five* (Leo Cooper, 1972).
6. '45 Vintage Newsletter' no. 2.
7. '45 Vintage Newsletter' no. 2, quoting a 1946 letter by Ian Beadle (E Troop).
8. '45 Vintage Newsletter' no. 2, Morris Steele (E Troop).
9. Young, D., *Op. cit.*
10. '45 Vintage Newsletter' no. 2.
11. '45 Vintage Newsletter' no. 5, Ray Hetherington (B Troop). The men who died were Cpl Arthur Robert Brooks and Marine Nathaniel McIntosh. The other man wounded was Marine John Jones.
12. Young, D., *Op. cit.*
13. The Four Five war diary gives the casualties in this incident as one man killed and another wounded, but Fred Harris insisted that there were two fatalities, which is confirmed by the unit's roll of honour. The dead men were Cpl Arthur Bidmead and Marine Robert 'Dinger' Bell. The wounded man was Marine 'Billy' Barclay.
14. Letter to Maud, 15 August 1944.
15. Interview with the author.
16. Mills-Roberts CBE, DSO, MC, Brig. D., *Clash by Night: A Commando Chronicle* (William Kimber, 1956).
17. Young DSO MC (2 bars), Lt Col P., *Storm From the Sea* (Wm Kimber, 1958).
18. Lt H. Muir Beddall, quoted in Young, D., *Op. cit.*

19. Mills-Roberts, D., *Op. cit.*
20. *Ibid.*
21. Lt H. Muir Beddall, *Op. cit.*
22. Interview with the author. The marine who died was John McFatter. He was one of six men from Four Five killed that day.
23. Day, Capt. J.E., *The Story of 45 Royal Marine Commando* (privately published).
24. '45 Vintage Newsletter' no. 9, Fred Harris (A Troop).
25. *Ibid.*
26. Samain, B., *Commando Men: The Story of a Royal Marine Commando in North-West Europe* (Stevens and Sons, 1948).
27. Letter to Maud, 31 August 1944.

Chapter 13: The Final Reunion

1. Letter to Maud, undated though clearly written on his return to Petworth at the end of September 1944.
2. Letter to Maud, post-dated 3 October 1944. Eric was referring in his letter to his brother-in-law, Ray, who was serving as an instructor, and Fred Draper, a friend and neighbour who lived with his wife Win opposite them in Colyer Road.
3. Letter to Maud, post-dated 9 October 1944.
4. Letter to Maud, undated from Bexhill.
5. Interview with author.
6. Letter to Maud, undated from Bexhill.
7. Letter to Maud, 24 November 1944.
8. Letter to 'Mum and All', undated from Bexhill late October or early November 1944.
9. Letter to Maud, October 1944.
10. Letter to Maud, post-dated 16 December 1944. Following a visit to the Winter Gardens, he wrote: 'There were very few there to what it used to be before we went to France. It didn't seem the same old place at all, and there were only half the old band there…'
11. Letter to Maud, post-dated 10 December 1944.
12. Letter to Maud, November 1944. It is not clear whether the incident referred to involved an enemy missile or an anti-aircraft shell that came down in Colyer Road, causing damage to a number of houses.
13. Letter to Maud, undated.
14. Letter to Maud, post-dated 1 January 1945.
15. *Ibid.*

Chapter 14: The Road to Brachterbeek

1. Letter to his mother, undated from Bexhill.
2. Letter to Maud, post-dated 5 January.
3. Letter to his mother, undated from Bexhill.
4. Interview with author.
5. '45 Vintage Newsletter' no. 6, an appreciation of the Rev Reginald Haw by John Tulloch.
6. Letter to Maud, post-dated 12 January. Hilda was Eric's younger sister, married to Harry.
7. Letter to Maud, stamped BLA January 45. The reference to going across a 'third time' remains something of a puzzle. It may be that he was counting the return trip from Normandy in September as well as the D-Day landing, but there is also the tantalising possibility that he may have been involved in some pre-invasion reconnaissance. In reply to his letter, Maud wrote: 'Why three times, dear, as if you count before D-Day it makes more than three...' Quite what she was referring to remains unclear. As yet no evidence has been found in support of the idea that he may have participated in earlier forays across the Channel.
8. Cakebread, D., 'My War Story from September 1944 to Demob in 1946' (unpublished manuscript).
9. Letter to Maud, 17 January 1945. During his brief time in Belgium, Eric found time to buy a decorative handkerchief for Maud and a Bruges lace bonnet for Julia, which he sent home.
10. Letter to his mother, 19 January 1945.
11. Day, Capt. J.E., *The Story of 45 Royal Marine Commando* (privately published).
12. Letter to Maud, 18 January 1945.
13. Letter to Maud, 19 January 1945.

Chapter 15: Advance to Contact

1. Robert Cory interview with author, 1994.
2. Essame, H., *The Battle for Germany* (Batsford, 1969).
3. Thompson, R.W., *The Battle for the Rhineland* (Hutchinson, 1958).
4. *Ibid.*
5. Samain, B., *Commando Men: The Story of a Royal Marine Commando in North-West Europe* (Stevens and Sons, 1948).
6. *Ibid.*
7. Cory, R., 'A Troop, 45 Commando RM, 23 January 1945' (unpublished recollections, passed to the author, 1994).
8. *Ibid.*

9. Recalling the action some fifty years later, Neil Patrick said of his failure to notice the presence of Cory's section: 'This may seem strange, but, in my experience, in situations like this one seems to have a tunnel vision and, consequently, end up fighting your own little war with the fellows immediately alongside you.'
10. Neil Patrick, letter to author, 1995. According to Fred Harris, the German shot by Thomas was one of a number of enemy soldiers seen running across the front of the station. For some unaccountable reason, he stopped midway and appeared to be pointing to something when he was 'dropped' by Thomas. 'I can still hear that peculiar laugh of his,' Harris recalled in a letter published in '45 Vintage Newsletter' no. 10, 'he was enjoying it, I'm sure!'
11. Walter Bigland, interview with author, 2012.
12. Neil Patrick, letter to author, 1995.
13. Fred Harris, interview with author, 2012; letter, 1995; and privately published memoir.
14. Letter to author, 1995.
15. *Ibid.* In a letter published in '45 Vintage Newsletter' no. 10, Patrick recalled that his efforts 'drew encouragement and applause from Mr Thomas who was in a building across the road'.
16. Letter to author, 1995.
17. Interview with author, 2012.
18. Cory, R. Op. cit.
19. *Ibid.*
20. *Ibid.*
21. *Ibid.*
22. *Ibid.* Though known in Four Five as Marine Frederick Edward Wales, his surname was actually Wale.
23. *Ibid.*
24. *Ibid.*
25. *Ibid.*

Chapter 16: No Greater Love

1. Letter to author, 1994.
2. While Johnny Haville and the subsequent citation for 'Doc's' Victoria Cross refer only to three journeys into no man's land, Bobby Cory and Reg Haw stated that he had braved the enemy fire on four separate occasions. Cory, in particular, was insistent in both his written account to me and his interview that Doc had risked his life four times. 'He came out to see us on the ground first and to attend to our wounds. Then he went back with poor old Wheeler. And then came back a couple of more

times,' he told me in 1994. TSM Wiggy Bennett, meanwhile, insisted that the number of trips was 'four known and possibly six'.

3. Based on correspondence with Johnny Haville, 1994.
4. Frank Middis in '45 Vintage Newsletter' no. 10. The men wounded in his jeep were Marine Ogden, the driver, and Marine George Moore. Another man, Marine Ken Adams escaped uninjured.
5. Harry Bennett, in Young, D., *Four Five* (Leo Cooper, 1972).
6. Letter to author, 1994.
7. The role of the tanks at Brachterbeek on 23 January 1945 is a contentious one. In an interview with the author in 1995, Bobby Cory stated that while they undoubtedly did 'take out' the windmill, which he described as the 'focal point' of the German defence, they gave no support during the advance into and beyond Brachterbeek during the morning. 'The ground was so frozen and snow-covered, manoeuvring the tanks was extremely difficult,' he said. 'They were sliding all over the place. It was partially because of this that it was 100 per cent an advance to contact infantry action.' The 1st RTR war diary states that C Squadron moved to support the Commando Brigade's advance into Maasbracht at 8.15 a.m., but made no move to Brachterbeek until 1 p.m. At 3 p.m., the squadron was preparing to support the Commandos (this was presumably the flanking move made by B and E Troops) and by 5.30 p.m. had 'completed its task' and returned to Schilberg, having suffered no casualties and claimed thirty Germans killed. John Day's recollection is taken from an account sent to the author in 1995.
8. Letter to author, 1994. Haville's account is at odds with the version published in David Young's history of Four Five which has Mason and Haville carrying the stretcher and Doc walking 'coolly' alongside, rendering aid to the badly injured Wales.
9. Letter to author, 1994. Although Haville made reference to it only after bringing in Marine Wales, TSM Bennett said it was after Doc returned with Wheeler that they first noticed his smock was 'ripped at the back by bullets'.
10. Letter to Maud Harden, 2 June 1945.
11. Johnny Haville, letter to author, 1994.
12. Cory, R., 'A Troop, 45 Commando RM, 23 January 1945' (unpublished recollections, passed to the author, 1994).
13. Johnny Haville, letter to author, 1994.
14. Cory, R., *Op. cit.*
15. Tulloch, J., unpublished memoir of his wartime service, passed to the author by his widow, 2012.
16. *Ibid.*
17. The reason the Germans agreed to the truce may have had something to do with the Commandos' willingness to allow them to recover the body of

the man shot by Tommy Thomas at the beginning of the action near the station. In a letter to the author, Neil Patrick stated that the enemy held up a white flag, 'requesting permission to remove Mr Thomas' victim, who still lay where he fell. This was granted and they produced a wheelbarrow into which they bundled the fellow in the white suit and black equipment and trundled him out of sight. This agreement stood us in good stead later in the day'.

18. Tulloch, J., *Op. cit.*
19. Captain John Day, who later saw the jeeps, thought that 'judging by the bullet holes in the windscreens and bodywork it was incredible that anyone in them could have survived' (Day, J., *A Plain Russet-Coated Captain* (Arthur H Stockwell, 1993)). Among the wounded marines brought out was Neil Patrick. He recalled being driven back 'at speed under a heavy concentration of fire' from the windmill. Fifty years on, he observed: 'The Red Cross obviously does not offer protection from morons.'
20. Based on John Tulloch's unpublished memoir.
21. Recalling that day in an interview for the Imperial War Museum, Frank Burton said of Nicol Gray: 'He wasn't a man who would stop at headquarters. He wanted to get out and move around and see how the troops were getting on in different positions. He used to say, "Come on Burton, we're going out after the Bad men." He never called them Germans.' At Brachterbeek, they followed along the line of a German trench dug-in along the Montforterbeek. 'We stayed down in the trench as far as it went,' said Burton. Emerging from it into open ground, they saw a few tanks moving up and then came under fire. 'I don't know if they were firing at the tanks or our little group. Anyway, I got hit in the arm. Didn't feel a great deal of pain, but my arm just became absolutely useless. I couldn't lift it... I carried on and eventually the CO realised that a one-armed signalman wasn't much good to him, so I went back to where our little dressing station was set up...' A bullet had cut through his right-hand breast pocket and been deflected into his arm by his cigarette tin. Another round was found embedded in one of the spare magazines for his 45 Colt automatic. Frank Burton was awarded the Military Medal for his bravery that day. See Appendix.
22. The men killed were Cpl John Cocks and Marine James Russell. Sgt Patrick Ahern died two days later, having been given the last rites by the chaplain, Reg Haw, at the regimental aid post.
23. Day, J., *A Plain Russet-Coated Captain* (Arthur H Stockwell, 1993).
24. The citation for Lt Riley's Military Cross gives a different version of events. See Appendix.
25. Cakebread, D., 'My War Story from September 1944 to Demob in 1946' (unpublished manuscript).
26. Interview with author.

27. See Appendix for the citation for the Distinguished Service Cross awarded to the Revd Reg Haw.
28. Donald Haskel Thomas, letter to author, 1994. Walter Bigland was another among the forward section who saw movement out in the field and drew his sergeant's attention to what he later discovered was Doc going among the wounded under heavy fire.
29. A 'Blighty' was a wound that necessitated evacuation back to England. The expression was a throwback to the First World War.
30. Cory, R., *Op. cit.*
31. Johnny Haville, letter to author, 1994.

Chapter 17: For Valour

1. Letter to Eric, 17 January 1945 (returned unread).
2. Letter to Eric, 22 January 1945 (returned unread).
3. *Ibid.*
4. *Ibid.*
5. Ethel Treadwell (*née* Harden), Eric's elder sister with whom he worked at the butcher's shop in Northfleet High Street.
6. May Gurney (*née* Pullen) and her daughter Jill. May was Maud's sister.
7. Eric had left for Belgium suffering from an earache.
8. Letter to Eric, post-dated January 26, 1945 (returned unread).
9. Letter to Lt Col Nicol Gray, undated.
10. Letter to Maud, 24 May 1945.
11. Sidney Gliddon, letter to Maud, 16 April 1945.
12. Letter to Maud, 7 February 1945. Subsequently, the Revd Haw wrote giving the precise location as 'Sheet number 37 Maasbracht SE, Map reference 711849'.
13. Letter to Maud, 16 April 1945.
14. In a letter to Maud dated 2 June 1945, Johnny Haville wrote: 'I felt glad somehow that it happened so quickly and he felt no pain. He never realised what happened for his face still remained calm.' Wiggy Bennett wrote in the same vein on 21 April, telling Maud that 'mercifully his death was sudden with no pain, his face had its usual serene look still which it always had in life...'
15. John Tulloch, unpublished memoir of his wartime service, passed to the author by his widow, 2012. Twenty-five years later at a Four Five dinner, Tulloch discovered that he had been the second person considered for a VC.
16. This was the ill-starred Operation Belle Island II. An intelligence-gathering 'prisoner snatch' mission mounted in the Merum area on the night of 27–28 January, it misfired badly with seventeen officers and men being

reported missing, of whom eleven were later found to be dead, and another thirteen wounded.

17. Letter to Maud, 7 February 1945.
18. Taken from *The Reporter*, Saturday 24 February 1945. In his account, Bennett stated that Doc had made four trips into no man's land, but his version of the story conflicted with those related by Haville and Cory. Bennett claimed that Doc had 'dressed the wounds of some of the men' in full view of the enemy during his first venture into no man's land and only after returning to his post did he learn that 'two other men were lying in the snow, badly wounded'. So, said Bennett, 'out he went again and administered morphia to the men, and then while all the battle and firing was raging, he put his arm under one wounded man's shoulder and zig-zagged back with him'. Later, before bringing in Lt Cory, Bennett said that he had asked Haville and Mason if they 'wanted a rest, but they said they would carry on'.
19. *Ibid.*
20. Private information passed to the author by Maud's daughter, Julia.
21. Lord Harris, MC, C St J, DL, letter to Maud, 23 February 1945.
22. Letter to Maud, 18 February 1945.
23. See Appendix for the full citation.
24. The other Blackcock VC was awarded to Fusilier Dennis Donnini, of the 4/5th Royal Scots Fusiliers. At 19, he became the army's youngest Victoria Cross recipient of the Second World War. Although gazetted twelve days after Doc Harden's cross, it was actually earned on 18 January 1945, during the fight for the German border village of Stein, a few miles south of Maasbracht.
25. Interview with the author, 2012.
26. *Ibid.*
27. Interview with the author, 1994.
28. Cory, R., 'A Troop, 45 Commando RM, 23 January 1945' (unpublished recollections, passed to the author, 1994). Cory felt the same way about Tim Cook and Marine Whitney. Cook subsequently received a mention in despatches. Cory wrote: 'I do not know whether Sgt Cook's "mention" was awarded for his gallantry that day, but I hope so.'
29. Wiggy Bennett's Military Medal recognised his 'sterling work' throughout the campaign in north-west Europe from June 1944 to May 1945. It was not gazetted until 12 February 1946. In a letter to Maud, written on 9 February 1947 while serving with 45 RM Commando in Hong Kong, Bennett wrote: 'I won it the same day as Eric's VC and was put in again afterwards but didn't get it until the end of the western war. I don't know what delayed it...' See Appendix for full citation.
30. Maj. Gen. L.O. Lyne, CB, DSO, letter to Maud Harden, 16 March 1945.
31. Hansard, vol. 409, p. 195

32. Letter to Maud Harden, 16 March 1945. Her husband was Admiral Sir Martin Dunbar-Nasmith VC, former C-in-C Plymouth and Western Approaches, who earned his Victoria Cross as a submariner during the 1915 Dardanelles campaign.
33. Brig. D Mills-Roberts, DSO, MC, Irish Guards, letter to Maud Harden, post-dated 14 March 1945.
34. Letter to Brig. Derek Mills-Roberts, 16 March 1945.
35. Letter to the Rev. Reginald Haw, undated.
36. Letter to unnamed correspondent, undated.
37. Letter to Maud, 21 February 1945.
38. Letter to Maud, post-dated 14 March 1945.
39. Letter to Maud, 2 June 1945.
40. Letter to Maud, 5 April 1945.
41. Letter to Maud, 21 April 1945.
42. Letter to Maud, 2 June 1945.
43. Letter to Maud, 24 May 1945.

Chapter 18: Acts of Remembrance

1. Harden, J., *Eric Harden VC, RAMC (45 RM Commando): My Family's Story* (Menin, 2011)
2. *Ibid.*
3. Maud married Ken Moody, co-proprietor of a Northfleet-based coach hire business, at Dartford Register Office on 16 September 1956. She later became a partner in the firm, as did her son Bobby when he left the Merchant Navy. When the local council compulsorily purchased their garage site in the 1970s, they bought a new coach business in Perthshire where they relocated.
4. Among the many Harden memorials are: Harden House, at Aldershot, once home to RAMC apprentices and now a sergeants' mess; Harden Bay in Selly Oak Hospital; Harden Barracks at Catterick (now defunct, with the memorial plaque destined for the Army Medical Services Museum); Henry Harden Medical Centre at the Defence College of Policing and Guarding, Southwick. There are also Harden Troops, for medical recruits at Aldershot and battle-recovering soldiers at Arbroath, and a Harden Cup, which is awarded annually to the top medical recruit. He has also been commemorated with a re-enactment of his courageous action at the Royal Tournament.

   Eric's Victoria Cross group of medals are among the treasures proudly displayed in the Army Medical Services Museum in Aldershot. They include a Defence Medal that was issued in 2007 following efforts undertaken by RAMC veteran Pat Higgins.

His operations jacket, biscuit rations tin and assorted personal possessions, are held by the Royal Marines Museum in Southsea, near Portsmouth.

5. Geocaching is a 'treasure-hunting' game where people use a GPS (Global Positioning System) to hide and seek containers of data.
6. Interview with the author.
7. Letter to author, 20 January 1995.
8. Letter to author, 5 February 1995.
9. Letter to author, 20 January 1995.
10. Letter to author, 5 August 1994.
11. Letter to author, 8 August 1994.
12. *Ibid.*
13. Harden, J., Op. cit.
14. *Ibid.*
15. Letter to Fred Harris, 27 June 1994.
16. *Ibid.*
17. Letter to Fred Harris, 6–9 February 1995.
18. *Ibid.*

Index

Places: